PRICE OF A PRECIOUS PEARL:

Religious Poverty Lived and Taught by Blessed Mother Teresa of Calcutta

PRICE OF A PRECIOUS PEARL:

Religious Poverty Lived and Taught by Blessed Mother Teresa of Calcutta

Paul Chungath

ISPCK

2009

Price of a Precious Pearl: Religious Poverty Lived and Taught by Blessed Mother Teresa of Calcutta – published by the Rev. Dr. Ashish Amos of the Indian Society for Promoting Christian Knowledge (ISPCK), Post Box 1585, 1654, Madarsa Road, Kashmere Gate, Delhi-110006.

ISBN: 978-81-8465-062-4

Imprimatur: Most Rev. Vincent M. Concessao, Archbishop of Delhi

Nihil Obstat: Most Rev. Franco Mulakkal, Auxiliary Bishop & Vicar General Archdiocese of Delhi

Cover design: Bro. Sijo Chungath

Laser typeset by

ISPCK, Post Box 1585, 1654, Madarsa Road, Kashmere Gate, Delhi-110006 • *Tel:* 23866323

e-mail: ashish@ispck.org.in • ella@ispck.org.in
website: www.ispck.org.in

Dedicated to

My beloved parents who gave me a strong foundation in my spiritual journey

Contents

Dedication ... *v*
Foreword ... *xi*
Preface ... *xiii*
Abbreviations ... *xv*

Introduction **1-5**
The Motivation 2
The Objective and Relevance 2
The Sources 3
The Structure of the Work 4

Chapter - 1:
Religious Poverty in the Life of Blessed Mother Teresa of Calcutta **6-52**

1. Renunciation 7
    1.1. At the Initial Stage of her Religious Life 7
    1.2. At the Second Stage of her Religious Life 8
2. Inspiration and Inner Strength for Religious Poverty 13
    2.1. Inspiration from the Bible 13
    2.2. Inspiration from Saints 16
        2.2.1. Inspiration from St. Francis of Assisi 16
        2.2.2. Inspiration from St. Ignatius of Loyola 19
        2.2.3. Inspiration from St. Therese of Lisieux 21
    2.3. Devotion to the Eucharist 23
    2.4. Life of Prayer 25
3. Trust in Divine Providence and Detachment from Money 27

- 3.1. Trust in Divine Providence 27
- 3.2. Free from Anxieties Over Money 31
- 3.3. Totally Free from the Possession of Money 33

4. Criteria to Accept Donations and Gifts 34
   - 4.1. Do not Accept the Object that is not Needed Immediately 35
   - 4.2. No Campaigns for Money, but Spontaneous Donations are Acceptable 36
   - 4.3. Donations should not be from Superfluous Funds 37
5. Her Life Style as Witness to Her Religious Poverty 40
   - 5.1. Simplicity in Personal Appearance 40
   - 5.2. Simplicity in the Food 43
   - 5.3. Simplicity in the Manner of Traveling 44
   - 5.4. Readiness to Live with Minimum Facilities 47
   - 5.5. Lowliest Acts 50

Chapter - 2:

Religious Poverty and Following of Christ 53-99

1. Following the Call of Christ 53
   - 1.1. Poverty for Discipleship 54
   - 1.2. Poverty for Holiness 59
   - 1.3. Poverty for Eternal Life 63
2. Following the Life of Christ 65
   - 2.1. Poor Birth of Christ 67
   - 2.2. Poor Life of Christ 69
   - 2.3. Poor Death of Christ 73
   - 2.4. Self Emptying Love of Christ (*Kenosis*) 76
3. Following the Teachings of Christ 81
   - 3.1. Poverty out of Loving Trust in God 82
   - 3.2. Poverty in Becoming a Humble Servant of All 85
   - 3.3. Poverty in Spirit 88
4. Following the Mission of Christ 91
   - 4.1. The Meaning and Purpose of Mission in the Light of Poverty 92
   - 4.2. The Role of Life-witness in the Mission 94
   - 4.3. Deliberate Choice of Simple and Lowly Means 98

Chapter - 3:

The Vow of Poverty and its Relation with Other Religious Vows 100-150

1. Vow of Poverty 102
   1.1. Poverty is Out of Free Choice 103
   1.2. Poverty is Freedom 106
   1.3. Poverty is Joy 109
   1.4. Poverty is Dowry 112
   1.5. Poverty for the Love of Christ and the Poor 114
2. Vow of Chastity and Poverty 118
   2.1. Meaning of Chastity in the Recent Church Teachings 118
   2.2. Meaning of Chastity in the Teachings of Mother Teresa 120
   2.3. Interrelation between Chastity and Poverty 126
3. Vow of Obedience and Poverty 128
   3.1. Meaning of Obedience in the Recent Church Teachings 129
   3.2. Meaning of Obedience in the Teachings of Mother Teresa 131
   3.3. Interrelation between Obedience and Poverty 138
4. Relevance of Religious Poverty and Its Practical Aspects 140
   4.1. Poverty is the Strength and Protection of Religious Life 141
   4.2. The Strict Observances of Religious Poverty 145
   4.3. Practical Aspects 147

Chapter- 4:

Religious Poverty in Relation with Charity 151-204

1. Meaning and Scope of Charity 152
   1.1. Meaning of Charity 153
   1.2. Scope of Charity 158
      1.2.1. Material Poverty 159
      1.2.2. Spiritual Poverty 160

2. Charity in its Theological Aspects 165
 2.1. Christological Dimension 166
 2.2. Vocational and Missionary Dimension 171
3. Charity in the Dimension of a Religious Vow 178
 3.1. Charity as the Fourth Vow 179
  3.1.1. Whole Hearted 180
  3.1.2. Free Service 181
  3.1.3. The Poorest of the Poor 182
 3.2. Importance of the Fourth Vow 184
 3.3. The Fourth Vow in Relation with Other Vows 186
  3.3.1. Charity and Chastity 186
  3.3.2. Charity and Obedience 188
4. Povery Strengthens the Role of Charity 188
 4.1. Vow of Poverty Safeguards the Vow of Charity 189
 4.2. The Life of Poverty to Understand the Poor 191
 4.3. The Life of Poverty to Welcome and Win Over the Hearts of the Poor 192
 4.4. Identification with the Poor as an Effective Means of Charity 194
5. Charity Strengthens Religious Poverty 197
 5.1. Vow of Charity Safeguards the Vow of Poverty 198
 5.2. Charity as a Motivation for Religious Poverty 199
 5.3. Life of the Poor as a Source of Inspiration for Religious Poverty 201
 5.4. Experience of God and Spiritual Enlightenment from the Poor 202

CONCLUSION **205-211**

BIBLIOGRAPHY **212-219**

Foreword

Ever since Jesus wandered around Palestine preaching the Good News and described riches as thorns which choke up the good seed, Christians have promoted poverty as something acceptable. Mother Teresa's celebration of poverty in Calcutta sprang not only from her own religious creed, but also from the dire social and economic conditions in that city. Like so many Christians before her, she was effectively adding a religious gloss to a social reality.

Mother Teresa was awarded the Nobel Prize "for work undertaken in the struggle to overcome poverty and distress, which also constitute a threat to peace." She refused the conventional ceremonial banquet given to laureates, and asked that the $6,000 funds be given to the poor in Calcutta. When Mother Teresa received the prize, she was asked, "What can we do to promote world peace?" Her answer was simple: "Go home and love your family."

In the life of Blessed Mother Teresa one can see the vow of poverty as the most important of all three evangelical vows. She taught more through her exemplary life than through her spoken words or written works. Her spirit in imitating the poor Jesus is something marvelous. Her conviction about poverty guided her to trust in Divine Providence and it remained the same from the beginning till the end.

Fr. Paul Chungath through his book - *Price of a Precious Pearl: Religious Poverty lived and taught by Blessed Mother Teresa of Calcutta* - sheds light on this eminent woman who taught the world to love the poor and hate poverty. She embraced the leper and comforted the dying. Her life and example may open new vistas for all men and women of good will. The world should be grateful to Fr. Paul Chungath for his scholarly work. I wish him every success.

Rev. Dr. Anthony Chirayath
Bishop of Sagar

Preface

This book is an outcome of my doctoral thesis in spiritual theology. An extract from my work was already published in 2007 to fulfill the formalities of doctorate studies with the title: *Religious poverty in the life and teachings of Blessed Mother Teresa of Calcutta.* This present book, *Price of a Precious Pearl,* is the revised edition in view of making it available to the general public as requested by many well wishers of Blessed Mother Teresa of Calcutta, particularly consecrated people belonging to various religious congregations.

I am immensely thankful to Bishop Rt. Rev. Dr. Joseph Pastor Neelankavil who sent me to Rome for my higher studies and my present bishop Rt. Rev. Dr. Antony Chirayath for his support and guidance in my studies. I gratefully acknowledge my gratitude to my beloved parents, who played a great role in inculcating in me a deep faith and a sound spirituality from my childhood.

In a very special way I am indebted to Rev. Prof. Manuel Belda my moderator. It is his constant encouragement, his incredible gift of time on my behalf, which helped me to complete this work. I am grateful to the Rector, the dean and professors of the faculty of theology of the Pontifical

University of Holy Cross, Rome, for their support and scholarly guidance during my studies in Rome.

I am grateful to H. E. Camillo Card. Ruini for giving me a nomination to assist in a parish through which I could get necessary economical support to continue my studies of doctorate. My stay in Rome was made comfortable by the Rector and staff of the Institute of *Maria Immacolata* in the initial two years and later by Don Giuseppe Grazioli by availing me a good stay in both of his parishes. I express heartfelt thanks to them for providing me a pleasant stay in Rome.

I express my sincere gratitude to Prof. Stanley Russell, Rev. Sr. Alice CSSJ and Rev. Sr. Philippa CSSJ for giving me necessary guidance and corrections to improve my thesis. I also gratefully acknowledge the support and encouragement I have received from the parishioners of *Parrocchia S. Andrea Avellino* and *Parrocchia S. Giuseppe Cottolengo* during my studies in Rome. I acknowledge the prayerful support and encouragement I have received from my well wishers and the priests and seminarians of my diocese, Sagar, India. Finally I acknowledge with gratitude to ISPCK, Delhi for publishing this book.

Abbreviations

AAS	*Acta Apostolicae Sedis*
AGD	*Ad Gentes Divinitus*
AIDS	Acquired Immune Deficiency Syndrome
Art.	Article
Cf.	Confer, compare
CIC	*Codex Juris Canonici*
ES	*Ecclesiae Sanctae*
ES	*Ecclesiae Suam*
ET	*Evangelii Testificato*
FAO	Food and Agriculture Organization of the United Nations
GS	*Gaudium et Spes*
Ibid.	*Ibidem*, in the same place
IL	*Instrumentum Laboris*
LG	*Lumen Gentium*
LM	*Lineamenta*
MC	Missionary of Charity
MCs	Missionaries of Charity
MD	*Mulieris Dignitatem*
PC	*Perfectae Caritatis*
RD	*Redemptionis Donum*
VC	*Vita Consacrata*
Vol.	Volume
v.	*Vide* (see)

Introduction

The awareness of one's own imperfection and the desire to achieve perfection is the beginning stage of our spiritual journey, a pilgrimage toward God the Father in heaven, from whom we all came and to whom we all should reach. It is natural to seek guidance and imitate the ways of others who have succeeded in attaining the goal of this pilgrimage by their exemplary earthly life. There are many great souls who, born into human nature like us, lived and left this world as any other human being. Some of them are canonised by the official Church and others are in process of being canonised. These great men and women left great lessons for us, so that we too, following their examples, may one day reach our final goal. These great lessons have become for us the subject matter of this research. I have chosen Blessed Mother Teresa of Calcutta, a great soul who was our contemporary . In this research a specific aspect, religious poverty, is chosen from her life and teachings.

Mother Teresa was canonised by religious-minded people in her lifetime itself by giving her the title 'Living Saint'; and in political and social circles she was well recognised internationally by being adorned with various prestigious awards. She was accepted and honoured by all, irrespective of religious, political and ideological differences. Pope John Paul II made this very clear in his Angelus

Message: "This sister, universally known as the Mother of the poor, leaves an eloquent example for everyone, believer and non-believer."[1] Her virtuous life opened all doors for her and enabled her to climb the steps of success rapidly.

THE MOTIVATION

This study grew out of personal interest and confusion regarding the meaning and place of poverty in the consecrated life. The question disturbed me during my priestly formation and thereafter in my priestly life; "What is the difference between my life and that of ordinary lay people in renunciation? Is there any way in which I can claim to be practising renunciation more than my own brothers at home who are married? These queries lead me to find some one who practised religious poverty and became a model for all religious in practising it. I found Blessed Mother Teresa. She suited my study, so I chose her life and teachings on religious poverty as the theme for my research. Therefore, in this work the title I have chosen is: "Religious poverty in the life and teachings of Blessed Mother Teresa of Calcutta".

THE OBJECTIVE AND RELEVANCE

The objective of this book is to present the importance of religious poverty in the spiritual journey toward Christian Perfection, through the detailed study of that virtue as practiced and taught by a contemporary soul. The most

---

[1] These words Pope John Paul II spoke about Mother Teresa, after receiving the news of her death, in his Angelus Message, September 7, 1997. This message is published in the official book of Missionaries of Charity on the occasion of the Beatification of Mother Teresa of Calcutta (*Come Be My Light: Blessed Teresa of Calcutta,* official commemorative edition, Missionaries of Charity, Rome 2003, p. 8).

remarkable aspect of Mother Teresa's teachings was her exemplary practice of strict religious poverty. Its practicality and effectiveness are proven by her life and the lives of her followers. This work is an attempt to unveil the secrets of her success in practicing the renunciation demanded by Jesus of a religious.

Renunciation of and detachment from material comforts are the conditions put forward by Jesus for following him. To be successful in practising this virtue, and to follow Jesus with undivided love, we need conviction to sacrifice very many things in life. In the present world there is a tendency to avoid hardships and to settle for an easy life. This is apparent even in the realm of religious vocation, to the extent that the younger generation finds difficulty in coming forward to join the religious life. In consequence, there is a general decrease in the number of vocations. However in the Missionaries of Charity, founded by Mother Teresa, there is a rapid growth in the increasing number of members who lead a life of strict religious poverty. Therefore, this theme has relevance in the balancing of religious vocation and the aspect of renunciation for discipleship of Jesus, properly understood.

The originality of the present work is in its specific concentration on the religious vow of poverty in the life and teachings of Blessed Mother Teresa. Thus this work has relevance in the sense that it can serve as a resource work for all those who aspire to learn more about the religious vow of poverty lived and taught by Blessed Mother Teresa.

THE SOURCES

There are certain limits to this study. First of all, Mother Teresa had very little interest in writing or keeping records of her own life or her own ideals. Her congregation members, too, did not concern themselves with the writing and publishing of books. This is clear from the words of Brother Angelo Devananda: "The Missionaries of Charity Sisters have specified in their constitutions: 'We shall proclaim the word of God through our personal presence and not by writing books or articles.'"[2] Mother Teresa, their foundress, followed these words of the constitutions very strictly. Therefore we do not have a full knowledge of her vision. However, there are books in her name as the author which are collections of her words compiled by her admirers.

For the sources of my study I have used mainly the Constitutions of Missionaries of Charities, letters of Blessed Mother Teresa, her words compiled by others in various books, and the numerous books written on her life and teachings.

THE STRUCTURE OF THE WORK

The whole work is divided into six chapters. This published work is only an extract of the thesis which consists of the last four chapters of the entire work. In this published work the first chapter deals with the way in which Mother Teresa practiced evangelical poverty throughout her life and proved the practicality of her teachings about this virtue. It is divided into five parts, which include the following themes: renunciation, inspiration and inner strength for religious poverty, trust in divine providence and detachment from money, criteria to accept donations and gifts, and her life style as witness to her religious poverty.

---

[2] A. D. Scolozzi, *Mother Teresa: Contemplative in the Heart of the World*, Servant Books, Ann Arbor, Michigan 1985, p. 9.

The second chapter is an analysis of her teachings on religious poverty and following the example of Christ. Here emphasis is placed on how the practice of religious poverty enables a religious to follow Christ as a close disciple. For our consideration it is divided under various themes and subtitles within the chapter. These are classified into four aspects on the following of Christ: following the call of Christ; following the life of Christ; following the teachings of Christ; and following the mission of Christ.

In the third chapter we analyse the vow of poverty in its relation with other religious vows, as taught by Mother Teresa. The first part deals in detail with the meaning and characteristics of poverty as a religious vow. Then her view on other religious vows, namely obedience and chastity, and their relation to the vow of poverty is dealt with. At the end of this chapter there is a discussion on the relevance of religious poverty and its practical aspects.

The fourth chapter deals with religious poverty in relation to charity. Charity will be seen here mainly in the dimension of a religious vow introduced by Mother Teresa– the fourth vow. Evangelical counsels of chastity, poverty and obedience are common to all religious orders. The fourth vow is specific to the Missionaries of Charity and this vow demands a wholehearted free service to the poorest of the poor. In this chapter Mother Teresa's teaching on the meaning and scope of charity with its theological and religious dimensions is dealt with. The main emphasis will be given to the relationship between the vow of poverty and the vow of charity. These aspects will be analysed under two sub titles: religious poverty strengthens the role of charity, and charity strengthens religious poverty.

CHAPTER 1

Religious Poverty in the Life of Blessed Mother Teresa of Calcutta

It is easy to preach but difficult to practice. This famous dictum we have heard several times. One may write volumes on virtues but if one does not practice them in one's own life it will not have much effect on others. Rather a person who practises a virtuous life, whatever he or she does or says may have a great effect on others. Such a life can become an open book for others to read, through which they might come to understand and assimilate various values that characterise that life.

The life of Mother Teresa was an example for others in the practice of religious poverty. She practised religious poverty very strictly in her life and then instructed other members of her congregation to practice it. Her followers imbibed the very spirit of poverty from her. Those who met Mother Teresa during her life-time were all taken up by her simplicity and her dedication to poverty. In this chapter I deal with the practical aspect of religious poverty that was reflected in her life.

1. RENUNCIATION

Renunciation is one of the demands put forward to the disciples by Jesus, when He called them to a special mission. "Whoever does not renounce all that he has, cannot be my disciple" (Lk.14:33). The first disciples responded well by leaving everything and following him immediately. "Immediately they left the boat and their father, and followed him" (Mt. 4:22). Peter answered to Jesus: "We have left everything and followed you" (Mk.10:28) that should be the case for anyone who receives a call to be his disciple. We can see this kind of renunciation in Mother Teresa when she received the call from Jesus. Her renunciation can be divided into two stages. The first, at the time of her leaving of her home to join a religious congregation, and the second at the time when she left the Loreto Convent to become poor and serve the poorest of the poor.

1.1. At the Initial Stage of her Religious Life

One of her poems, composed on December 9, 1928, on board the ship to India, expresses her renunciation at the initial stage of her religious vocation:

> I leave the house that gives light to my heart,
> My country, my entire family.
> My goal is Bengal, prostrate with suffering,
> A land dear to me, although it is a foreign land.[1]

Mother Teresa left everything she had in life in order to respond to the call from Jesus and entered the religious Congregation of our Lady of Loreto. She left her beloved parents, near and dear ones, birth place and all the family

---

[1] This poem is quoted by F. Zambonini in his book (F. Zambonini, *Teresa of Calcutta: A Pencil in God's Hand*, translated by J. Aumann, Alba House, New York 1993, p. 147).

comforts to join a religious order. It was a sacrifice she made in order to follow Jesus, who, in her view, is the King of the whole world. It was clear from her answer to her brother Lazar who wrote her a somewhat imperious letter as to whether she really knew what she was doing. She replied:

> You think you are important, because you are an officer serving a king with two million subjects. But I am serving the King of the whole world.[2]

1.2. At the Second Stage of her Religious Life

As in the case of Abraham, the man of faith, a deep trust and profound faith can be seen in Mother Teresa. She committed herself fully to God, sacrificed all she had, her security, even her religious Congregation, to put herself blindly in God's hands, not knowing what her fate would be.[3]

She courageously renounced her familial and social security, even the religious habit of her old religious congregation, and took a humble form of dress. It was something like a great leap into the unknown, a leap into darkness, with total trust in God. To do so required extraordinary courage and deep faith in God. Renunciation of material comfort is rather easy when compared to leaving behind all social security and leaping into a situation where the only companion is God.

---

[2] K. Spink, *Mother Teresa: An authorised Biography*, Harper and Collins, London 1997, p. 11. On 1 September 1928 Albania became a monarchy under King Zog I, and the young second Lieutenant Bojaxhiu enlisted in the army of the newly crowned king. The news of his sister's vocation came as a surprise to him. So he enquired her about it through a letter (Cf. *Ibid.*).

[3] Cf. E. Le Joly, *We do it for Jesus: Mother Teresa and the Missionaries of Charity*, Oxford University Press, Calcutta 1977, p. 93; cf. M. Muggeridge, *Something Beautiful for God: Mother Teresa of Calcutta*, Ballantine Books, New York 1973, p. 67.

The Archbishop of Calcutta understood the seriousness of the risk Mother Teresa was taking in leaving Loreto convent at Calcutta and he made her wait. He was aware of the possible irresponsibility of allowing a woman to live and work alone in the slums of India, a woman who wanted to trust entirely in Divine Providence for the provision of her own needs and needs of those who might join her. It was a time of strong Indian nationalist feeling. Mother Teresa was a European. New congregations were more usually begun when a group was already established. He also had a fear about the possible criticism from the Church circle itself by allowing a foreign woman to step out alone to undertake what in human terms might appear an act of folly.[4]

To understand the gravity of the renunciation made by Mother Teresa at this stage we should go to Entally, the Convent and well-organised school run by the congregation of Loreto, with an impressive collection of buildings sited in a sizeable compound enclosed by high walls, from where she left everything to follow the inner call of Jesus. One can imagine that she enjoyed very good facilities and security as a religious nun and teacher.[5] Mother Teresa renounced

---

[4] Cf. K. Spink, *Mother Teresa: An Authorised Biography*, p. 26.

[5] Cf. K. Spink, *Mother Teresa: An Authorised Biography*, p. 16; cf. R. Allegri, *Teresa of the Poor: The Story of Her Life*, Servant Publications, Ann Arbour, Michigan 1996, p. 40; cf. N. Chawla, *Mother Teresa: The Authorized Biography*, Element, Boston 1992, p. 10. Michel Gomes, in whose house Mother Teresa stayed in the beginning stage of new venture, said: "Have you been to Entally? Have you seen that beautiful comfortable convent? Then you can understand what I am about to tell you….From the window of her room on the first floor of the convent she could see the street and how the people lived there – cooking their meals and sleeping on the sidewalk, and the naked children around in the filth of the

the wall of self-protection and embraced poverty in order to serve Jesus in the poorest of the poor. The word "wall" even appears in her conversation:

> Our sisters must walk on the Street, take the streetcar as our people do, and enter the houses of the poor. We cannot enclose ourselves behind walls and wait for the poor to knock at our door.[6]

The extraordinary decision Mother Teresa took gave pain to the superior and other sisters in her convent. For them her decision was something unimaginable; the new step Mother Teresa took was a great leap into insecurity. Secondly, she was well accepted and had enjoyed a good reputation in the community. When the decree of exclaustration from Rome arrived and Fr. Van Exem read it out in the convent, the superiors reacted to it with deep sorrow. The superior Mother de Cenacle reacted with tears and spoke about her innocence. The reaction of the Provincial, Mother Columba, seemed more moderate. She put the following notice on the bulletin board: 'Dear Sisters: Teresa is leaving the convent. Do not praise. Do not criticize. Pray'. In the recollection of Sister Marie Téresè Breen, many were saddened because they had all been very friendly.[7]

---

city street. I believe that for a long time she had prayed and meditated until she was to make her great decision." (F. Zambonini, *Teresa of Calcutta: A Pencil in God's Hand*, pp. 44, 45).

[6] Mother Teresa spoke these words to F. Zambonini during her conversation with him and he quoted this in his book (F. Zambonini, *Teresa of Calcutta: A Pencil in God's Hand*, p. 10).

[7] Cf. K. Spink, *Mother Teresa: An Authorised Biography*, p. 31; also cf. F. Zambonini, Teresa of Calcutta: A Pencil in God's Hand, pp. 33-34. "She was a very hard worker. Up to time on this, up to time on that. She never wanted to shirk anything, she was always ready. Always a very pious person, she was just herself. She did not force it on anybody, if you like, she was just what

Mother Teresa left the Loreto convent not from dissatisfaction with life in the community. It was a great sacrifice for her to leave, and it was painful for her to leave the place where she enjoyed love and all she wanted. But for the sake of Christ and the poorest of the poor she made a sacrifice, a renunciation by leaving all that she had in her life. This can be well understood from the words of Mother Teresa:

> To leave Loreto, was my greatest sacrifice, the most difficult thing I have ever done. It was much more difficult than to leave my family and country to enter religious life. Loreto, my spiritual training, my work there, meant everything to me.[8]

The determination of Mother Teresa in accepting the poverty for the sake of Christ is reflected in the way she left the Loreto convent at Calcutta. Her strong decision in accepting poverty can be well understood by analysing the selection of materials and facilities from the very initial period of her second stage of call, or her call within a call. Her promptness in making decisions and putting them into practice at once was something extra ordinary. She always knew what she wanted. On the following day she went to the market and bought two white cotton sarees with a blue border. They were the kind worn by the poor people in India. She went

---

she felt she had to be. She fitted in very well; we were all very happy, very happy." This was an answer given by Sr. Marie-Théresè Breen, who was with Mother Teresa at Loreto Convent, to a question: "How did Mother Teresa fit into Loreto?" She responded in this way during an interview by N. Chawla, biographer. Later biographer quoted in his book (N. Chawla, *Mother Teresa: The Authorized Biography*, p. 12).

[8] Mother Teresa acknowledged these words about leaving the Loreto convent to K. Spink and she quoted in her book (K. Spink, *Mother Teresa: An Authorised Biography*, p. 32).

all alone, after taking off the habit of the Sisters of Loreto and putting on the sari. All she had was her train ticket and five rupees. She had asked not to be accompanied to the train for Patna, nor did her new condition of poverty permit her to take a taxi or a rickshaw. She headed to the railway station on foot, carrying her rosary, her train ticket and five rupees. She was truly God's vagabond and had risked everything to answer His call.[9]

In the midst of struggles and the deprivation of the poor people whom she served she remembered the comfort she had experienced in the Loreto Convent. She remembered her school, her nice bed, the fans that ventilated the rooms, and the clean mosquito nets. She felt as though she had passed from heaven to hell. But it was there in that hell that the poor were living, the beloved brothers and sisters of Jesus, the people whom she wanted to serve. It is clear from her words:

> The change was extremely difficult. In the convent I had lived without knowing what difficulties were. I had lacked nothing. Now everything was different. I slept where I happened to be, on the ground, often in hovels infested by rats. I ate what the people I was serving, ate, and only when there was a little food. [10]

---

[9] Cf. F. Zambonini, *Teresa of Calcutta: A Pencil in God's Hand*, pp. 34-35; cf. K. Spink, *Mother Teresa: An Authorised Biography*, p. 31; cf. M. Muggeridge, *Something Beautiful for God: Mother Teresa of Calcutta*, pp. 51, 54.

[10] Mother Teresa told these words to R. Allegri in the conversation and he quoted in his book (R. Allegri, *Teresa of the Poor: The Story of Her Life*, p. 62).

2. INSPIRATION AND INNER STRENGTH FOR RELIGIOUS POVERTY

A virtue is born and nurtured in a person in accordance with the inspiration received. Further, it is maintained by the continuous support of strengthening elements. In the life of Mother Teresa poverty as a virtue and a religious vow was rooted by inspiration from the Bible and the life history of saints. Her inner strength in the practice of strict religious poverty was her devotion to the Eucharist and an ardent life of prayer.

The influence of St. Francis of Assisi and St. Teresa of Child Jesus is not seen explicitly in the life of Mother Teresa, but in her instructions and speeches, especially on religious poverty, she used the examples of these two saints. From this we can come to an understanding of the extent to which Franciscan poverty and the humility of St. Teresa of Child Jesus were rooted in her. Inspiration of St. Ignatius of Loyola is brought out from the assumption of the spiritual formation she had received from the Jesuit priests. The name of St. Ignatius of Loyola is not cited in her instructions or speeches. It is rather the natural influence of her spiritual directors and confessors that is reflected in the formation of her spiritual life. When we see the strictness with which she practiced the life of religious poverty, which was also a special feature in the life of St. Ignatius of Loyola, we may naturally draw conclusions about its source.

2.1. Inspiration from the Bible

Mother Teresa's inner strength came from her meditation of the Word of God and an urge to practice in her life the inspiration she received from it. Once she strongly expressed her conviction that the inspiration she had received was Biblical in nature:

> The call of God to be a Missionary of Charity is the hidden treasure for me, for which I have sold all to purchase it. You remember in the gospel, what the man did when he found the hidden treasure – he hid it. This is what I want to do for God.[11]

The conception of poverty developed by MCs is in line with the biblical conception of poverty. The biblical conception of poverty is that of the poor of Yahweh. It is the attitude of opening up to God. It is the ready disposition of one who hopes for everything from God. Such a person values the goods of this world, but does not become attached to them and recognises the higher value of the riches of the kingdom of God. Therefore the MCs Constitution states:

> We will first allow ourselves to be God's providence to His people by seeking first His kingdom and His righteousness, by labouring wholeheartedly to bring God into their lives.[12]

The poverty of the poor of Yahweh is the same poverty blessed by Christ. Blessed are the poor means blessed are those who are totally at the disposition of the Lord. It means to have no other sustenance than the will of God. Poverty is not to be found in the book but in the lives, Mother Teresa used to say. Poverty gives complete and real freedom from everything. Poverty is one of the greatest gifts granted by the Church to their congregation. They must have the joy of being poor and have a burning desire for poverty. Once they see God in the poor, poverty will become a joy for them.

---

[11] Mother Teresa spoke these words to her biographer while explaining about the call within the call and the biographer quoted in the biography (K. Spink, *Mother Teresa: An Authorised Biography*, p. 22).

[12] *MCs Constitutions*, Art. 54.

They must protect it as they protect a great and precious treasure.[13]

When Mother Teresa talked about her voluntarily chosen life of poverty, she said it was in order to live out the gospel:

> I had chosen that lifestyle in order to literally live out the gospel, especially where it says, 'I was hungry and you gave me to eat, I was naked and you clothed me, I was in prison and you came to find me.' Among the poorest of the poor of Calcutta, I loved Jesus. When I love like that, I don't feel suffering or fatigue.[14]

Mother Teresa chose a very strict kind of poverty for her congregation, in imitation of Jesus, born in a stable, dying on a cross. During His public ministry He lived on the alms people offered for the sustenance of the little company of his disciples. The Missionaries of Charity own nothing, live on what they receive, and are ready to beg in case of need, for the poor and for their own food. Their poverty unites them to Jesus, poor by choice; "Though he was rich, he chose to be poor" (2 Cor. 8: 9). It makes them more similar to their Master.[15]

---

[13] Cf. A. Savarimuthu, *Spirituality of Mother Teresa of Calcutta*, Ph.D. diss., Pontifical University of St. Thomas Aquinas, Rome 1999, p. 142; cf. Mothers Instructions: *Let us make Our society Something Beautiful for God*, Printed as a gift to the Missionaries of Charity by the Knights of Columbus, for private circulation, no date, Vol.1, pp. 57, 62, 168.

[14] Mother Teresa told these words to R. Allegri in a conversation and he quoted in his book (R. Allegri, *Teresa of the Poor: The Story of Her Life*, p. 62).

[15] Cf. E. Le Joly, *Mother Teresa: Messenger of God's Love*, St. Paul's Publications, Bombay 1998, p. 48.

2.2. Inspiration from Saints

Mother Teresa received inspiration from the saints and requested the members of her congregation to imitate them in the practice of the vow of poverty. They can learn from St. Ignatius of Loyola to have a painful and fruitful love of poverty and to love it as dearly and tenderly as a mother. As St. Francis of Assisi was in love with lady-poverty, so the MCs must find the joy of being poor. From St. Bernard they can also draw inspiration to accept the vow of poverty with cheerfulness.[16]

2.2.1. *Inspiration from St. Francis of Assisi*

Mother Teresa left the Loreto convent and started a new congregation of her own under the inspiration and influence of the spirituality and personal life of St. Francis of Assisi. This fact is very clear from the letter she wrote to the Cardinal Prefect of the Congregation for Religious requesting permission to leave her religious congregation and to begin a new congregation on her own with new inspiration and vision. In the request letter she mentioned specially her intention to dedicate her life to the service of the poor, following in the footsteps of St. Francis of Assisi.[17]

---

[16] Cf. *Mother's Instructions: Let us make Our Society Something Beautiful for God*, Vol. 1, p. 168; also Cf. Vol. 3, Supplement 1, p. 35.

[17] "Your Eminence, with the permission of my Mother General, I humbly ask permission to begin a life very different from that which I have lived in the convent until now, to dedicate my life to the poor in total service, following in the footsteps of St. Francis of Assisi. Since September, 1946, God has been calling me to this. To do this work in a spirit of prayer and sacrifice, it is necessary to be close to the poor on the streets and to become poor as they are, to see Christ in every poor person." Mother Teresa wrote this letter, on 7th February 1948, to the Cardinal

Mother Teresa while explaining the vow of poverty made many references of the religious poverty of St. Francis Assisi. From this we can conclude that St. Francis of Assisi had great influence in her life and that she drew inspiration from St. Francis with regard to the practises of religious poverty. She used to mention, in her instructions St. Francis of Assisi as an example to follow in the practice of poverty. In one of her instructions she says:

> It is said about St. Francis of Assisi that when he died, his habit, which he wore daily, had forty patches.[18]

Mother Teresa inspired by the poverty of St. Francis is clearly reflected in her speech at Assisi during the closing ceremony of the eight hundredth anniversary of the birth of St. Francis:

> Let us make a strong resolution in this beautiful city of Assisi that just like St. Francis 'love, complete, total surrender to God, to us, when he kissed the leper, was the beginning of his great love; because then he became free. Poverty is not only renunciation, poverty is joy, poverty is freedom.[19]

St. Francis was not afraid of property and riches, he chose not to have them because he loved Christ with an undivided love. As Christ came to give Good News to the poor, Francis was in love with his lady-Poverty. So too Mother Teresa

---

Prefect of the Congregation for Religious, Rome. F. Zambonini with the permission from Vatican saw the file, read the letter and later quoted it in his book (F. Zambonini, *Teresa of Calcutta: A Pencil in God's Hand*, pp. 29-30).

[18] *Mother's Instructions: Let us Make Our Society Something Beautiful for God*, Vol. 2, p. 35.

[19] Mother's Speech in Assisi for the closing of the eight hundredth anniversary of the birth of St. Francis of Assisi, June 1982, (*Supplement to Mothers Instructions*, Vol. 2, 85a).

followed his way.[20] When St. Francis met a leper completely disfigured, he drew back, but later overcoming himself kissed that terrible, disfigured face. The result was that he was filled with an untold joy.[21] Similarly Mother Teresa showed her love for the poorest of the poor.

To imitate the perfect joy of St. Francis in complete surrender to God and full trust in his divine Majesty, such is the programme of life Mother proposes to her sisters. Her spirituality owes much to St. Francis. She emulates him in the cult and practice of evangelical poverty. Like him she adopts a simple, unsophisticated approach to life and its problems.[22]

St. Francis of Assisi was not ashamed to beg for the poor and to receive the scraps of food he would share with them. Similarly the sisters are not to be ashamed to ask for the poor, even if begging represents a form of poverty that has come to be despised in the modern world. The constitution states: "We and our poor will rely entirely on divine providence. We are not ashamed to beg from door to door as members of Christ, who himself lived on alms during his public life and Whom we serve in the sick and the poor."[23]

During public functions or meetings Mother Teresa used to invite everyone to join her in prayer, the Prayer of

---

[20] Cf. *Mother's Instructions: Let us make Our Society Something Beautiful for God*, Vol. 2, p.112; cf. P. Gallela, *Christian Charity as Witnessed by Mother Teresa of Calcutta*, Ph.D. diss., Pontifical University of St. Thomas Aquinas, Rome 1999, p. 256.

[21] Cf. P. Gallela, *Christian Charity as Witnessed by Mother Teresa of Calcutta*, p. 256.

[22] Cf. E. Le Joly, *We Do it for Jesus: Mother Teresa and the Missionaries of Charity*, p. 154.

[23] *MCs Constitutions*, Art. 54, 56: quoted in *Ibid.*, p. 131.

St. Francis for Peace. At an International gathering at Oslo, when she received the Nobel Peace Prize, she invited the assembly to recite the prayer of St. Francis of Assisi with the special mention that she and her community recited this prayer everyday after Holy Communion."[24]

2.2.2. *Inspiration from St. Ignatius of Loyola*

Mother Teresa's religious training and formation as a Loreto nun was greatly influenced by the spiritual exercises of St.

---

[24] "As we have gathered here to thank God for the Nobel Peace Prize, I think it will be beautiful that we pray the prayer of St. Francis of Assisi, which always surprises me very much. We pray this prayer every day after Holy Communion, because it is very fitting for each one of us, and I always wonder that 400-500 years ago when St. Francis of Assisi composed this prayer, they had the same difficulties that we have today" (Mother's Noble Peace Prize Acceptance Speech, December 1979, quoted in Supplement to Mother's Instructions [*Supplement to Mother's Instructions* Vol. 1, 177a]; also cf. F. Zambonini, *Teresa of Calcutta: A Pencil in God's Hand*, p. 151).

Lord, make me an instrument of your peace:
Where there is hatred, let me so love;
Where there is injury, pardon;
Where there is discord, unity;
Where there is doubt, faith ;
Where there is error, truth;
Where there is despair, hope;
Where there is darkness, light;
Where there is sadness, Joy
O divine Master, grant that I may seek not so much
To be consoled as to console,
To be loved as to love.
For it is in giving that we receive,
It is in losing ourselves that we find ourselves,
It is in pardoning that we are pardoned,
It is in dying that we are born to eternal life (R. Allegri, *Teresa of the Poor: The Story of Her Life*, p. 135).

Ignatius of Loyola. She habitually had Jesuits as confessors, spiritual advisers and preachers at the yearly retreat. The most influential Jesuits who became her spiritual guides were Fr. Jambrenkrovic, Fr. Julien Henry and Fr. Celeste Van Exem.[25] It is understandable that these Jesuits might have had some influence on her in the line of spirituality of St. Ignatius of Loyola, the founder of Jesuits. For Mother, as for Ignatius, the end of all activity, of all apostolate, is the glory of God and the good of souls. Perfection consists in doing all things according to the will of God; the will of God is our sanctification. The glory of God and the good of souls require of the religious, among other qualities and as part of his complete self-denial and surrender to God's guidance.[26]

Ignatian poverty as featured in the Formula of the Society of Jesus makes it very clear that the members cannot acquire any civil right to stable goods, but be content with whatever is given them out of charity.[27] The strict and unchangeable

---

[25] Fr. Jambrenkovic S. J. was the pastor of Sacred Heart Church. He guided her in the childhood and even gave her inspiration to become a missionary (Cf. E. EGAN *Such a Vision of the Street: Mother Teresa – The Spirit and the Work,* Doubleday & Company, Inc., Garden City, New York 1985, p. 9). Fr. Julien Henry S. J. was the pastor of the Church of St. Teresa. He influenced her through his spiritual guidance through Marian Sodality. He also celebrated daily mass in her Loreto convent (Cf. *ibid.*, p. 22) Fr. Celeste Van Exem was a Belgian Jesuit who became Mother Teresa's spiritual director when she was in a Loreto convent in Calcutta and eventually he continued his guidance when she came out from Loreto Convent to start a new religious order. He continued to support her in all her decisions to form a new religious community (Cf. K. Spink, *Mother Teresa: An Authorised Biography,* pp. 20-21).

[26] Cf. E. LE Joly, *Mother Teresa: Messenger of God's Love,* p. 144.

[27] Cf. G. E. Ganss, translated, *Formula of the Institute, The Institute of Jesuit Sources,* St. Louis 1970, no. 5.

nature of poverty in the constitution gives us the understanding of the importance of religious poverty in Ignatian spirituality: "Poverty as the strong wall of religious life, should be loved and preserved in its integrity as far as possible with God's grace...All those who make profession in this society should promise not to take part in altering what pertains to poverty in the constitutions, unless it is in some manner to make it stricter, according to the circumstances in the Lord."[28]

When we study religious poverty in the life of Mother Teresa we have to consider the probable sources or inspirations in her life that might have influenced her to take such a strong stand on religious poverty. In this regard as indicated earlier Jesuits as her confessors, spiritual directors and the main collaborators at the time of her starting a religious congregation certainly had strong influence. So we conclude that St. Ignatius of Loyola and his spirituality were not just an inspirational source but provided the inner strength for Mother Teresa to develop a certain way of religious poverty.

2.2.3. *Inspiration from St. Therese of Lisieux*

St. Therese of Lisieux had an influence in the life of Mother Teresa, who repeatedly claimed this saint as her patron saint. On many occasions she repeated that she was not named after the big St. Teresa of Avila, but the little one. She says:

> St. Teresa of Avila? Oh no! I haven't called myself after the big Teresa, but after the little one, Teresa of Lisieux.[29]

---

[28] G. E. Ganss, translated, *The Constitutions of the Society of Jesus*, The Institute of Jesuit Sources, St. Louis 1970, Part VI, Ch. 2, no. 1.,

[29] Mother Teresa of Calcutta, *A Gift for God: Prayers and Meditations*, compiled by M. Muggeridge, Harper & Row, New

Mother Teresa had a high esteem and respect for St. Therese of Lisieux.[30] A saint whom she gives to her sisters as an example to imitate and of whom she loves to speak is the Little Flower, whose autobiography portrays her as a wonderful example of trust in God, humility, simplicity, love of poverty, surrender to divine Providence, acceptance of suffering, penitential life, zeal for souls and burning love for Jesus.[31] Mother Teresa herself confessed:

> We all want to love God, but how? The Little Flower is a most wonderful example. She did small things with great love – ordinary things with extraordinary love. That is why she became a great saint.[32]

In instructing her nuns, Mother Teresa compared Jesus' humility and the humility of the Little Flower. Jesus, the Son of God loved us so much that he became one with us by taking human life and humbling himself. At the passion he

---

York 1975, p. 70; N. Chawla, *Mother Teresa: The Authorized Biography*, p. 8; cf. S. CONROY, *Mother Teresa's Lessons of Love and Secrets of Sanctity*, Our Sunday Visitor, Indiana 2003, pp. 216, 218; cf. J. L. Gonzalez – Balado, *Always the Poor: Mother Teresa Her Life and Message*, p. 15.

[30] When she came to know that St. Therese was going to be declared a Doctor of the Church, she explained: "It is truly amazing that little soul who was so hidden and unknown during her brief life on earth is so known and loved by so many people throughout the world and is being lifted to such heights! God's ways are so wonderful!" and she exclaimed: "Oh very nice! I am also Teresa!" Mother Teresa expressed these words to S. Conroy in the conversation and she quoted in her book (S. Conroy, *Mother Teresa's Lessons of Love and Secrets of Sanctity*, pp. 216-217).

[31] Cf. E. LE Joly, *Mother Teresa: Messenger of God's Love*, p. 149.

[32] Mother Teresa expressed these words to S. Conroy in the conversation and she quoted in her book (S. Conroy, *Mother Teresa's Lessons of Love and Secrets of Sanctity*, pp. 216-217).

was humiliated, spat upon, given a crown of thorns; all this he suffered for us. For this reason St. Therese of the Child Jesus said that the greatest grace she received was the realization of smallness, her nothingness before God, and that her realization of this was the greatest truth in her life.[33]

Thus St. Therese of Lisieux and her spirituality had a certain influence in forming the spirituality of Mother Teresa, especially the humility and simplicity in the practice of religious poverty.

2.3. Devotion to the Eucharist

The Eucharist was Mother Teresa's daily spiritual nourishment and strength for her life of extreme poverty. She could not go a single day without the Holy Eucharist.[34] Once she stated that the Holy Eucharist is the spiritual food that sustains her, without which she could not get through one single day or hour in her life. She elaborated further by saying that in the Mass we have Jesus in the appearance of bread, while in the slums we see Christ and touch him in the broken bodies and in the abandoned children.[35] She was so convinced in this matter and repeated it on different occasions to show its importance. On another occasion she stated: "Jesus feeds us with his love; he becomes our spiritual nourishment in the Eucharist."[36] According to her the most

---

[33] Cf. *Mother's Instructions*, Vol. 1, p. 98; cf. P. Gallela, *Christian Charity as Witnessed by Mother Teresa of Calcutta*, p. 259.

[34] Cf. S. Conroy, *Mother Teresa's Lessons of Love and Secrets of Sanctity*, p. 114; cf. M. Muggeridge, *Something Beautiful for God: Mother Teresa of Calcutta*, p. 37; cf. P. Chetcuti, *Choosing to Serve the Destitute*, Irish Messenger Publications, Dublin 1980, p. 11.

[35] Cf. Mother Teresa Of Calcutta, *A Gift for God: Prayers and Meditations*, p. 76; also in cf. M. Muggeridge, *Something Beautiful for God*, pp. 56, 108.

[36] Mother Teresa expressed these words to her congregation members and one of them, A. Devananda quoted in his book

important time of the day is the time of Holy Mass in which a King has humbled Himself to come among us and make Himself the Bread of Life.[37]

When Mother Teresa was invited to start her community in Yemen, a Muslim country that for the first time in 800 years had opened its doors to Catholic nuns, she accepted the invitation but on one condition, namely, that she was to have her priest.[38] She said: "We cannot do without the Holy Communion."[39] In her instructions to her nuns, Mother Teresa spoke on the Eucharist saying that they should get their strength from the bread of life. In one of her instructions she said:

> We cannot separate our lives from the Eucharist, the moment we do, something breaks. People ask, 'Where do the sisters get the joy and energy to do what they are doing?' Eucharist is not just receiving, it is also the hunger of Christ we are satisfying.[40]

Adoration of Jesus in the Blessed Sacrament exposed another way she expressed her devotion to the Eucharist, which gave her inner strength for her religious life, especially for her strict poverty. She also insisted that her sisters follow this devotion one hour in the morning and one hour in the

---

(A. D. Scolozzi, *Mother Teresa: Contemplative in the Heart of the World*, p. 29).

[37] Cf. *Mother's Instructions; Let us Make Our society Something Beautiful for God*, Vol.1, p. 150.

[38] Cf. P. Gallela, *Christian Charity as Witnessed by Mother Teresa of Calcutta*, p. 237.

[39] Mother Teresa expressed these words to Desmond Doig and he quoted this in his book (D. Doig, *Mother Teresa: Her People and Her Work*, Collins, Glasgow 1976, pp. 101-103).

[40] *Mother's Instructions; Let us Make Our Society Something Beautiful for God*, Vol.1, p. 110.

evening.[41] She was convinced of its importance in her life, which can be well understood from her expression:

> Every moment of prayer, especially before our Lord in the tabernacle, is a sure, positive gain. The time we spend in having our daily audience with God is the most precious part of the whole day.[42]

On another occasion Mother Teresa explained how Eucharistic adoration strengthens her in carrying out the activities:

> With Jesus we start our walk every day. As we come back at sunset, we have an hour of adoration in the presence of Jesus exposed in the Eucharist. The ten or twelve hours of service to the poor that we carry out every day suffers no interruption because of this.[43]

2.4. Life of Prayer

The day begins for Mother Teresa with prayers and meditation at 4.30 am. For her everything has to begin with prayer, which is the inner strength for all the sacrifices; and she used to remind her co-workers of this principle repeatedly.[44] The inner strength for extreme poverty is

---

[41] Cf. Mother Teresa, *A Life for God*, comp. L. Neff Servant Publications, Ann Arbor, Michigan 1995, p. 168; cf. P. Chetcuti, *Choosing to Serve the Destitute*, p. 10.

[42] Mother Teresa, *Heart of the World: Thoughts, Stories, and Prayers*, ed. B.Benenate, New World Library, Novato, California 1997, pp. 103-104.

[43] Mother Teresa, *Heart of Joy: The Transforming Power of Self-Giving*, ed. J. L. González – Balado, Servant Publications, Ann Arbor, Michigan 1987, p. 7.

[44] Cf. M. Muggeridge, *Something Beautiful for God: Mother Teresa of Calcutta*, p. 32; cf. S. Conroy, *Mother Teresa's Lessons of Love and Secret of Sanctity*, p. 113; cf. J. L. Gonzalez – Balado, *Always the Poor: Mother Teresa – Her Life and Message*, Liguori Publications, Liguori, Missouri 1980, p. 42; cf. J. L. Gonzalez – Balado, *Stories*

sustained by the life of prayer. It can be noticed in her own words in an interview:

> We are contemplative sisters who live in the world. Prayer, then, is fundamental for us. We always pray, whether it is walking down the street, during our work, or wherever. If we're not continually united with God, it would be impossible to make the sacrifices that are required for living among those who have been forsaken.[45]

She had unlimited confidence in prayer and considered it to be the great inner force through which she could do everything. When she spoke about the importance of prayer to the soul, she compared it to the role of blood to the body – prayer feeds the soul and it brings us closer to God.[46] According to her God is the power and she gets strength from this power through the means of prayer so without prayer she is nothing. This fact is clear from her expressions:

> I am only a little wire – God is the power.[47] Without prayer I could not work for even half an hour. I get strength from God through prayer.[48]

---

of Mother Teresa: Her Smile and Her Words, Liguori Publications, Missouri 1983, p. 84.

[45] Mother Teresa spoke these words as an answer to the question, what's a typical day for the sisters? in an interview by R. Allegri and he quoted in his book (R. ALLEGRI, *Teresa of the Poor*, pp. 77-78); cf. S. Conroy, *Mother Teresa's Lessons of Love and Secret of Sanctity*, p. 113.

[46] Cf. Mother Teresa, *A Simple Path*, compiled by L. Vardey, Rider, London 1995, p. 7.

[47] *Ibid*., p. xi.

[48] *Ibid*., p. 8.

3. TRUST IN DIVINE PROVIDENCE AND DETACHMENT FROM MONEY

Trust in the providence of God enables a person not to be worried about the future. Mother Teresa had this trust in a great measure and it helped her in the practice of radical poverty. From this trust she was free from the anxieties over money and also free from the possession of money. There are very many examples we can draw from her life, and some of them are shown below to support my argument.

3.1. Trust in Divine Providence

Deep trust in the divine providence is visible in the life of Mother Teresa in the way she came out from the Loreto convent to begin her own congregation and begin a new life. Her superiors were ready to give her more money and accompany her at least up to the railway station. She left everything and took only five rupees and her train ticket in hand and walked out. Thus her basic capital for founding of a new congregation and to manage her life was just five rupees and a train ticket.[49] We can call this childlike faith and trust in the Father. The intimacy of Jesus helped her to believe blindly in divine providence. The teaching of Jesus on trust in God, as narrated in the St. Matthew's Gospel, she fully and literally practiced in her life: "Do not be anxious. . . Your heavenly Father knows that you need them all. But seek first his kingdom and his righteousness, and all these things shall be yours as well" (Mt.6:31-33).

In the life of Mother Teresa there were situations leading to financial stringency. To be responsible, as she was, for houses in different parts of the world, and all the activities

---

[49] Cf. F. Zambonini, *Teresa of Calcutta: A Pencil in God's Hand*, p. 34.

associated with them, as well as for an ever-growing number of Sisters at different stages in their formation, without any fixed income or source of revenue, would make most people worry.[50] But with her deep trust in divine providence she overcame all these economical struggles.[51]

Towards the end of her life her prestige and international reputation opened all doors for her, but we must remember that she began her work with only five rupees. From a vagabond she had been transformed into an entrepreneur of charity. Millions of dollars passed through her hands, but she did not permit anyone to collect funds in her name. She trusted and waited for the helping hand of God through some human beings. Many thought that after her death all her work would collapse, and they used to ask her what would happen to her congregation after her death. Trusting in God's providence she used to answer that, if it is a work of God, He will take care of it.[52]

With great trust in God she totally depended on divine providence for her own maintenance, for the members of her congregation and for the poor people who were entrusted

---

[50] Cf. M. Muggeridge, *Something Beautiful for God: Mother Teresa of Calcutta*, p. 19.

[51] An incident from her life would suffice at this point: A sister telephoned from Agra to say that a children's home which would cost 50,000 rupees was desperately needed there. Mother Teresa was compelled to tell her that because of lack of funds it was impossible. The telephone rang again shortly afterwards, however, to inform her that she had been awarded the Magsaysay Award from Philippines. The award money amounted to some 50,000 rupees. So she called back to the sister to tell her that God must want a children's home in Agra (K. SPINK, *Mother Teresa: An Authorised Biography*, p. 94).

[52] Cf. F. Zambonini, *Teresa of Calcutta: A Pencil in God's Hand*, pp. xiii, 34.

to her care. The members of the congregation and the institutions increased day by day, but she had no problem of getting the funds to maintain them. Materials and money poured in according to the need.[53] She never accepted money for what was not needed for her immediate purpose. She did not accumulate money, thinking about the future, but always trusted in divine providence. An author narrates an incident whereby Mother Teresa sent back the money received as security fund for her congregation: "Once she actually sent back a check for $500.00 because of a stipulation that the money was to be a security fund for her Missionaries of Charity. Since the very poor do not have security funds, neither would she. God would provide."[54] She exposed a life with freedom from the worries of the future, which she left in the hands of God; her field of action was the present.[55]

Her poverty did not allow having any government assistance, church subsidies, salaries or fixed income. She

---

[53] Cf. S. Vazhakala, *Life with Mother Teresa*, Servant Books, Ohio 2004, p. 109. (Fr. Sebastian Vazhakala. M. C. was the first priest ordained as a Missionaries of Charity. He has thirty years of friendship with Mother Teresa. He is Co-founder and Superior General of the Missionaries of Charity contemplative brothers and priests and founder and spiritual director of the lay Missionaries of Charity). There was the time in the life of Mother Teresa when there appeared to be no food with which to feed seven thousand people who were expected for the next two days. For some unanticipated reason the Government closed down the schools for those days, and all the bread that would have been provided for the schoolchildren was sent to the Missionaries of Charity for their seven thousand dependants (K. SPINK, *Mother Teresa: An Authorised Biography*, p. 94).

[54] J. L. Gonzalez – Balado, *Always the Poor: Mother Teresa Her Life and Message*, p. 9.

[55] Cf. E. Le Joly, *Mother Teresa: Messenger of God's Love*, p. 165.

lived without worrying about the future, leaving everything in the hands of God and living with a total trust in God's care. On one occasion when she saw something was going against this conviction, she announced publicly:

> We do not accept any government assistance or church subsidies, salaries or fixed income. The birds of the air and the flowers of the field do not have an income, but God takes care of them. Therefore, will not God also take care of us, who are more important than flowers and birds?[56]

Once as she came out of a government office, reporters asked her whether the government gave any money for her project. Her answer was: "God will provide". This was an act of faith. It meant God could provide for somebody through the instrumentality of the government making a grant for the purpose. But she knew what she meant, as she did not prefer to take government grants. "God will provide", if it is for the glory of God; in case it does not happen that way, then it is the sign that God does not want that particular work; better then to forget about it.[57] Once she said:

---

[56] Mother Teresa spoke these words to the people who collected modern equipments and home furnishings for the new house of MCs at San Francisco. First she made them remove all those things then she spoke through the microphone. Gjon Sinishta narrated this incident to the writer F. Zambonini and the writer quoted in his book (F. Zambonini, *Teresa of Calcutta: A Pencil in God's Hand*, pp. 120 – 121). This was the same answer she gave to those who asked what would happen to the Missionaries of Charity after her death: "If it is a work of God, He will take care of it. Otherwise it is just as well that it should disappear" (*ibid.*, p. xiii).

[57] Cf. E. Le Joly, *Mother Teresa: The Glorious Years*, St. Paul's, Mumbai 1998, pp. 101-102.

> We and the poor will depend entirely on divine providence both for material and spiritual needs.[58]

3.2. Free from Anxieties Over Money

Trusting in divine providence, Mother Teresa bothered least about money matters for the continuation of her work. It was not only at the initial stage of her founding a new congregation but even after fifteen years her attitude with regard to money problems remains the same. It is clear from one of her dialogues with Edward Le Joly and narrated in his book *We do it for Jesus*:

> Money, Father, I never think of it. It always comes. The Lord sends it. We do His work; he provides the means. If He does not give us the means that shows that He does not want the work. So why worry?[59]

Again after fifteen years, her attitude is the same, as is clear from her conversation with the same author on another occasion. As he was enquiring about the progress of her work, Mother Teresa explained that money never becomes

---

[58] Mother Teresa, *A Life for God*, compiled by L. Neff, p. 214; Mother Teresa, *Essential Writings*, selected with an introduction, J. Maalouf, Orbis Books, Maryknoll, New York 2001, p. 23.

[59] Mother Teresa spoke these words to E. Le Joly during the conversation and he quoted in his book (E. Le Joly, *We Do it for Jesus: Mother Teresa and the Missionaries of Charity*, p. 104). The author narrates an incident: "When Mr. Thomas, the chairman of Hindustan Lever came to see Mother Teresa, to offer her a property in Bombay, he first asked her: 'Mother, how is your work financed?' She answered him very gently: 'Mr. Thomas, who sent you here?' 'I felt an urge inside me…' 'Well, other people like you come to see me and say the same; that is my budget. It was clear: God sent you, Mr Thomas, as he sends Mr X., Mrs Y., Miss Z., and they provide the material means we need for our work. The grace of God is what moved you. God sees to our needs, as Jesus promised'" (*Ibid.*).

a problem for her work, as she always does God's work, and if God does not provide money, it is the sign that God does not want that particular work. He enquired about whether she has any financial problems. She answered:

> Money? I never give it a thought. It always comes. We do all our work for our Lord; He must look after us. If He wants something to be done, He must give us the means. If He does not provide us with the means, then it shows that He does not want that particular work. I forget about it.[60]

With total trust in divine providence and conviction, on money matters, Mother Teresa succeeded very well. It was never heard that any of her work was blocked or not realised in time due to lack of money. Instead, God provided her needed money in due time through somebody. She got donations for her work and she spent them for the service of the poorest of poor, as it was her motto.

On 15.1.1986 Fr C.J. Schwalm, Pastor of Our Lady of the Airways parish – so called because the Toronto airport is in his parish – came to Calcutta. He had brought a check of $3400, a gift from his parishioners. As Mother was absent he gave it to Sister Priscilla, who had been in charge in the U.S. and was accustomed to big donations. She casually put the cheque aside. On another day, the morning paper announced that an American lady who had been a librarian in Oklahoma, and widowed for many years, had left her savings of $ 300,000 to Mother.[61] The more she got the more she gave, and the more she gave the more she received.

---

[60] *Ibid.*, p. 164; cf. J. L. Gonzalez – Balado, *Stories of Mother Teresa: Her Smile and Her Words*, p. 70.

[61] Cf. E. Le Joly, *Mother Teresa: The Glorious Years*, pp. 96-97.

Thousands wanted to be associated with her charitable work: there was a halo surrounding it.[62]

For Mother Teresa, lack of money never became an obstacle in starting up a new house anywhere in the world. She never bothered about it and went ahead with the same trust as when she began her work with five rupees. Once her sisters wrote to her saying that she was welcome to start a house in a particular place, but could not expect any financial aid from the bishop, as he was very poor. In this case, again, Mother expresses her strong trust in divine providence and lack of bother about money. She answered:

> That never stands in the way. We shall get help from elsewhere. Lack of money is never an obstacle; we do not consider it. We went to New Guinea because the Bishop is poor and the people are poor. We have opened four houses there already. The work progresses very well.[63]

3.3. Totally Free from the Possession of Money

Mother Teresa was a living model of poverty. During her lifetime, all who came into contact with her were taken up by her simplicity and poverty. Detachment from money and handling money without actually possessing it are the outstanding features of her poverty. She used to teach this to her sisters through her instructions.[64]

---

[62] Cf. *Ibid.*, p. 104.

[63] Mother Teresa spoke these words to E. Le Joly during the conversation and he quoted in his book (E. Le Joly, *Mother Teresa: Messenger of God's Love*, p. 134).

[64] It is stated in her instructions to her sisters: "Let me tell you something. When I go out, my drawers are all completely empty. And when I come back, I ask for what I need, 'May I have'. May I have a pad to write or may I have a pencil or a pen etc. Why? Because I am a Sister and I have made my vow of poverty and I am bound to live it. I must live it. I made my vow to God alone

When the government of India sent two men from New Delhi to have an inspection as to what Mother Teresa had done with all the money she received, she expressed her detachment from money plainly. She showed them all the records and then she said to them:

> I will tell you more. I have nothing. When I go out somewhere I go to this Sister (Sister Camilus was with her) and I ask, 'May I have'. In my room there is nothing. Open everything, there is nothing there. Not because I can't have, but because I choose not to have – for greater love, like Jesus, having all things, being rich became poor.[65]

Moreover, there was no stipend, salary or pocket money for Mother. It shows that she had not even a single penny over which she had full authority.[66] Whatever she used was for the congregation and necessarily accountable.

4. CRITERIA TO ACCEPT DONATIONS AND GIFTS

Mother Teresa offered to the world a special teaching through her life in the field of practicing poverty as in the matter of accepting donations and gifts. In other words, the criteria for accepting donations and gifts should not water down the religious poverty of one's own religious order. There is a tendency among the religious who have taken the vow of poverty that all free gifts and donations can be accepted because while accepting such gifts they are not spending any money so it is not against the vow of poverty to accept it. Accumulating more than they need, they

---

and I live it for Him. I never take money without asking. The moment I arrive, I put everything on Sister Camilus' desk and I have nothing with me." (*Mother's Instructions: Let Us Make Our Society Something Beautiful for God,* Vol.1, p. 61).

[65] *Ibid.*, Vol. 2, p. 72.

[66] Cf. S. Vazhakala, *Life with Mother Teresa*, p. 109.

therefore give an impression of living in luxury. Mother Teresa had fixed certain criteria by which she controlled the mitigation of religious poverty. It is a lesson for all religious who have taken the vow of poverty. There are mainly three elements in the criteria for accepting donations and free gifts as such: (1) do not accept any object that is not needed immediately; (2) there should be no campaigns for money, but spontaneous donations are always acceptable; (3) donations should not be from superfluous funds.

4.1. Do not Accept the Object that is not Needed Immediately

By her life style and the way she rejected certain free gifts and donations, even if it was a good amount, she taught a lesson not to accept any object that is not needed immediately. Nor should there be accumulation of gifts with reference to the future or with the intention of selling. There are number of examples of this in her life. I should like to mention two.

It happened in 1985 that the novices and tertians in Calcutta became so numerous that the Mother-House and the house in Park Street were overcrowded. There was an urgent need of another house. A rich lady offered a house she owned on Park Street that would have been ideally located, being close to the other two houses of formation. But the grand style of the house and its location were judged by Mother to be unfit for training nuns, who would have to live, and work, and pray, during their whole life, among the poor. So the property was not accepted. Nor did Mother think of accepting it to sell it or exchange it for another more suitable one, something that might have pained the owner. If Mother Teresa did not need an object, she did not accept it, which was her style. When it was needed, the Lord would provide it.[67] In the same year a Buddhist lady donated to Mother a property at Tindheria, in the hills of Darjeeling district. It was a nice house with very good furniture and extensive grounds, worth 100,000 dollars. Mother was not willing to accept the donation, because she already had five houses in the diocese and there was not much work among the poor people in that particular area.[68]

4.2. No Campaigns for Money, but Spontaneous Donations are Acceptable

With the intention to avoid unnecessary accumulation, to stand firm in radical poverty and to teach the people to give something that touches their hearts she avoided organised begging or any campaigns or any sales of articles to collect funds. She encouraged the people to make spontaneous donations out of sacrifices, a gift that comes from the heart of the giver.[69] Once in an interview she expressed this matter clearly:

> I always insist on people doing the work with us, and for us, and for the people. I never speak to them of money or ask for things from them. I just ask them to come and love the people, to give their hands to serve them and their hearts to love them.[70]

---

[67] Cf. E. Le Joly, *Mother Teresa: The Glorious Years*, p. 102.

[68] Cf. *Ibid.*, p. 96.

[69] Cf. *Ibid.*, p. 100. In particular, she banned fund-raising: "I want to make it very clear I do not want our co-Workers to be involved in fund raising. . . . Let us avoid publicity under that fund raising name because it has become like a target with other organizations and people are beginning to doubt, and so let us not give them a chance."(K. Spink, *Mother Teresa: An Authorised Biography*, p. 135).

[70] Mother Teresa spoke these words to Malcolm Muggeridge in an interview and he quoted in his book (M. Muggeridge, *Something Beautiful for God: Mother Teresa of Calcutta*, p. 96).

On fund-raising her vision was to raise money of love in the sense of giving people an opportunity to love people, and she rejected the term "fund-raising group" for her mission. She said:

> We are not a fund-raising group nor are we begging people to give us money. We are giving people an opportunity to love people: it is a chance given to them. I could like more people to give their hands to serve and their hearts to love – to recognize the poor in their own homes, towns, and countries, and to reach out to them in love and compassion giving where it is most needed.[71]

Even in the midst of financial struggles she did not encourage the collection of money through campaigns. She did not want to make her works the means for the collection of money. Instead she trusted in divine providence. She encouraged people to make spontaneous donations out of love of God. Once she expressed this in the words: "Not even in the early times did I ever ask for money. I wanted to serve the poor exclusively out of love for God."[72]

4.3. Donations should not be from Superfluous Funds

The third element in the criteria of accepting the donation according to Mother Teresa is donations should not be from superfluous funds. The mental disposition of the donor while giving the donation is important for both parties. She did not encourage giving or receiving from any one from excess funds. The particular gift should come from the donor as a fruit of sacrifice. In other words it should cost the donor by

---

[71] These words of Mother Teresa was collected by E. Le Joly and quoted in his book (E. LE Joly, *Mother Teresa: A Women in Love*, Ave Maria Press, Notre Dame, Indiana 1993, p. 108.

[72] Mother teresa Of Calcutta, *The Blessings of Love*, ed. N. Sabbag, Servant Publications, Michigan 1996, p. 56.

giving a little pain which touches his life. This disposition enables the donor to receive spiritual benefits from the act of giving.[73]

Mother Teresa received very many gifts and donations in this spirit. One such donation she received from a beggar. She considered the contribution of the beggar a great sacrifice, for he had to sit in the sun all day and whatever he had received he contributed for the service of the poor. She narrates:

> I was once walking down the street and a beggar came to me and he said, 'Mother Teresa, everybody's giving to you, I also want to give to you. Today, for the whole day, I got only twenty-nine paise and I want to give it to you'. . . .if I don't take it I will hurt him. So I put out my hands and I took the money.[74]

She narrated the story of another contribution received in the spirit of sacrifice, which she considered of great value. A newly married couple came to her with the money they had saved by making their marriage celebration very simple. They gave all the money they had saved to Mother Teresa.

---

[73] Cf. E. Le Joly, *We do it for Jesus: Mother Teresa and the Missionaries of Charity*, p. 105; also cf. E. Le Joly, *Mother Teresa: The Glorious Years*, p. 105; cf. F. Zambonini, *Teresa of Calcutta: A Pencil in God's Hand*, p. xiii; cf. M. Muggeridge, *Something Beautiful for God: Mother Teresa of Calcutta*, p. 95; cf. K. Spink, *Mother Teresa: A Complete Authorised Biography*, p. 135.

[74] Mother Teresa, *A Simple Path*, Compiled by L. Vardey, p. 100. Once she described the contribution of that beggar as valued much more than the Nobel Prize: "In my heart I felt that the poor man had given me more than the Nobel Prize because he gave me all he had. In all probability, no one gave him anything else that night and he went to bed hungry" (J. L. Gonzalez – Balado, *Stories of Mother Teresa: Her Smile and Her Words*, p. 21).

She expressed her sentiments about this contribution in the following ways:

> They were sharing their love with the poor. Something like this happens every day. By becoming poor ourselves, by loving until it hurts, we become capable of loving more deeply, more beautifully, more wholly.[75]

She not only received contributions in the above spirit of sacrifice but also gave in the same spirit. One day, while she was walking along the streets of Calcutta, a priest came up to her asking her to give a contribution for a collection for promoting some worthy project. That morning she had left the house with all the money she had, five rupees, which amounted to about thirty cents. During the day, she had spent four on the poor. She had only one rupee to live on the next day and the following days if something didn't happen. Trusting in God, she gave her last rupee to that priest.[76]

---

[75] Mother Teresa, *A Simple Path*, Compiled by L. Vardey, p. 101; cf. K. Spink, *Mother Teresa: A Complete Authorised Biography*, pp. 135-136. Mother Teresa once shared an experience from her life to clarify this view: "Some time ago, we in Calcutta underwent a period when sugar was very scarce: Somehow the story spread that Mother Teresa had no sugar for her orphans. A child said to his parents, 'For three days I won't eat sugar: what I save I want to give to Mother Teresa.' So his parents, who had never been to our house, brought the child with a can of sugar. He was four years old and could barely speak, but that small child had a great love: he loved with sacrifice" (Mother Teresa, *Heart of Joy: The Transforming Power of Self-Giving*, ed. J. L. González – Balado, p. 35).

[76] Cf. Mother Teresa spoke about this incident in a conversation with R. Allegri and he quoted in his book (R. Allegri, *Teresa of the Poor: The Story of Her Life*, p. 64).

5. HER LIFE STYLE AS WITNESS TO HER RELIGIOUS POVERTY

Mother Teresa chose a lifestyle for herself and for the congregation that was very simple and austere for two reasons: (a) To identify with Jesus, that others might become rich out of that poverty, and (b) To have conformity with the kind of apostolate she and her congregation members were called to undertake. She wanted the poorest of the poor to feel at home with the Missionaries of Charity.[77]

Life examples of Mother Teresa are equal to volumes of books, as her every action came through with conviction and always provided a lesson for others, whoever came in touch with her. In this section we are going to see how her simple lifestyle became witness to her religious poverty, in such matters as personal appearance, food, manner of travelling, readiness to live with minimum conveniences, and her most humble gestures.

5.1. Simplicity in Personal Appearance

A) Dress: A white cotton sari with blue border covering the head serving as the veil has become the symbol by which to recognise Mother Teresa and her sisters all over the world. After leaving the Loreto congregation and going out to start a new congregation, with her new vision she embraced the life style of the very poor. She left the traditional religious habit and adapted it, wearing a cotton sari, a cheaper style of dress,[78] as worn by poor Indian women. Besides that her

---

[77] Cf. S. Vazhakala, *Life with Mother Teresa*, p. 108.

[78] Cf. F. Zambonini, *Teresa of Calcutta: A Pencil in God's Hand*, p. ix. The sari which Mother Teresa used to wear costs only $ 1.00 (J. L. Gonzalez – Balado, *Always the Poor: Mother Teresa Her Life and Message*, p. 86); the fabric of her sari was the cheapest she could find (Cf. K. Spink, *Mother Teresa: A Complete Authorised*

saris had a blue border, which is the sign of the uniform of the women who carry the night soil in the city of Calcutta. These women are considered very poor and of the lower class in society, according to the nature of their work. In India a person with a western background and lifestyle coming down to the standard of these women who are the lowest class of society is something unimaginable. Above all, the transition from a 38 year old Irish nun to an Indian nun dressed as a humble woman, shows a perfect transformation.[79] While explaining the reason for choosing the white cotton sari, made of the poorest fabric, as the habit for her and Sisters in the MCs, she said:

> The sari allows the Sisters to feel poor among the poor, to identify with the sick, with the children, with the homeless aging, and to share in the way of life of the dispossessed of this world by sharing in the same dress.[80]

Again, the number of the clothes she had was kept to a very minimum. Mother had just three sets of clothes, one of which was used only on Sundays and special occasions.[81]

B) Sandals: She always wore thin sandals on her naked feet, which was another quality of simplicity in her life style.[82]

Biography, p. 31; cf. M. Muggeridge, *Something Beautiful for God: Mother Teresa of Calcutta*, p. 5).

[79] Cf. E. Le Joly, *Mother Teresa: The Glorious Years*, p. 76; cf. F. Zambonini, *Teresa of Calcutta: A Pencil in God's Hand*, p. 34.

[80] Mother Teresa explained these to J. Gonzalez and he quoted in his book (J. L. Gonzalez – Balado, *Always the Poor: Mother Teresa Her Life and Message*, p. 24); cf. M. Muggeridge, *Something Beautiful for God: Mother Teresa of Calcutta*, p. 10.

[81] Cf. S. Vazhakala, *Life with Mother Teresa*, p. 109; cf. Mother Teresa, *No Greater Love*, ed. B. Benenate and J. Durepos, New World Library, California 1997, p. 55.

[82] Cf. F. Zambonini, *Teresa of Calcutta: A Pencil in God's Hand*, p. ix ; also cf. E. Le Joly, *Mother Teresa: The Glorious Years*, p. 76.

The greatness of simplicity is not in wearing the sandals but in the person who wears them and what her background was previously. In India, women who live in rural areas usually use sandals. In urban areas they may use them only inside the house. In the case of Mother Teresa, who came from western culture and background and, above all, as a Loreto nun, adopting this standard is something to be appreciated greatly.

C) Bag: A shopping bag with wooden handles is another peculiarity of Mother Teresa's.[83] In this modern world there are many varieties of vanity bags, brief cases, suit cases etc., available, and there is a natural tendency of human beings to use these convenient things with rather good appearance. But Mother Teresa went around the world with this shopping bag, again demonstrating her simplicity and poverty.

Mother Teresa appeared everywhere in the same style of dress whether to receive the Nobel prize or to do some service among the poorest of the poor. Dressed in a white sari with a border of three blue stripes and a small crucifix on the left shoulder, wearing a grey sweater against the cold and thin sandals on her naked feet, and carrying a cloth shopping-bag with wooden handles – that is how Mother Teresa arrived in Oslo to receive the Nobel prize and in New York to open a house for AIDS patients. That is also the way in which she appeared on the podium at the United Nations headquarters and amid the ruins of Beirut. In thousands of photographs she always looks the same, whether in the slums of a large city or in the offices and residences of the powerful and wealthy.[84]

---

[83] Cf. F. Zambonini, *Teresa of Calcutta: A Pencil in God's Hand*, p. ix, 31; cf. J. L. Gonzalez – Balado, *Stories of Mother Teresa: Her Smile and Her Words*, p. 69.

[84] Cf. F. Zambonini, *Teresa of Calcutta: A Pencil in God's Hand*, p. ix.

An author once remarked on the simplicity and humility in the appearance of Mother Teresa and its consequent impression created in whoever came into contact with her. He states: "The simplicity and humility of Mother Teresa is always impressive. She radiates the indescribable inner happiness of Jesus' presence everywhere, from the moment of first contact."[85]

5.2. Simplicity in the Food

"My food is to do the will of him who sent me, and to accomplish his work" (Jn.4:34). Jesus expressed this to the disciples as they brought food for Him. The disciples wondered, when they brought food to Jesus to eat, why He did not show any interest. The intimacy with the Father and enthusiasm to do the will of the Father lessened the interest towards the material needs in the life of Jesus. It is the same with anyone who is a devoted follower of Jesus and ever ready to do His will. Material needs are given secondary importance, even one's own food. The practice of restricting oneself to simplicity in food is to experience poverty as poor people do, a kind of sacrifice in order to be more effective in the mission. This sense of sacrifice of food is not easily understood by secular people. Mother Teresa once expressed this view:

> To the world, it seems foolish that we delight in poor food, that we relish rough and insipid bulgur (wheat).[86]

There was simplicity and practice of poverty in the matter of food so as to identify with the poor.[87] But Mother Teresa

---

[85] J. L. Gonzalez - Balado, *Stories of Mother Teresa: Her Smiles and Her Words*, p. 70.

[86] Mother teresa, *No Greater Love*, ed. B. Benenate and J. Durepos, p. 55.

[87] Cf. M. Muggeridge, *Something Beautiful for God: Mother Teresa of Calcutta*, p. 10.

worked very hard. She ate very little and her food was almost devoid of fats. Her nourishment consisted of rice and vegetables; she drank water or tea; she did not sleep more than three hours a night, taking time from rest in order to work, to think of the Sisters, to answer letters, to do whatever was necessary. She never ate or drank anything outside the convent, even when she was on a long journey; and she never accepted anything in the places she visited. Toward this behaviour she was of the opinion that it was done out of respect for the poor.[88]

Mother Teresa chose a very simple style of food for her and for the members of her congregation, but always ensured that it should be sufficient to sustain one in one's daily duties. The testimony of Father Sebastian Vazhakala, MC, who was closely related with her for 30 years and was the co-founder of the Contemplative Brothers, confirms that the simplicity and keen attention not to waste food gives us a better understanding of Mother Teresa: "The food was very simple but sufficient to sustain the members to do their difficult work. Many times I observed Mother at the table. She ate very naturally, without making any fuss and choosing. She picked up small particles of bread from her plate . . . she knew that many people die each day because of malnutrition or starvation." [89]

5.3. Simplicity in the Manner of Traveling

Mother Teresa always used the cheapest means of travel possible.[90] She usually travelled by train in third class, lower

---

[88] Cf. F. Zambonini, *Teresa of Calcutta: A Pencil in God's Hand*, pp. xii-xiii, 135.

[89] S. Vazhakala, MC, *Life with Mother Teresa*, pp. 108-109.

[90] Cf. *Ibid.*, p. 109; cf. M. Muggeridge, *Something Beautiful for God: Mother Teresa of Calcutta*, p. 5.

class.[91] In India to travel this class is almost a penance because compartments are so crowded that there one cannot even find a place to stand. Though she enjoyed a free pass granted her by the Railway Minister to travel in the higher class, she liked to travel with the poor and experience their inconveniences. Indira Gandhi, former prime minister of India, gave Mother a free pass for the Indian Airlines, but she used it only in unavoidable circumstances.[92]

When travelling around the world, Mother Teresa always carried a coarse cotton bag containing everything she might need, which was very little. Even though there was nothing of value in that little bag, she cared for it because it was made by her favourite children, the lepers. She never carried books, agendas and briefcases with her. She always travelled the world in complete poverty and evangelical simplicity.[93]

She travelled everywhere without money, cheques or currency. Her friends and co-workers met her at the airports with their cars. She had no money in her bag. She managed

---

[91] Cf. K. Spink, *Mother Teresa: An authorised Biography*, p. 92; cf. Mother Teresa, *No Greater Love*, ed. B. Benenate and J. Durepos, p. 55.

[92] Cf. E. LE Joly, *We Do it for Jesus: Mother Teresa and the Missionaries of Charity*, p. 115; cf. M. Muggeridge, *Something Beautiful for God: Mother Teresa of Calcutta*, P. 5.

[93] Cf. R. Allegri, *Teresa of the Poor: The Story of Her Life*, pp.103, 119. Her simplicity in the style of travelling impressed many. An author writes of one such experience: "I was deeply impressed one time when Mother Teresa arrived at the Belgian National Airport in Zaventem. She had been in Rome and the only baggage she carried was a small hand bag and a cardboard box which served as a suit case" (O. Tanghe, *For the Least of My Brothers: The Spirituality of Mother Teresa and Catherine Doherty*, translated by J. Mac Donald, Alba House, New York 1989, p. 29).

her affairs by the generosity of others. Everywhere she was treated as a VIP.[94]

She did not prefer to call a 'coolie' to carry the luggage. In India at railway stations and bus stands there are no facilities of small self-driven carts as we see in western countries. So travellers have to depend on the coolies, who do this work for payment. Once mother expressed this fact very frankly: "We carry all our goods ourselves," said Mother, laughing. "They call us the coolie-sisters, because we always do without porters."[95]

In this regard Father Julien Henry shared an experience with E. Le Jolly. In February 1978, Mother went to the Calcutta docks to take delivery of a lorry-load of bales of goods donated by friends for the poor. She drove back through the streets of Calcutta, sitting on top as the local workmen do. This was no mean feat for a lady in her late sixties. Wrapped in her white sari, uncomfortably perched atop bales of goods, praying to her Lord Jesus Christ, she formed a truly Franciscan picture.[96]

A similar incident happened in Tirana, Albania, on the vigil of Easter in 1991. Mother Teresa had just received a shipment of sacks of rice from Caritas, but the truck was too big to enter the Ali Pasha quarter where she had recently opened a house. With the help of some officials from the Italian Embassy, a plan was worked out: the huge truck could

---

[94] Cf. E. Le Joly, *Mother Teresa: The Glorious Years*, p. 96.

[95] Mother Teresa expressed these words to E. Le Joly and he quoted in his book (E. Le Joly, *We Do it for Jesus: Mother Teresa and the Missionaries of Charity*, p. 173).

[96] Fr. Julien Henry narrated this incident to E. Le Joly and he quoted in his book (Cf. E. Le Joly, *Mother Teresa: Messenger of God's Love*, p. 50).

be parked in front of the Embassy and a smaller truck would shuttle back and forth with the bags of rice. Mother Teresa supervised the transfer to the smaller truck and then climbed up on top and travelled with it.[97]

5.4. Readiness to Live with Minimum Facilities

Mother Teresa had everything in her religious life as a Loreto nun, but as she accepted the special call of Jesus to serve the poorest of the poor she forced herself to live with minimum facilities for the love of the poor so as to identify with them and to experience their difficulties of life. She stripped herself first, lived a life as simple as possible, with minimum belongings. Time and again in the early days she went hungry so that others could eat, or she gave people the little money she had and silently walked home instead of riding. On certain occasions she begged Micheal Gomes, the owner of the house where she stayed at the beginning of her mission, to get some food for her as she was so hungry. She lived in that house with the minimum furniture and house articles.[98]

She was even ready to live in a small hut and never bother about a better convenience. Once at Casilina Street, Roma, she was lodged in a small hut at the rear of the kitchen garden; perhaps it was once a chicken-coop.[99] She was satisfied with bare facilities so long as she could do her work. Her parlour, where very many VIPs were welcomed and

---

[97] Cf. F. Zambonini, *Teresa of Calcutta: A Pencil in God's Hand*, p. 50.

[98] Cf. J. Moniz, *No Greater Service: Mother and the Mahatma*, Better Yourself Books, Mumbai 1998, p. 60; also cf. K. Spink, *Mother Teresa: An Authorised Biography*, p. 38.

[99] Cf. F. Zambonini, *Teresa of Calcutta: A Pencil in God's Hand*, p.140.

had conversation with her, was very simple. It was a tiny room with a small table and simple wooden chairs.[100]

In the chapel she always sat down on the floor and never bothered about a chair or any other furniture to sit on.[101] After her death someone donated a statue of Mother Teresa in the squatting position, and the sisters placed it in the chapel at General house, Calcutta, in the same place where she used to sit on the floor for the prayer and other ceremonies. Now, whoever goes to see her tomb can see this statue in the chapel.[102] It is one of the signs of her simplicity. This simplicity was appreciated by many. In the chapel there is no furniture except the simple and neat altar.[103] Certainly one can understand that this simplicity in the arrangement of the chapel was directed by her.

---

[100] Cf. E. Le Joly, *We Do it for Jesus: Mother Teresa and the Missionaries of Charity*, 10; also cf. E. Le Joly, *Mother Teresa: Messenger of God's Love*, p. 168.

[101] Cf. F. Zambonini, *Teresa of Calcutta: A Pencil in God's Hand*, p. 4.

[102] When I visited the tomb of Mother Teresa in the Chapel of MC's General house, Calcutta, sisters explained this matter to me, as I showed interest in knowing about the beautiful statue placed at the back of their chapel.

[103] Cf. M. Muggeridge, *Something Beautiful for God: Mother Teresa of Calcutta*, p. 23; cf. R. Hess, *Passage Way to Heaven*, Sacred Heart League, walls 1987, p. 12. Susan Conroy, after spending many days with Mother Teresa and her Sisters, writes a testimony about their simplicity in following manner: "The chapel was a simple and beautiful place. There were no pews, chairs, or cushions. Everything in Mother Teresa's life seemed to be stripped down to the bare essentials. Each day, dozens of volunteers and hundreds of Sisters would gather in prayer. We would remove our sandals and enter the chapel barefoot" (S. Conroy, *Mother Teresa's Lessons of Love and Secrets of Sanctity*, p. 112).

Though she was the founder and superior general she never enjoyed special facilities in the community but lived just like any other sister in the community. She had no reserved seat in the chapel in spite of her position in the congregation, but sat or knelt on the floor. Usually in the religious communities the mother superior is revered, served, and treated in a special way. She considered herself equal to her fellow sisters, equal even to the newly arrived postulants and novices.[104] Once in an interview in answer to a question on this topic, she said: "I am a sister just like the others."[105]

Mother Teresa refused, on principle, to make any of her works of charity into an institution. For example, she refused to have hospitals. In her home for the dying in Calcutta she refused to employ a full-time doctor and was happy simply to have the free service of one or two doctors who volunteered to come. She never allowed modern equipment in her homes, even a simple microscope, which could have been useful for the rapid diagnosis of certain sicknesses. In her eyes this would have been the first step toward the establishment of an institution for sick people. And in future the institution would then become more important than the patients. Later, it might have followed that certain cases would be rejected according to the criteria of curability of diseases and the economic means of the person.[106] Even in the midst of work load she never appointed a personal

---

[104] Cf. R. Allegri, *Teresa of the Poor: The Story of Her Life*, p. 84.

[105] Mother Teresa replied to R. Allegri in an interview when he asked her whether she keeps up the regular time table of other sisters in her community (*Ibid.*, p. 79).

[106] Cf. J. L. Gonzalez - Balado, *Stories of Mother Teresa*, pp. 90-91; cf. P. Chetcuti, *Choosing to Serve the Destitute*, p. 15.

secretary with typewriter to do correspondence work for her. She wrote most of her letters in her own hand.[107]

Mother Teresa always refused the admittance of material comforts in her homes. Once she vigorously expressed this matter to Father E. Le Joly:

> Some priests would like me to change things. For example, they have told me we ought to hang curtains in the communal rooms. I do not want them; the poor we serve have none. Most of the nuns come from peasant homes, where there are none either. They ought not to have more comfortable lives here than they had in their own homes.[108]

She voluntarily accepted inconveniences in order to help others by sacrificing her little comforts. One such incident is noted in her diary and later recorded by her spiritual director:

> Met N., who said there was nothing to eat at home. I gave him the fare for my tram, all the money I had, and walked home.[109]

5.5. Lowliest Acts

Performing the humblest act is one of the fruits of evangelical poverty. Out of humility one becomes ready to do any menial job willingly and joyfully, as Jesus being the master washed the feet of the disciples and proved his readiness to come

---

[107] Cf. M. Muggeridge, *Something Beautiful for God: Mother Teresa of Calcutta*, p. 19.

[108] Mother Teresa expressed these words to E. Le Joly and D. Porter took this and then quoted in his book (D. Porter, *Mother Teresa: The Early years*, SPCK, London 1986, p. 80).

[109] This is a diary note of Mother Teresa recorded by her spiritual director in his writings and the author quoted in his book (D. Porter, *Mother Teresa: The Early Years*, p. 70).

down to the level of a servant. In the life of Mother Teresa we can find very many such occasions whereby she won over the hearts of others by her humble acts. Even after she had become internationally famous she kept up this style.

She was a model for others in doing menial jobs. She used to lead the way by pulling up her sleeves, washing, cleaning the convent toilet, salving and bandaging wounds, washing the dirty and smelly bodies of lepers.[110]

One Sister remembers an action of Mother Teresa that taught her a lesson for her entire life. As a newcomer she had found the toilet dirty one day and had hidden herself away in disgust. Mother Teresa happened to pass by without seeing the Sister. She immediately rolled up her sleeves and took a broom and cleaned the toilet herself.[111]

Loading and unloading the truck is one of her lowliest services noted by some of her biographers. As mentioned earlier in 1991 at Tirana, Albania, as she received food materials from Caritas and trucks were unloading, she joined with the workers to unload the sacks of rice from the truck. We can imagine in her advanced age how much she could do. Here the point for us to reflect on is her readiness to pitch in at any level. International awards and reaching up to the height of success did not in any way relieve her from doing menial jobs, even loading and unloading the materials from the truck.[112]

---

[110] Cf. J. L. Gonzalez – Balado, *Always the Poor: Mother Teresa Her Life and Message*, p. 82.

[111] Cf. K. Spink, *Mother Teresa: An Authorised Biography*, p. 48.

[112] Cf. F. Zambonini, *Teresa of Calcutta: A Pencil in God's Hand*, p. 50.

Jesus became a servant of all as a sign of his poverty. He washed the feet of his disciples (cf. Jn.13: 5-12); he made clay by his own hand to give sight to a blind (cf. Jn.9:6); he begged food to feed the hungry (cf. Mt.14:16-18), touched the sick people (cf. Mt. 9:29) and became friendly with all, irrespective of their status. We can find these humble services of Jesus in the life of Mother Teresa.

She washed feet, like Jesus; she bathed sores and bandaged wounds like the good Samaritan; she pressed babies to her heart as Christ did; she lifted up the cripple; she visited the slums; she begged for the hungry and the sick. She experienced hunger, thirst and tiredness, all for the love of Jesus.[113]

---

[113] Cf. E. Le Joly, *We Do it for Jesus: Mother Teresa and the Missionaries of Charity*, p. 125.

CHAPTER 2

Religious Poverty and Following of Christ

In the previous chapter, the way Mother Teresa practised the religious poverty in her life was dealt with in detail. In this chapter I shall deal mainly with the teaching aspect, especially following Christ through religious poverty. This chapter is divided into four parts with subtitles. The first part deals with following the call of Christ in and through the practice of poverty. In the second part, following the life of Christ in the light of voluntary poverty is treated in detail. In the third part, her view of following the teaching of Christ through the theme of voluntary poverty is dealt with. In the fourth part, her conviction of religious poverty as an effective means for the success of the mission of Christ is emphasised.

1. FOLLOWING THE CALL OF CHRIST

The call is an invitation from one person to another person for a specific goal, with certain commands to be followed. In the religious sphere, the call comes from Christ to a person to become his disciple and participate in his salvation economy, also known as vocation. The call of Christ also involves certain demands and one of them is renunciation, which is also the basic condition of becoming a disciple of Christ. This renunciation in the life of religiously consecrated people is known as religious poverty. In this section we are going to deal with the importance of religious poverty in following the call of Christ as taught by Blessed Mother Teresa of Calcutta. We can also notice two other dimensions as objectives to be achieved when Christ calls someone to be a religious, to become holy and to achieve eternal life. Thus, there are three dimensions of objectives in the call of Christ to become a religious: discipleship, sanctification and eternal life. Voluntary poverty enables one to achieve these dimensions of the call and they are seen below.

1.1. Poverty for Discipleship

Evangelical poverty is a condition put forward by Jesus to any one who wishes to be his disciple: "None of you can be my disciple, unless he gives up all his possessions" (Lk. 14:33). A total renunciation of material things, of desire and ambition for power, of worldly honour and glory are the condition for following Him and also the condition for entering the Kingdom of God (cf. Mt. 10:23-27); that is, you must renounce your very self (cf. Lk. 9:23), sell all your possessions (cf. Lk.12: 33) in order to love Him above everything, love Him in everything and everything in Him.[1] To be a disciple of Jesus, it is necessary to have undivided love for Jesus and be detached from all earthly matters (cf. Mt. 19: 16-21). Mother Teresa narrated the example of the rich young man from the Gospel who could not respond to the invitation of Jesus to become his disciple, due to his attachment to wealth. In her words:

---

[1] Cf. *Constitutions and Directory of Contemplative Brothers*, Art. 64, p. 33.

> Let us not be like the rich young man in the Gospel. Jesus saw him and loved him and wanted him but he had given his heart to something else to his riches. He was rich, young, and strong. Jesus could not fill him.[2]

We cannot serve two masters at the same time. In order to become a disciple of Jesus, detachment from money is essential. Attachment to money may take away our love and fidelity to Jesus our master. She was convinced that money is one of the keys of the devil that will open any heart, and it is the beginning of great evil. Thus attachment to money becomes the greatest cause of destroying our joy in loving Jesus.[3]

Mother Teresa was of the opinion that once longing for money comes into our life, longing also comes for the things that it can bring into our life: the superfluous, luxury in eating, luxury in dressing, trifles etc. Our needs increase, because one thing calls the other, resulting in uncontrollable dissatisfaction in life.[4]

---

[2] Mother Teresa, *Total Surrender*, ed. A. D. Scolozzi, Servant Books, Ohio 1985, p. 51; A. D. Scolozzi, *Mother Teresa: Contemplative in the Heart of the World*, p. 66.

[3] Cf. Mother Teresa, *Thirsting for God: A Year Book of Prayers, Meditations and Anecdotes*, compiled by A. D. Scolozzi, Servant Books, Ohio 2000, p. 168.

[4] Cf. Mother Teresa, *Jesus, The Word to be Spoken*, compiled by A. D. Scolozzi, Claretian Publications, Bangalore 1999, p. 104; cf. Mother Teresa, *Total Surrender*, ed. A. D. Scolozzi, p. 56; cf. Mother Teresa, *Essential Writings*, selected with an introduction by J. Maalouf, p. 107; cf. Mother Teresa, *No Greater Love*, ed. B. Benenate and J. Durepos, p. 95; cf. Mother Teresa, *Love: A Fruit Always in Season – Daily Meditations*, ed. D. S. Hunt, Ignatius Press, San Francisco 1989, p. 180; cf. Mother Teresa, *The Love of Christ: Spiritual Counsels*, eds. G. Goree and J. Barbier, p. 106; cf. Mother Teresa, *The Joy in Loving*, compiled by J. Chalika and E. Le Joly, Viking, New Delhi 1996, p. 246; cf. A. D. Scolozzi, *Mother Teresa: Contemplative in the Heart of the World*, p. 71.

When money and material comforts increase in our life, we have less time to spend for Jesus. The increase of material goods leads us to be busy in caring and protecting these things, and this takes away our time in caring for and loving the poor. Thus we have no time to give our love to Jesus, who is present among the poor.[5]

She analyzed the reason for the decrease in religious vocations in the Church, compared to an earlier time, as the increase of comfort in life. Her reflections stress that a life of luxury becomes the cause of the lack of religious vocation. She considered the main cause for the lack of vocations in general for the religious life as due to extravagance in the life both of the lay families and religious. She said:

> I think that if today there are no vocations in the church, or if they are scarce, it is partly due to the fact that there is too much wealth, too much comfort, too high a standard of living, not only in families but even in religious life.[6]

Her reflections and consequent convictions with regard to the significance of radical poverty in religious life led her to be stricter in practicing and inspiring others to this virtue. Thus she emphasized religious poverty in her teachings and did not fail to speak of this whenever she visited a house belonging to her religious community.[7] Once when she was preparing for a trip, she gave special instructions with regard to poverty, especially to the novices, an invitation really to a life of poverty, in order to become a disciple of Jesus. She said:

---

[5] Cf. Mother Teresa, *One Heart Full of Love*, ed. J. L. González – Balado, Servant Books, Ohio 1984, p. 100.

[6] Mother Teresa, *Heart of Joy: The Transforming Power of Self-Giving*, ed. J. L. González – Balado, p. 87.

[7] Cf. E. LE Joly, *Mother Teresa: Messenger of God's Love*, p. 50.

> Strive for poverty in desires, in attachments, in tastes and distastes, for Jesus, rich as he was, became poor for our sake.[8]

She was also of the opinion that many were attracted to become living examples of Christ's poverty, a disciple of Christ in a true sense. For example, many well-off young people from all parts of the world came to India to take on a very poor life. This phenomenon was due to their desire to be free from their environment of wealth and to lead a life following the living example of Christ's poverty.[9] She expressed this view from her experience, as she received more vocations from Europe and America in this spirit of search for the genuine poverty of Christ. In an era when in general the religious vocation was deteriorating in Europe and America she received more vocations from these continents. There was also the special attraction of becoming a living example of Christ's poverty.[10]

She believed that the increasing number of vocation to the MCs was occurring, not because the young people were attracted to a life of action, but rather to the life of poverty. They were searching for a life of poverty without compromise.[11] It would be natural to assume that the activities of Mother Teresa, being so attractive, may continue to encourage modern youth to enter the MCs. There is also a possibility, however that her radical poverty may keep modern youth away from entering MCs. But from her experience, she believed the young people saw in her

---

[8] Mother Teresa, *Heart of Joy: The Transforming Power of Self-Giving,* ed. J. L. González - Balado, pp. 87, 121.

[9] Cf. *Ibid.,* p. 87.

[10] Cf. *Ibid.,* p. 88.

[11] Cf. Mother Teresa, *One Heart Full of Love,* ed. J. L. González - Balado, p. 52.

congregation a genuine life of poverty, and it became the real cause for them to request entering as a member in the religious order.[12] She expressed it in these words:

> You will be very surprised to know what these young girls write, 'I want a life of poverty, prayer, and sacrifice that will lead me to serve the poor.' It is beautiful to see how these young people give without counting the cost.[13]

The growing tendency among the younger generation in search of the genuine spirit of religious poverty was explained further with examples from her life. Once a young man from a rich family in New York came in his car to the residence of Mother Teresa and told her that he had given everything to the poor and had come to follow Christ. Thus she proved that today's youth are looking for the challenge of self denial.[14] In another instance, a rich young woman expressed her desperation in finding a genuine spirit of poverty among the religious orders, because she could not find any difference in her present life and in the life of some religious orders with regard to poverty:

> A very rich young woman wrote to me. She said, 'Jesus has been inviting me to become a religious sister for several years. I have tried to find out where Jesus wants me to go. I have seen that in some places the sisters have the same things that I have, so I would not have to give up anything.[15]

---

[12] Cf. Mother Teresa, *Heart of Joy: The Transforming Power of Self-Giving*, ed. J. L. Gonzalez-Balado, p. 122.

[13] Mother Teresa, *Loving Jesus*, ed. J. L. González – Balado, Servant Books, Ohio 1991, pp. 33-34; Mother Teresa, *One Heart Full of Love*, ed. J. L. González – Balado, pp. 13, 52.

[14] Cf. Mother Teresa, *Heart of Joy: The Transforming Power of Self-Giving*, ed. J. L. Gonzalez-Balado, p. 135.

[15] Mother Teresa, *One Heart Full of Love*, ed. J. L. González – Balado, p. 52.

Spiritual life after the special call is also a union with Jesus in which the divine and the human give themselves completely to one another. According to Mother Teresa, all that Jesus demands of us for this union is to give ourselves to Him in all our poverty and nothingness.[16] A life of voluntary poverty and consequent detachment from material comforts are prerequisites for becoming a genuine disciple of Jesus. Any one who aspires to enter in the discipleship of Jesus has to make a personal decision to deny that which may become an obstacle to this union with Jesus. In this respect she said:

> Get rid of anything that's holding you back. If you want to be all for Jesus, the decision has to come from within you.[17]

1.2. Poverty for Holiness

Jesus invited all his followers to a life of holiness. This is a call from Jesus which all Christians should aspire to. In acquiring holiness in one's religious life, voluntary poverty has a role to play. Voluntarily accepted poverty becomes a means toward achieving holiness. Mother Teresa was convinced of the call of Jesus to lead a holy life. She invited others to this call of holiness. Once she asserted:

> I will pray for you to grow in holiness. Jesus has said very clearly, 'Be holy as the Father in Heaven is holy!'[18]

The call to holiness was explained well by Mother Teresa to the members of her religious order. According to her all must be saints in this world, and holiness is not a luxury for only

---

[16] Cf. Mother Teresa, *No Greater Love,* ed. B. Benenate and J. Durepos, p. 85.

[17] Mother Teresa, *Total Surrender,* ed. A. D. Scolozzi, p. 61.

[18] Mother Teresa, *Loving Jesus,* ed. J. L. González – Balado, p.14.

a few but it is a duty for everyone. Therefore we have to become saints and give glory to the Father. In order to make us holy and give us a share in the happiness of God in eternity, Jesus being rich became poor.[19] She also reminded them never to forget about the obligation towards perfection, and that everyone should aim ceaselessly at it.[20]

Mothers Teresa was of the opinion that only holiness can perfect one's religious commitment, and she invited her sisters to this holiness. She insisted her sisters not strive to become only good religious but also strive to achieve holiness through perfect sacrifice, because she would not be satisfied to see them good religious sisters without being holy. According to her, the soul that has made such a decision to be holy is exposed to renunciation, to temptation, to struggle, to persecution and to all sorts of sacrifice.[21]

The state of holiness is union with Jesus, which consists of mutual giving – human effort and divine grace. An essential element to achieve holiness is the willingness on the part of a person to become holy and be ready to carry out God's will with joy. This willingness is the first step toward holiness. The only thing Jesus demands from us is the commitment to Him, in total poverty. Without a great

---

[19] Cf. Mother Teresa, *One Heart Full of Love*, ed. J. L. González – Balado, p. 29; cf. Mother Teresa, *Thirsting for God: A Year Book of Prayers, Meditations and Anecdotes*, compiled by A. D. Scolozzi, p. 80; cf. Mother Teresa, *Love: A Fruit Always in Season – Daily Meditations*, ed. D. S. Hunt, pp. 181, 231; cf. J. L. Gonzalez – Balado, *Always the Poor: Mother Teresa – Her Life and Message*, p.7.

[20] Cf. Mother Teresa, *No Greater Love*, ed. B. Benenate and J. Durepos, p. 5.

[21] Cf. Mother Teresa, *Heart of Joy: The Transforming Power of Self-Giving*, ed. J. L. González – Balado, p. 86.

effort of renunciation we cannot become saints.[22] Mother Teresa emphasised the point of sacrifice in her conception of voluntary poverty; and it is clear from her later teachings what she meant by holiness. She said:

> The words 'I want to be holy' mean: I will divest myself of everything that is not of God; I will divest myself and empty my heart of material things; I will live in poverty and in privation: I will renounce my own will, my inclinations, my whims, my fickleness; and I will become a generous slave girl to God's will.[23]

Renunciation and all kinds of sacrifices are what surround the soul that has opted for holiness. Thus it costs him much who resolves to become a saint.[24] Poverty as important for our sanctification was taught by Christ himself through his life, though He did not have to lead a life of poverty. He chose poverty as the companion of His life on earth as He

---

[22] Cf. *Ibid.*, p. 92; cf. Mother Teresa, *No Greater Love,* ed. B. Benenate and J. Durepos, p. 85; cf. Mother Teresa, *Love: A Fruit Always in Season – Daily Meditations*, ed. D. S. Hunt, p. 230; cf. Mother Teresa, *The Love of Christ: Spiritual Counsels,* eds. G. Goree and J. Barbier, p. 20.

[23] Mother Teresa, *Heart of Joy: The Transforming Power of Self-Giving*, ed. J. L. González – Balado, p. 86; Mother Teresa, *Jesus, The Word to be Spoken,* compiled by A. D. Scolozzi, p.54; Mother Teresa, *Total Surrender*, ed. A. D. Scolozzi, p. 32; Mother Teresa, *No Greater Love,* ed. B. Benenate and J. Durepos, p. 54; S. D'cunha, *Mother of the Motherless: A Short Sketch of the Life and Work of Mother Teresa,* St. Paul Publications, Bangalore 1978, p. 53.

[24] Cf. Mother Teresa, *In My Own Words*, compiled by J. L. Gonzalez-Balado, Liguori Publications, Liguori 1996, p. 3; cf. Mother Teresa, *Essential Writings*, selected with an introduction by J. Maalouf, pp. 31-32; cf. Mother Teresa, *Jesus, the Word to Be Spoken,* compiled by A. D. Scolozzi, p. 45.

came to live among us. We must imitate Him in the practice of poverty to acquire holiness.[25]

Our attachment to money will become the cause of losing contact with God, if we allow it, and thus will keep us far from holiness. Mother Teresa preferred death to losing contact with God and a life of holiness. She insisted on praying to God that He keep us away from the inclination toward the attachment to money. She was also not in favour of collecting surplus money in the bank.[26] Our holiness consists in loving God and giving Him the utmost devotion. If we show excessive care for money, then it shows that we are serving two masters, which Jesus himself discouraged (cf. Mt. 6:24). She taught that a religious totally belongs to Christ and should remain in this belongingness. She expressed her conviction in this regard through the following words: "Our vocation is nothing else but to belong to Christ."[27]

Mother Teresa reminded priests, both religious and secular, about the demand of priestly consecration as living in poverty and achieving a holy life. She said priests are not ordained to become social workers but to lead a life of holiness through consecrated obedience and poverty.

---

[25] Cf. Mother Teresa, *Total Surrender*, ed. A. D. Scolozzi, p. 58; cf. Mother Teresa, *Essential Writings*, selected with an introduction by J. Maalouf, p. 108.

[26] Cf. Mother Teresa, *Heart of Joy: The Transforming Power of Self-Giving*, ed. J. L. González – Balado, p. 95; cf. Mother Teresa, *Love: A Fruit Always in Season – Daily Meditations*, ed. D. S. Hunt, p. 180; cf. Mother Teresa, *The Love of Christ: Spiritual Counsels*, eds. G. Goree and J. Barbier, p. 106.

[27] Mother Teresa, *Loving Jesus*, ed. J. L. González – Balado, p.33.

It is clear from her statement:

> I say to you all priests: Your have not become priests to be social workers. You must have a life of holiness, and consecrated obedience and poverty. Everything you do must spring from your consecrated life.[28]

1.3. Poverty for Eternal Life

In the parable of the rich man and Lazarus, Jesus gave the message that eternal life is given according to one's ability to practice voluntary poverty and one's sensitivity towards poor fellow brethren. "Son, remember that in your life time you received your good things . . . now he is comforted here you are in anguish" (Lk.16:25) The rich man's lack of awareness about the people around who were in utter poverty and his lack of concern for them shown by his not sacrificing his material comforts voluntarily for them created an obstacle for attaining eternal life. He was punished not merely because he was rich, but because of his lack of understanding that all his belongings were from God and that some of his brethren below were suffering due to utter poverty. He failed to come down to Lazarus. Coming down to the lower level by one's own action is essential to obtain eternal life – voluntary poverty. No one has a choice to be born into a particular family and economic background, but all have freedom to come down to work for their own salvation and the salvation of others.

Mother Teresa considered our voluntary poverty as equally important as serving Jesus in the poor. She referred to our hardship in becoming poor and serving the poor as expressing our love of God, for which our heavenly reward would be eternal life. Therefore she said:

---

[28] *Ibid.*, p. 46.

> Our life of poverty is as necessary as the work itself. Only in heaven will we see how much we owe to the poor for helping us to love God better because of them.[29]

As an essential part of the Divine Plan Jesus underwent a life of voluntary poverty and finally sat on the throne in heaven. We recall his words; "Alas for you who are rich, you are having your consolation now" (Lk.6:24); "It is easier for a camel to go through the eye of a needle than for a rich man to enter the kingdom of God" (Mt. 19: 24); "Enter by the narrow gate . . . For the gate is narrow and the way is hard, that leads to life" (Mt. 7:13-14). He invites us to understand the importance of voluntary poverty as the way, the means to reach the eternal life. According to Mother Teresa, Jesus not only taught this value of poverty as the means for attaining eternal life but he practiced it in his life. Once she said:

> He (Jesus) chose poverty because he knew that this was the authentic means for possessing God and for bringing God's love on earth.[30]

She taught that poverty must be seen as beautiful in heaven. She affirmed her statement with the argument that Jesus could have had wealth, but instead chose poverty. If Jesus could choose to become so small, so poor, then poverty must

---

[29] Mother Teresa Of Calcutta, *A Gift for God: Prayers and Meditations*, compiled by M. Muggeridge, p. 35; Mother Teresa, *Essential Writings*, selected with an introduction by J. Maalouf, p. 111; Mother Teresa, *Love: A Fruit Always in Season – Daily Meditations*, ed. D. S. Hunt, p. 159.

[30] Mother Teresa, *Essential Writings*, selected with an introduction by J. Maalouf, p. 110; L. Gjergji, *Mother Teresa: To Live, to Love, to Witness – Her Spiritual Way*, translated by J. Aumann, New City Press, New York 1991, p. 53; Mother Teresa, *Heart of Joy: The Transforming Power of Self-Giving*, ed. J. L. González – Balado, p. 130.

be seen as an experience of heaven.[31] Thus for her, the practice of poverty is a heavenly experience which she practiced with cheerfulness, and she invited others to have this same state of joy. The joy from poverty has two dimensions, in the present life and in future life – eternal life.

When Jesus spoke about the Last Judgement and entrance into eternal life, he made clear the acceptance of his presence in the disguised poor (Mt. 25: 31ff.). Whoever could see Jesus and serve him in the poorest of the poor would be rewarded eternal life. He identifies himself with the hungry, the naked, the homeless etc. His voluntarily accepted image of poverty becomes a way for humanity to accept Him in this situation, to serve him and be rewarded at the end. According to Mother Teresa, this is a call to recognize Him in the poor and serve Him and be prepared for our eternal life. She said:

> He became hungry. He became naked. He became poor one dying in our streets. He wants us to love him in those who are hungry, in those who are naked, in those who are homeless. This is what you and I are called to do.[32]

2. FOLLOWING THE LIFE OF CHRIST

The religious, the close followers of Christ through evangelical counsels,[33] are expected to follow the example of the poverty of Christ. Christ who practised poverty from birth to death in his earthly life is a model for all those who follow Him. Mother Teresa drew inspiration from the life of

---

[31] Cf. Mother Teresa, *Thirsting for God: A Year Book of Prayers, Meditations and Anecdotes*, compiled by A. D. Scolozzi, p. 180.

[32] Mother Teresa, *One Heart Full of Love*, ed. J. L. González – Balado, p. 91.

[33] Cf. PC 13b.

Christ and also taught others to follow a Christ-like poverty in religious life. She was an ardent preacher on this theme. She cautioned her sisters: "Each of us has given our word to God to follow Christ in poverty."[34] She admonished them on the same matter on another occasion with the following words:

> It would be a shame for us to be richer than Jesus, who for our sake endured poverty.[35]

Though Christ was God, all throughout His earthly life, He depended on His heavenly Father and Joseph and Mary. He led an ordinary and simple life. That is why people were surprised when He worked miracles. Jesus was known not only by His miracles but also by His poverty. So every MC must be poor like Jesus and imitate His poverty of Bethlehem, Nazareth and Calvary and must renounce everything for the sake of God's kingdom.[36]

---

[34] Mother Teresa, *Total Surrender*, ed. A. D. Scolozzi, p. 59.

[35] Mother Teresa, *Heart of Joy: The Transforming Power of Self-Giving*, ed. J. L. González – Balado, p. 137; Mother Teresa, *No Greater Love*, ed. B. Benenate and J. Durepos, p. 96.

[36] Cf. *Mother's Instructions: Let Us Make Our Society Something Beautiful for God*, Vol.1, p. 52; cf. *Mother's Letter*, 20 August 1968; 5 February 1979; 20 May 1980; 22 March 1981; cf. January 1983. When her Congregation started establishing foundations different places, Mother Teresa communicated to her Sisters through official letters. She wrote all the letters with her own hand. Later they were all typed and kept in two volumes. In the beginning she wrote them on First Fridays of the month because of her great devotion to the Sacred Heart of Jesus. After some years, due to others factors, as and when the necessity arose she wrote them. At present about 246 letters are available. In this work hereafter the references will be made to theses letters by date, month and year and sometimes without date and month when they are not found in the letters; A. Savarimuthu, *Spirituality of Mother Teresa of Calcutta*, p. 146.

2.1. Poor Birth of Christ

Mother Teresa reflected deeply on the poor birth of Christ and invited others to reflect on this fact. Christ doesn't love riches or greatness; He didn't come to dwell in a palace. When He came into the world He became so very small – He became a child, born to a virgin, placed in a manger. Mary did not expect Him to be born in this humble way. It seems strange that we must stop and ask ourselves why He did so. Though He could have had wealth, He chose poverty.[37] Christ's poverty is out of personal choice and the desire to become totally one among us:

> It was not necessary for Jesus to practice this absolute poverty. There is only one reason: because he desired it. He wanted to be to the fullest 'one' of us.[38]

Her reflections on the poverty of the family to which Jesus was born is explained very well. Jesus was born into a poor family, and deeper poverty was seen at the time of His birth since His parents could not even find a dignified place for His birth. This fact showed well the light of poverty. The appearance of Mary and Joseph might have revealed that they had no money to pay rent, so the inn keeper and others denied them a room. The way they were begging for a simple dwelling place and how they were denied a room are reflected in her teachings, as she said:

> Before His (Jesus') birth his parents asked for a simple dwelling place and they were given none because they

---

[37] Cf. Mother Teresa, *Thirsting for God: A Year Book of Prayers, Meditations and Anecdotes*, compiled by A. D. Scolozzi, p. 180.

[38] Mother Teresa, *Total Surrender*, ed. A. D. Scolozzi, p. 56-57; Mother Teresa, *Essential Writings*, selected with an introduction by J. Maalouf, p. 108.

> were poor. The innkeeper probably looked at Joseph the carpenter and decided that he would not be able to pay. So he refused. But Mother Earth opened a cave and took in the Son of God.[39]

The poor surroundings and lack of necessary materials lead us to understand the helplessness of the situation at the time of the birth of Jesus. The Son of God chose birth in the poorest condition and environment. He has gone down to the bottom level of poverty at the time of becoming man. The pathetic situation into which Jesus was born paves the way for understanding the gravity of his nothingness. This fact was explained in Mother Teresa's simple words:

> Jesus was born in Bethlehem. All he had was a piece of cloth, some straw. Picture the animals gathering around the child.[40]

The birth of Christ was like that of the poorest of the poor. Even our poorest of poor have someone assist them at the time of giving birth and immediately after the delivery. But in the case of Mary the mother of Jesus, no one was there to assist.[41] Jesus could have come down from heaven as a full grown man, but He came to us as an infant. Everything had to be done for Him. He willed to be born in this way out of His love for humanity.[42] The inexplicable poverty found in the birth of Christ leads us to understand the ineffable love of God toward us.

Jesus was brought up in a poverty which no human being will ever be able to experience, because 'being rich He made

---

[39] Mother Teresa, *Total Surrender*, ed. A. D. Scolozzi, p. 130.
[40] *Ibid.*, p. 60.
[41] Cf. *ibid.*, pp. 56-57; Mother Teresa, *Essential Writings*, selected with an introduction by J. Maalouf, p. 108.
[42] Cf. Mother Teresa, *Total Surrender*, ed. A. D. Scolozzi, p. 60.

Himself became poor.'[43] The criterion by which to measure the seriousness of one's poverty depends on the nature of the place from where he chose to become the poorest of the poor. As Jesus in his incarnation became one of us in everything except sin, religious should follow the path of Jesus, especially in mission through the adaptation of local culture and language – a new situation at incarnation, so to speak. It is a kind of detachment of oneself from one's own land, culture and language.[44]

Religious should learn to live with the minimal facilities of the poor to imitate the life of Jesus in His incarnation in executing the mission given by His Father.

2.2. Poor Life of Christ

For a number of years at Nazareth, Jesus was simply, to the people of his village, "the carpenter, the son of Mary, the brother of James and John, and Jude and Simon" (Mk. 6:3; Jn. 6:42); an ordinary workman, like so many of the young men of his age, though he had an advantage over the very poor among them: his father had a profession, and therefore a source of income. In a sense, as C. H. Dodd puts it, his class was that of "the petit-bourgeois small farmer or independent craftsman, equally removed from the well-to-do and from the proletariat . . . If at a later stage He was poor and homeless,

---

[43] Cf. *Ibid.*, p. 59; Mother Teresa, *No Greater Love,* ed. B. Benenate and J. Durepos, p. 96; cf. Mother Teresa, *Jesus, the Word to Be Spoken,* compiled by A. D. Scolozzi, p. 99; Mother Teresa, *Essential Writings,* selected with an introduction by J. Maalouf, p. 113; cf. Mother Teresa, *A Life for God,* compiled by L. Neff, Servant Publications, p. 210.

[44] Cf. Mother Teresa, *Jesus, the Word to Be Spoken,* compiled by A. D. Scolozzi, p. 121.

this was a voluntary poverty."[45] Reflecting on this view point of Jesus' life, Mother Teresa said:

> Jesus was born into a family and stayed in Nazareth for thirty years. He had come to redeem the world, yet he spent thirty years in Nazareth, doing the humble work of an ordinary person.[46]

In her opinion, Jesus was a real labourer and known as the son of a carpenter; He lived a life of hard labour for nearly twenty years, never hesitating, never doubting the will of God, though He came to bring souls to God. In the hard work of his foster father's shop, He showed the greatest virtues that a human being can have: humility, obedience, poverty. Always keeping Himself above material preoccupations, He – the master of everything – worked not for the work itself but for Him who sent Him, for His Father in heaven.[47]

During His public ministry He appeared as a travelling Rabbi whose life was so often of such privation that "he had nowhere to lay his head" (Mt. 8:20; Lk. 9:58); He himself carried no money (Mt. 17:24-27) and He depended a great deal on charity (Lk. 8: 1-3); He was also helped, at least occasionally, by the work of his disciples, the fishermen of the lake, who, would go back to their boats and try their luck. Jesus' life was then hard, austere; hunger (Mk. 11:12), thirst (Jn. 4:7), fatigue (Jn. 4:6) were his companions as they seem to have been the companions of so many other Rabbis.[48]

---

[45] S. pierre, *Poverty, Celibacy, Obedience,* Gala Publications, Kenya 1976, p. 13; C. H. Dodd, *The Founder of Christianity,* p.527.

[46] Mother teresa, *Loving Jesus,* ed. J. L. González – Balado, p.107.

[47] Cf. Mother Teresa, *Jesus, the Word to Be Spoken,* compiled by A. D. Scolozzi, p. 104.

[48] Cf. S. Pierre, *Poverty, Celibacy, Obedience,* Gaba Publications, Kenya 1976, p. 13; cf. J. Jeremias, *Jerusalem in the Time of Jesus,* SCM Press, London 1969, p. 116.

Jesus had experienced uncertainty about His residence during his public ministry. "Foxes have holes and the birds have nests; but the Son of man has nowhere to lay his head" (Lk. 9: 58). Jesus had deliberately made his own poverty far more complete than what He had become accustomed to as a boy and a man in the carpenter's home. As the Apostles had left their nets and family security, Jesus had left a carpenter's profession and his family. He became a wandering preacher without a fixed abode. Reflecting on this theme of Christ's poverty with regard to residence Mother Teresa said:

> Our Saviour's poverty is greater even than that of the poorest of the world's beast. 'The foxes have holes and birds of the air their nests but the Son of Man has nowhere to lay his head.' So it was in fact. He had no house of his own, no fixed abode. The Samaritans had just turned him away and he must seek for shelter. Everything was uncertain: lodging and food.[49]

Mother Teresa had imbibed this spirit of Christ's poverty in her life and left a lesson for her followers. When she left the Loreto convent, we noted that there was an uncertainty about her future residence. Where would she be staying? Above all, the acceptance of the society about her new way of life was a question mark. Her diary records this hardship in practising Christ's poverty in her life, and it provides an inspiration and encouragement for whoever wishes to follow Christ through the life of poverty.[50]

---

[49] Mother Teresa, *Jesus, the Word to Be Spoken*, compiled by A. D. Scolozzi, p. 99.

[50] "Today I learned a good lesson. The poverty of the poor must be so hard for them. While looking for a home I walked and walked till my arms and legs ached. I thought how much they must ache in body and soul, looking for home, food and health. Then the comfort of Loreto came to tempt me. 'You

Uncertainty over food was another matter she meditated upon from the life of Christ. She began her reflection from the childhood of Christ. His parents were poor, and the poor do not feast on the good things of the table.[51] In public life, He experienced the scarcity of food in a severe way, as there was no certainty in the matter of food. Together with his Apostles he became totally dependent on others' generosity for his livelihood, especially for daily bread.[52] The seriousness of the lack of food in the life of Christ can be found in a deeper sense in the following words of Mother Teresa:

> The Lord sometimes suffered real indigence, as can be understood from the multiplication of bread and fish and the picking of grain at the edge of the path. This thought should serve as a comfort to us when our food is scarce.[53]

The life of Christ and his Apostles was a life of real want in the matter of food, which is clear from the instances of multiplication of food and the act of the plucking the ears of grain on walks through the fields. Mother Teresa made use of this thought on the poverty of Christ to teach her followers to have the proper spirit of poverty in the matter of food. When meals are meagre or dishes are not tasty, one should accept it with a joyful heart as an opportunity to share the poverty of Christ. In this respect she taught the right attitude one should have in the midst of poor food:

---

have only to say the word and all that will be yours again'." (K. Spink, *Mother Teresa: An Authorised Biography*, p. 37).

[51] Cf. Mother Teresa, *Jesus, the Word to Be Spoken*, compiled by A. D. Scolozzi, p. 105.

[52] Cf. *Ibid.*, p. 99.

[53] Mother Teresa, *Heart of Joy: The Transforming Power of Self-Giving*, ed. J. L. Gonzalez-Balado, p. 129; Mother Teresa, *Essential Writings*, selected with an introduction by J. Maalouf, p. 107.

> If dishes taste good, thank God; if not, thank him still and thank him even more because he has given you an opportunity to imitate our Saviour in his poverty. It would be a defect to speak about food or to complain about what is served; to be occupied with such thoughts at any time is disedifying.[54]

Christ experienced great poverty as a beggar, a condition of life he had freely chosen. He was living on alms; a life dependent on the charity of others. It is a great poverty when we consider the original state of Christ, the God-Man, the Lord of heaven and earth. He might have possessed many things, but he left everything and chose a poor life. This made his poverty majestic and rich. He chose this poverty out of his love for us and with the intention to enrich us. We are blessed in being called to share in our own little way the great poverty of this great God.[55] Mother Teresa also taught her community members to aspire to the same spirit of poverty and readiness to become beggars for the sake of Christ who lived on alms in his public life. She stated:

> The brothers and Sisters should not be ashamed to beg from door to door if necessary, becoming beggars for the poor members of Christ, who himself lived on alms during his public life and whom they serve in the sick and poor.[56]

2.3. Poor Death of Christ

Mother Teresa was taken up by the poverty of Christ at the time of His death, especially the aspect of His poverty on the Cross. It is reflected in her words while leaving the Loreto convent: "Our Lord wants me to be a free nun, covered with

---

[54] Mother Teresa, *Jesus, the Word to be Spoken: Prayers and Meditations for Every Day of the Year*, compiled by A. D. Scolozzi, p. 105.

[55] Cf. *Ibid.*, p. 99.

[56] *Ibid.*, p. 103.

the poverty of the cross."[57] She was deeply moved by the meditation on the poor death and burial of Christ and taught her reflection on this theme to her religious community. Jesus was stripped of everything before crucifixion and remained naked. He had nothing of his own other than his naked body. The necessary things were given by others; the cross, the nails, the crown, the tomb and other materials for burial.[58] Thus in the scene of death and burial of Jesus, utter poverty is found, which was a free choice on the part of Christ, despite the fact He could have had a burial in the style of a king. She explained her reflections in these words:

> On the cross Christ was deprived of everything. The cross itself had been given him by Pilate; the nails and the crown, by the soldiers. He was naked. When he died he was stripped of the cross, the nails, and the crown. He was wrapped in a piece of canvas donated by a charitable soul, and he was buried in a tomb that did not belong to him. Despite all that, Jesus could have died like a king and could even have been spared death.[59]

---

[57] Mother Teresa recorded these in her diary which K. Spink quoted in her biography (K. Spink, *Mother Teresa: An Authorised Biography*, p. 37).

[58] Cf. Mother Teresa, *Essential Writings*, selected with an introduction by J. Maalouf, p. 110; L. Gjergji, *Mother Teresa: To Live, to Love, to Witness – Her Spiritual Way*, translated by J. Aumann, p. 53; cf. Mother Teresa, *Total Surrender*, ed. A. D. Scolozzi, p. 56; cf. Mother Teresa, *Love: A Fruit Always in Season – Daily Meditations*, selected and ed. D. S. Hunt, p. 104; cf. Mother Teresa, *The Love of Christ: Spiritual Counsels*, eds. G. Goree and J. Barbier, p. 108.

[59] Mother Teresa, *Heart of Joy: The Transforming Power of Self-Giving*, ed. J. L. Gonzalez-Balado, pp. 129-130; Mother Teresa, *Essential writings*, selected with an introduction by J. Maalouf, p. 107; Mother Teresa, *Jesus, The Word to be Spoken*, compiled by A. D. Scolozzi, p. 103; Mother Teresa, *No Greater Love*, ed. B. Benenate and J. Durepos, p. 96.

The absolute poverty of Jesus on the cross can be understood when we reflect on the way He hung on the cross; naked, mournful, despised by all. The great suffering He underwent for the love of humanity during the passion and death was a concrete sign of His love for humanity. He accepted a poor death for the love of His Father and humanity; poverty for the love of God and man. The pitiful situation of Jesus on the cross was expressed by Mother Teresa in these words:

> The God-man naked on the cross, mournful, despised by all, the man of suffering crushed like a worm by the scourging and the crucifixion.[60]

On the cross, Jesus felt a thirst, a thirst for love and sacrifice, the last wish expressed by Jesus towards humanity. This was a request he made to all of us while He was on the cross, deprived of every consolation and dying in absolute poverty. He experienced thirst and expressed it in words to the people who were present. According to Mother Teresa, this thirst of Christ was not for water but for love and sacrifice.[61] If we wish to receive the fruits of sacrifice of Jesus then we have to respond to His last wish, love and sacrifice in life – accept poverty for the love of Jesus and the poor. Despite of the fact we can have everything, we sacrifice our material comforts for the sake of Jesus and the poor. Whatever we sacrifice out of our free choice for the love of others in the spirit of Christ's sacrifice will be rewarded with the ultimate aim of Christ's sacrifice – a share of eternal life.

Renunciation and poverty of the cross is a demand of Jesus for his disciples. "Whoever wishes to follow me let him deny himself, take up his own cross and then follow

---

[60] Mother Teresa, *Total Surrender*, ed. A. D. Scolozzi, p. 116.

[61] Cf. A. D. Scolozzi, *Mother Teresa: Contemplative in the Heart of the World*, p. 29.

me" (Mt. 16:24) Mother Teresa was convinced of the necessity of renunciation and poverty of the cross for religious, especially those who are carrying out their work among the poor. Therefore she said:

> When Our Lord asked His religious Sisters to carry on their work among the poor, He then explicitly asked them to accept the poverty of the cross.[62]

Besides the material aspect of poverty at the time of the death of Christ, the very fact of suffering is reflected upon by Mother Teresa with regard to poverty. According to her, by suffering with Christ we can have a share in the sufferings of the poor. In this regard she said:

> We have to suffer with Christ. In doing this we will share in the sufferings of the poor.[63]

2.4. Self Emptying Love of Christ (*Kenosis*)

Mother Teresa, taking various levels of self emptying aspects of Christ, taught us to follow his example in emptying oneself in the practice of religious poverty. According to her, the humility of Jesus can be seen in the crib, in the exile in Egypt, in the hidden life, in the inability to make people understand Him, in the desertion of his apostles, in the hatred of His persecutors, in all the terrible suffering and death of His passion, and now in His permanent state of humility in the tabernacle, where He has reduced Himself to such a small particle of bread that a priest can hold Him with two fingers.

---

[62] These words of Mother Teresa are quoted by O. Tanghe in his book (O. Tanghe, *For the Least of My Brothers: The Spirituality of Mother Teresa and Catherine Doherty*, p. 35).

[63] Mother Teresa, *Heart of Joy: The Transforming Power of Self-Giving*, ed. J. L. González – Balado, p. 64.

The more we empty ourselves, the more room we give to God to fill us.[64]

The self emptying of Jesus through his hidden life in the womb was a matter meditated upon by Mother Teresa. According to her, the Son of God wanted to feel what it meant to be a human being, to be locked up, so to speak, for nine months, entirely dependent on a mother.[65] She considered this act of Christ as the beginning of true poverty. The nature of this self emptying and absolute poverty she conveyed through the following words:

> The first true poverty was when 'Christ emptied himself'. For nine months he was lost in the little space of Mary's bosom: not even St. Joseph knew who he was. Having all things, yet possessing nothing.[66]

Jesus claims His presence in the world in the distressing disguise of the poor, and thus He makes Himself one among the poor. Jesus said: "Whatever you did for the least of these my brethren you did it to me" (Mt. 25: 40). Jesus made Himself as one with the naked, hungry, homeless, sick, dispossessed etc. Thus Jesus made Himself the poorest of the poor.[67]

---

[64] Cf. Mother Teresa, *Jesus, the Word to Be Spoken,* compiled by A. D. Scolozzi, p. 55; cf. Mother Teresa, *Love: A Fruit Always in Season – Daily Meditations,* ed. D. S. Hunt, p. 25; cf. Mother Teresa, *Life in Spirit,* ed. K. Spink, Harper & Row, San Francisco 1983, p.48.

[65] Cf. Mother Teresa, *Total Surrender,* ed. A. D. Scolozzi, p. 24.

[66] *Ibid.*, p. 56; Mother Teresa, *Essential Writings,* selected with an introduction by J. Maalouf, p. 107.

[67] Cf. Mother Teresa, *Loving Jesus,* ed. J. L. González – Balado, p. 18; cf. Mother Teresa, *Heart of Joy: The Transforming Power of Self-Giving,* ed. J. L. Gonzalez-Balado, pp. 107-108; cf. Mother Teresa, *One Heart Full of Love,* ed. J. L. González – Balado, p. 16;

Jesus not only became poor like us, but also he transformed himself into the Bread of the Eucharist. And He said, "Unless you eat my flesh and drink my blood, you cannot live, you cannot have eternal life" (Jn. 6:54). He was aware of the hunger of man, both physical and spiritual. Therefore He emptied himself and took on a poor form, a piece of bread, so as to satisfy our hunger. Bread is usually the cheapest and the simplest food for people everywhere. The form of His choice to be present in the Eucharist was so small that just two fingers can hold it, so fragile even a baby or a dying person can eat it.[68] Once, Mother Teresa expressed the poverty, humility and self emptying love of Jesus in the following words:

> Think of it! Bread – even a little child can eat it. This is the humility of God, the poverty he chose by becoming one of us. He made himself the Bread of life to satisfy your hunger for love.[69]

Following the footsteps of Christ, the religious should attempt to empty the self while practicing poverty. Christ being rich emptied himself. If anyone wants to be poor like

---

cf. Mother Teresa, *Jesus, the Word to Be Spoken,* compiled by A. D. Scolozzi, p. 74; cf. Mother Teresa, *Thirsting for God: A Year Book of Prayers, Meditations and Anecdotes,* compiled by A. D. Scolozzi, p.168.

[68] Cf. Mother Teresa, *One Heart Full of Love,* ed. J. L. González – Balado, pp. 2-3, 91,128; cf. Mother Teresa, *No Greater Love,* ed. B. Benenate and J. Durepos, pp. 82-83; cf. Mother Teresa, *Jesus, the Word to Be Spoken,* compiled by A. D. Scolozzi, p. 74; cf. Mother Teresa, *Thirsting for God: A Year Book of Prayers, Meditations and Anecdotes,* compiled by A. D. Scolozzi, p. 51.

[69] Mother Teresa, *Loving Jesus,* ed. J. L. González – Balado, p.17.

Christ – who became poor even though he was rich – He is obliged to do the same.[70]

The more the space created through self-emptying the more one can be filled by God. Unless a person is empty of various preoccupations of worldly matters, there is no place for God. In the personal life of every religious, material detachment is necessary to reserve a place for God. The measure of material detachment determines how much place a person leaves for Jesus in his or her life. Mother Teresa expressed her feelings on this matter through the following words:

> Riches, both material and spiritual, can choke you if you do not use them fairly. Let us remain as empty as possible so that God can fill us up, for not even God can put anything in a heart that is already full.[71]

Jesus chose poverty because that was the means of possessing God and bringing His love to the people. God desires our littleness and our emptiness not our fullness.[72] The greatest humility rests in one's acceptance of one's own nothingness or emptiness. This acceptance clears the way

---

[70] Cf. Mother Teresa, *Total Surrender*, ed. A. D. Scolozzi, p. 57; cf. Mother Teresa, *Essential Writings*, selected with an introduction by J. Maalouf, p. 108; cf. Mother Teresa, *No Greater Love,* ed. B. Benenate and J. Durepos, p. 96; cf. Mother Teresa, *Heart of Joy: The Transforming Power of Self-Giving*, ed. J. L. González – Balado, p. 79.

[71] Mother Teresa, *Heart of Joy: The Transforming Power of Self-Giving*, ed. J. L. Gonzalez-Balado, p. 89; Mother Teresa, *No Greater Love,* ed. B. Benenate and J. Durepos, p. 95; Mother Teresa, *Love: A Fruit Always in Season – Daily Meditations*, ed. D. S. Hunt, p. 196; Mother Teresa, *The Love of Christ: Spiritual Counsels,* eds. G. Goree and J. Barbier, Harper & Row, London 1982, p. 60.

[72] Cf. O. Tanghe, *For the Least of My Brothers: The Spirituality of Mother Teresa and Catherine Doherty*, p. 35.

for God to fill it with Himself in everyone who has this sort of humility.[73]

For Mother Teresa, emptying the self in order to make a place for Jesus in our heart does not mean mere detachment from material preoccupations, but detachment even from inner feelings, such as, our self-sufficiency, selfishness and intellectual pride. The basic argument for this thought is the same as we have seen above – 'God cannot fill what is already full'. Every one must keep one's own heart empty so God may fill it with Himself. Where there is emptiness, there is a room for God to fill us with Himself.[74] When our self is devoid of all other preoccupations and attachments, then there is a vacuum, and this space can be filled by Jesus enabling us to have His life in us. Our emptiness is more important than what we have to give him. Therefore she said:

> God cannot fill what is full - He can only fill your emptiness - deep poverty - and your 'yes' is the beginning of your becoming empty. It is not how much we really 'have' to give but how empty we are – so that we can receive fully in our life and let Him live His life in us.[75]

---

[73] Cf. Mother Teresa, *Thirsting for God: A Year Book of Prayers, Meditations and Anecdotes*, compiled by A. D. Scolozzi, p. 153.

[74] Cf. Mother Teresa, *Heart of Joy: The Transforming Power of Self-Giving*, ed. J. L. Gonzalez-Balado, pp. 80,102; cf. Mother Teresa, *Thirsting for God: A Year Book of Prayers, Meditations and Anecdotes*, compiled by A. D. Scolozzi, p. 155; cf. Mother Teresa, *Jesus, the Word to Be Spoken*, compiled by A. D. Scolozzi, p. 55; cf. Mother Teresa, *No Greater Love*, ed. B. Benenate and J. Durepos, p. 149; cf. Mother Teresa, *Love: A Fruit Always in Season – Daily Meditations*, ed. D. S. Hunt, p. 195; cf. Mother Teresa, *Life in the Spirit*, ed. K. Spink, p. 48.

[75] Mother Teresa wrote these words in her letter to a priest and later she gave this text to Omar Tanghe which he published in his book (O. Tanghe, *For the Least of my Brothers: The Spirituality*

3. FOLLOWING THE TEACHINGS OF CHRIST

When we think of the teaching of Christ on evangelical poverty, a number of well known texts come to mind: "Alas for you who are rich, you are having your consolation now" (Lk. 6:24); "How hard it is for those who have riches to enter the kingdom of God . . . It is easier for a camel to pass through the eye of a needle than a rich man to enter the kingdom of God" (Mk.10:23,25). Jesus' words on riches are radical, and some of them sound like a condemnation without appeal! (See also Lk. 12: 13-21, 14: 25-27, 16: 9-13, 18:18-30). In the Sermon on the Mount, Jesus began with the beatitude on poverty (cf. Mt. 5:3; Lk. 6:20). There is a difference in the characterization of the poor in the account of Matthew and of Luke.[76] In the first the emphasis is on the material poverty where as in the second the emphasis is one the spiritual poverty. Jesus was so radical when he spoke about the need for material poverty. This aspect is found in the twin parable of the treasure and of the pearl (cf. Mt. 13:44-46). The need of detachment from material possessions is revealed in Jesus' teaching when he said that nobody can serve two masters at the same time (cf. Mt. 6:24). We have already seen some of the teachings of Christ on voluntary poverty in following the call of Christ, which need not repeat here.

Thus Christ taught various aspects of voluntary poverty, and the religious who made a commitment to follow him have to pay special regard in following his teachings. Some

---

of Mother Teresa and Catherine Doherty, p. 16); Mother Teresa, *Thirsting for God: A Year Book of Prayers, Meditations and Anecdotes*, compiled by A. D. Scolozzi, p. 69; Mother Teresa, *Love: A Fruit Always in Season – Daily Meditations*, ed. D. S. Hunt, p. 195; E. Egan, *Such a Vision of the Street*, p. 388.

[76] In the Gospel of Luke: "Blessed are you poor" (Lk.6:20); while Mathew has, "Blessed are the poor in spirit" (Mt. 5:3).

of those aspects taught by Mother Teresa frequently are: poverty out of loving trust in God (cf. Mt.6:25-34; Lk.12:22-31), poverty in being a humble servant of all (cf. Mt. 20:26-27; Jn.13:14) and poverty in spirit (cf. Mt. 5:3), each of which shall be dealt with in detail in what follows.

3.1. Poverty out of Loving Trust in God

We have seen in the third chapter how total trust in the providence of God was practised in the life of Mother Teresa, with various examples on different occasions. In this chapter, I shall deal with the theoretical aspect of that trust. She explained what it meant to have a loving trust in God. For her, loving trust is a total reliance on our Heavenly Father with spontaneous abandonment like children, totally convinced of our utter nothingness but trusting to the point of rashness with courageous confidence in his fatherly goodness.[77] Her definition of loving trust in God is based on the teaching of Christ, whereby He explained how to remove our over-preoccupation with accumulation for the future. In her teaching on poverty out of loving trust in God,

[77] Cf. Mother Teresa, *Jesus, the Word to Be Spoken,* compiled by A. D. Scolozzi, p. 122. According to her, we have to learn this child like trust in the Father from Jesus. Her constitution article no. 23 expresses this view: "Jesus trusted His Father with an unshakable trust. His trust was the fruit of His intimate knowledge and love of the Father. He trusted His Father so completely that He entrusted His whole life and the mission for which He was sent into the hands of the Father. He was fully confident that His Father would work out His plan of salvation in spite of the ineffectual means used and the apparent failure." (*MCs Constitutions,* Art. 23); also in the Rule of life and covenant of the Universal Brothers of the Word, Association of Christian Faithful Founded by Mother Teresa, and it is published by A. Devananda in the appendix of his book (A. D. Scolozzi, *Mother Teresa : Contemplative in the Heart of the World,* p. 135).

she emphasises the words of Jesus, that we are much more important than the grass and other creatures of the earth. We should have a deep trust in the Father. She said:

> Jesus Christ has said that we are much more important to his Father than the grass, the birds, and the flowers of the earth; and so, if he takes such care of these things, how much more would he take care of his life in us. He cannot deceive us; because life is God's greatest gift to human beings.[78]

She explained further about this loving trust in the care of God as a firm and lively faith that God can and will help us. That He can is evident because He is almighty. That He wills is certain because He promises to help in so many passages of Holy Writ and because He is infinitely faithful to all His promises.[79] While explaining the need of renunciation out of trust in God, she insisted not to engage in money-making business, nor have bank accounts, nor store money or things in the house more than the immediate need, but rather to have a simple trust in the Heavenly Father and like the poor not to worry about tomorrow.[80] She very well expressed the

---

[78] Mother Teresa Of Calcutta, *A Gift for God: Prayers and Meditations,* compiled by M. Muggeridge, p. 40; She repeated similar idea in a different occasion: "Do not let money so preoccupy you as to forget that we and our poor are more important to God than all the lilies of the field and the birds of the air" (Mother Teresa, *Love: A Fruit Always in Season – Daily Meditations,* ed. D. S. Hunt, p. 181; J. L. Gonzalez – Balado, *Always the Poor: Mother Teresa – Her Life and Message,* p. 7).

[79] Cf. Mother Teresa, *Thirsting for God: A Year Book of Prayers, Meditations and Anecdotes,* compiled by A. D. Scolozzi, p. 122.

[80] Cf. *MCs Constitutions,* Art. 54; in another occasion she confirmed the necessity of Trust in God in these words: "Trust God. Feel the security of divine providence. Trust Him. He knows. He will provide." (Mother Teresa, *Love: A Fruit Always in Season – Daily Meditations,* ed. D. S. Hunt, p. 27).

need of trust in God and avoidance of future worries about material needs:

> We must never get into the habit of being preoccupied with the future. There is no reason to do so. God is there.[81]

A spirit of renunciation out of loving trust in God should be there even in the midst of economic struggle and uncertainty. Such a situation can be a trial for our faith in God. A person who has a genuine trust in God will not be affected by financial crisis. We have seen this strong character in the life of Mother Teresa in the first chapter. She taught others to have this firmness:

> Jesus wants us to put all our trust in him. We have to renounce our desires in order to work for our own perfection. Even if we feel like a boat without a compass on the high seas, we are to commit ourselves fully to him, without trying to control his actions.[82]

Besides the members of her religious order, she also offered the same teachings to the universal Church.[83] Thus, following

---

[81] Mother Teresa, *Total Surrender*, ed. A. D. Scolozzi, p. 56; *Mother Teresa: Essential Writings*, selected with an introduction by J. Maalouf, p. 107; Mother Teresa, *Love: A Fruit Always in Season – Daily Meditations*, ed. D. S. Hunt, p. 180; Mother Teresa, *The Love of Christ: Spiritual Counsels*, eds. G. Goree and J. Barbier, p. 106.

[82] Mother Teresa, *Heart of Joy: The Transforming Power of Self-Giving*, ed. J. L. Gonzalez-Balado, p. 126; Mother Teresa, *Essential Writings*, selected with an introduction by J. Maalouf, p. 39.

[83] A bishop approached Mother Teresa with his worries, as he had to write an article on the topic – the future of the Church. He wanted to know her opinion. She answered: "The future is not in our hands. We have no power over it. We can act only today. . . Our Lord told us not to fret about tomorrow which is in God's hands. So we do not worry about it. Then Jesus is the same yesterday, today and tomorrow. Jesus is the same. He is the same today and tomorrow, and only He matters'." Mother

the teaching of Christ, she taught a lesson to all of us that religious poverty should be based on the loving trust in the Heavenly Father, a trust that can free a person from future worries and have him remain joyful even in absolute poverty.

3.2. Poverty in Becoming a Humble Servant of All

Christ invited his disciples to become servants of one another through humble service (Jn.13:14) and declared it as the condition for becoming great among others (Mt. 20: 26), for serving others with the attitude of unworthy servants (Lk.17:10). He also taught that becoming a slave to others was the way to become first among others (Mt. 20:27). Thus, becoming a humble servant is a model Christ taught his disciples to follow. Humble service to the least of society is one of the elements of religious poverty; i.e., coming down from one's original status to the least through humble service is also a form of renunciation.

Mother Teresa taught this aspect of becoming a servant through the lessons from the life and teachings of Christ. Christ took the form of a poor servant in order to make us rich and called us to follow Him. He did this in order to make the poor rich. Religious are to follow this teaching of Christ through becoming humble servants to others.[84] She illustrated the way the religious should practice poverty through humble service in one's own community. Once a

---

Teresa spoke these words to the bishop of Rotterdam in a conversation, on 15th August 1977 – inauguration day of a new house there. During this conversation E. Le Joly was present with them and later he quoted in his book (E. LE Joly, *Mother Teresa: Messenger of God's Love*, pp. 170-171).

[84] Mother Teresa wrote this in her letter to contemplative brothers on 8th November 1979 and it is quoted by S. Vazhakala, the co-founder and superior general of contemplative brothers, in his book (S. Vazhakala. MC, *Life with Mother Teresa*, p. 109).

week all members, including superiors, should be ready to clean the drains and toilets, and also be ready to give a helping hand in the kitchen. Once a month they must all help clean the store-room where food and relief goods are kept. Wherever there is a plot of land, make sure that they work in the garden and plant as many fruit trees as possible so that they can give food to the poor.[85] She considered humble service a privilege, and it is reflected in the constitution of the Missionaries of Charity.

> We consider it an honour and privilege to serve Christ in the distressing disguise of the poorest of the poor with our humble work, and we do it with deep gratitude and profound reverence in a spirit of fraternal sharing, convinced that in accepting our humble service they make our existence as Missionaries of Charity possible.[86]

According to her, the life of sacrifice that comes from the life of poverty should lead to a love of humble works. She instructed the members of her congregation through letters that this teaching of humble work is the outcome of the spirit of sacrifice drawn from the life of poverty. She wrote:

> Do not think it is a waste of time to feed the hungry, to visit and take care of the sick and dying, to open and receive the unwanted and homeless. Oh, no, this is our love of Christ in action. The humbler the work, the greater will be your love and efficiency. Be not afraid of the life of sacrifice that comes from the life of poverty.[87]

The basic reason by which she insisted on doing humble work was her conviction that usually there are none willing to do such work; rather, there are very many who wish to do great things. Because we human beings consider certain

---

[85] Cf. Mother Teresa, *Total Surrender*, ed. A. D. Scolozzi, p. 92.

[86] *MCs Constitutions,* Art. 71.

[87] *Mother's Letter,* Melbourne, Victoria, 17th May, 1970.

works as low, we refuse to do them. God does not look at things as we do. We are so small that we look at things in a small way. But God, being Almighty, sees everything as great. Whatever is small in our sight is great in the sight of God. So we should not shy away from doing humble works.[88] She explained this matter further with certain examples:

> Even if you write a letter for a blind man or you just go and sit and listen, or bring a flower to somebody – small things – or wash clothes for somebody, or clean the house. Very humble work, that is where you and I must be, for there are many who can do big things but there are very few people who will do the small things.[89]

She taught us the core of humility in the context of living a simple life. She emphasized the humility of God in becoming man, taking the form of the servant despite the fact that He possessed the fullness of the Godhead. She emphasised the fact that even today God shows His humility by making use of instruments as deficient as human beings, who are weak, imperfect, inadequate instruments.[90] She considered each one of us a small instrument in the hands of God.[91] With this conviction she instructed her sisters to do the humblest services for the poorest of the poor in the slums:

> In the slums the sisters should find a place where they will gather street children, who ever they may be. Their very first concern is to make them clean, feed them and

---

[88] Cf. Mother Teresa, *Love: A Fruit Always in Season – Daily Meditations,* ed. D. S. Hunt, p. 26; cf. Mother Teresa, *Life in Spirit*, ed. K. Spink, p. 49.

[89] Mother Teresa, *Love: A Fruit Always in Season – Daily Meditations,* ed. D. S. Hunt, p. 26.

[90] Cf. E. Le Joly, *We Do it for Jesus: Mother Teresa and the Missionaries of Charity*, p. 167.

[91] Cf. Mother Teresa, *No Greater Love,* ed. B. Benenate and J. Durepos, p. 67.

> only then teach them, and prepare them for admission into regular schools. The love of God must be proposed to them in a simple, interesting and attractive way.[92]

When someone remarked that she seemed to be shrinking to become smaller and smaller as if she were not feeling well, her answer was that she wanted to become so small that she could enter into the Heart of Jesus.[93] Again, on another occasion she remarked: "I am just a little pencil in the hands of God."

3.3. Poverty in Spirit

Jesus' teaching on the poor in spirit appears in the St. Matthew's version of the Beatitudes, the inaugural message of Jesus during his Sermon on the Mount. Jesus began His preaching with the beatitude on the poor in spirit: "Blessed are the poor in spirit, for theirs is the kingdom of heaven" (Mt. 5:3). Mother Teresa meditated upon these words of Jesus and taught the members of her religious community to imbibe the spirit of poverty. According to her, this is a personal disposition in the midst of material discomforts and is also an internal attitude each one should develop in the use of the things in the world. Her interpretation of the poor in spirit also covers the interpretation of spiritual poverty as an acceptance with humility of the state of our nothingness and sinfulness. Once she expressed the remarkable sign of a true spirit of poverty as the internal attitude in the midst of discomforts:

> Those who have the true spirit of poverty rejoice if the worst things of the house are given to them for use while the good things which were given by some of their friends

---

[92] *Ibid.*, p. 153.

[93] Cf. E. Le Joly, *Mother Teresa: The Glorious Years*, p. 83.

> are being used by some other sister or given to some other house.[94]

She was careful to maintain the spirit of poverty in her communities and always advised her sisters not to go after comforts and attractive material objects. In the line of keeping the spirit of poverty in the community, she instructed her sisters to be moderate in purchasing things because good example in saving will safeguard in them the spirit of poverty. Some of the practical ways she advised were as follows: a religious must buy things of cheaper quality;[95] while shopping pick up the simplest things;[96] and instead of living in a private room live in a common dormitory.[97] One should have the sense of detachment both in the time of comforts and in the time of discomforts, while receiving things and also when nothing is given. She said:

> Even if you beg, show your detachment by feeling comfortable, both when nothing is given to you and when you receive generously.[98]

In order to save sinful mankind Christ became poor, and in this we can find God's love in action. For Mother Teresa what makes us poor is our sinfulness, our attachments, our jealousy and our pride. This is our poverty, and Christ came to save us from this poverty.[99]

---

[94] *The Little Book of Mothers Letter's*, pp. 82, 85.

[95] Cf. Mother Teresa, *Jesus, the Word to Be Spoken*, compiled by A. D. Scolozzi, p. 104; cf. Mother Teresa, *Love: A Fruit Always in Season – Daily Meditations*, ed. D. S. Hunt, p. 160.

[96] Cf. Mother Teresa, *Heart of Joy: The Transforming Power of Self-Giving*, ed. J. L. González – Balado, p. 95.

[97] Cf. Mother Teresa, *Jesus, the Word to Be Spoken*, compiled by A. D. Scolozzi, p. 104.

[98] Mother Teresa, *Heart of Joy: The Transforming Power of Self-Giving*, ed. J. L. González – Balado, p. 128.

[99] Cf. *Mother's Instructions: Let Us Make Our society Something Beautiful for God*, Vol. 3, Supplement 1, p. 8.

The spirit of poverty is considered an acknowledgement of one's own nothingness before God. A kind of dependence on God is essential for the success of life. It is clearly spelt out in the constitution of the MC Fathers:

> The spirit of poverty is the recognition of our sinfulness, the acceptance of our helplessness and nothingness before God, and the acknowledgement of Him 'without whom we can do nothing' (Jn.15:5). It is also a spirit of joyful hope in Him, of interior detachment from material and spiritual goods, and of openness to receive all things from God our Father.[100]

It is not the amount of wealth one has that makes him rich or poor but the attachment toward what he has. If one has an undue attachment to whatever one has, he is spiritually poor. This sort of attachment and failure to respond to the call can also be seen in the case of the rich young man in the Gospel. Jesus counselled him to give up his wealth and give to the poor, advice to which he could not respond; and so he went away sad (Mk.10: 21-22). Whereas, in the case of Zacheus, the contact with Jesus slowly melted his heart and he even became ready to share his wealth with the poor (Lk.19:1-10). Mother Teresa, while speaking about the spirit of poverty, time and again mentioned avoiding undue attachment towards one's own property. She said:

> There is not only material poverty but also spiritual poverty, which is harder and deeper, harbouring even in the hearts of very wealthy men. Wealth is not only property and money, but our attachment to these things and our abuse of them.[101]

---

[100] *Constitution and Directory of Missionaries of Charities - Fathers,* Tijuana, 1992, Art. 41.

[101] Mother Teresa, *Heart of Joy: The Transforming Power of Self-Giving,* ed. J. L. González – Balado, p. 123.

One should not remain satisfied just with the knowledge of the spirit of poverty but go beyond it and practice the spirit of poverty concretely in daily life. Through the life of poverty one should give witness to the world the real meaning of poverty. The climax of the spirit of poverty has to be reflected in the life of a person who claims to have the spirit of poverty. In this regard Mother Teresa said:

> It is not enough to know the spirit of poverty; you have to know poverty itself. Poverty means not having anything. Today everyone, even those who come from well to do environments, want to know what it really means to have nothing.[102]

4. FOLLOWING THE MISSION OF CHRIST

The proclamation to the poor is the finest hour of Jesus' mission, and the option for the poor is the benchmark of Jesus' call to radical discipleship, His call to let oneself be sent. The option for the poor is more than a simple way of life. Its most authentic expression is solidarity with the poor, participation and involvement in their struggle for human dignity.[103] The missionary vocation of the religious is revealed in the mission of Jesus as stated in Luke's Gospel: "To proclaim the good news to the poor . . . to set free the oppressed" (Lk. 4:18-19). Religious poverty can be an effective means for the mission of Christ of preaching the Gospel to all the nations. His missionary command also consists of certain demands of poverty on the part of disciples, and all three synoptic writers record this account (cf. Mt. 10:9-10; Mk. 6: 8-10; Lk. 9:3). Radical aspects of poverty prescribed by Jesus are rigorous in all three gospels.

---

[102] *Ibid*., p. 88.

[103] Cf. A. Karokaran, "Discipleship: A Participation in Jesus' sending", in *Review for Religious*, Vol. 58 (1999), p. 618.

Mother Teresa emphasised the life-witness of the missionaries rather than the mere preaching without practicing gospel values in one's own life.[104] Jesus became a success in His mission by His voluntary poverty from birth to death, with His incarnation and approach to the people, since he came down to the lower level of human misery with regard to material poverty. Mother Teresa emphasised this approach in her mission and taught others to do the same. Hence, in the following section we shall deal with the mission of Christ by following the voluntary poverty of Christ as a way to achieve success in mission.

4.1. The Meaning and Purpose of Mission in the Light of Poverty

Christ's mission was to proclaim to the poor the good news of God's salvation (cf. Lk. 4:18). Mother Teresa taught that the mission of the religious is to take part in the work of God in converting and sanctifying souls. In this task irrespective of most abandoned places, poor facilities, filth and squalor, they should be ready for their mission. They must be willing to go all over the world and should not be attached to one place.[105] She clarified her vision on mission by stating:

> A missionary is one sent with a mission – a message to deliver. Just as Jesus was sent by His Father, we too are sent by Him and filled with His Spirit to be witness of His

---

[104] "There should be less talk; preaching point is not a meeting point. What do you do then? Take a broom and clean someone's house. That says enough" (Mother Teresa OF Calcutta, *A Gift for God: Prayers and Meditations,* compiled by M. Muggeridge, pp. 44-45).

[105] Cf. Mother Teresa, *Total Surrender*, ed. A. D. Scolozzi, pp. 15, 139; cf. Mother Teresa, *Heart of Joy: The Transforming Power of Self-Giving*, ed. J. L. González – Balado, p. 97.

> gospel of love and compassion, first in our communities and then in our apostolate among the poorest of the poor all over the world.[106]

She taught her followers about the specific nature of mission of the MCs as becoming 'a messenger of God's love'. She also pointed out how in Yemen her sisters are known as 'carriers of God's love'. Yemenites realized that these are women of God, messengers of his love on earth. They experience how sisters convert their love for Christ into deeds.[107] According to her, the holy faith is nothing but a gospel of love. It reveals to us God's love for us and in return, our love for God, who is love. Therefore, a missionary must be a missionary of love,[108] as she made it clear concerning the nature of MCs mission:

> Our mission is a mission of love. It is a mission of kindness especially for today, when there is so much hunger for God . . . a Missionary of Charity is a messenger of God's love.[109]

Mother Teresa was of the opinion that a religious who opted for the mission of Jesus should be ready to face any hardships in life, even unto death. Therefore, she advised her sisters that they must be ready to pay the price Jesus paid for souls, to walk in the way he walked. Similarly, missionaries must

---

[106] Mother Teresa, *No Greater Love,* ed. B. Benenate and J. Durepos, p. 145; Mother Teresa, *Total Surrender*, ed. A. D. Scolozzi, p. 15.

[107] Cf. Mother Teresa, *One Heart Full of Love*, ed. J. L. González – Balado, pp. 13, 23; cf. Mother Teresa, *No Greater Love,* ed. B. Benenate and J. Durepos, p. 147.

[108] Cf. Mother Teresa, *Thirsting for God: A Year Book of Prayers, Meditations and Anecdotes,* compiled by A. D. Scolozzi, p. 114.

[109] Mother Teresa, *Heart of Joy: The Transforming Power of Self-Giving,* ed. J. L. González – Balado, p. 51.

die everyday if they want to lead souls to God.[110] Missionary zeal and enthusiasm to present Christ and his message all over the world was deep-rooted in Mother Teresa. This is clear from her words:

> Once, someone asked me, 'Why do you go abroad? Don't you have enough poor in India?' So I answered, "Jesus told us to go and preach to all the nations.' That is why we go all over the world to preach His love and compassion.[111]

4.2. The Role of Life-witness in the Mission

Religious who chose to experience material poverty in a radical way as an evangelical witness are a constant source of amazement and admiration to both believers and non-believers alike.[112] Gospel values on voluntary poverty can be effectively preached through the life-witness of religious. Life-witness has greater effect than preaching by words. Thus practice of radical poverty comes under the effective means of evangelization. Mother Teresa paid much attention to teach this missionary value to others by her words and her life examples. She insisted that, for the members of her congregation, the practice of radical poverty is a way to realize this missionary vision.

---

[110] Cf. Mother Teresa, *Total Surrender*, ed. A. D. Scolozzi, p. 141; cf. Mother Teresa, *Heart of Joy: The Transforming Power of Self-Giving*, ed. J. L. González – Balado, p. 99.

[111] Mother Teresa, *No Greater Love*, ed. B. Benenate and J. Durepos, p. 61.

[112] Cf. O. Tanghe, *For the Least of My Brothers: The Spirituality of Mother Teresa and Catherine Doherty*, p. 27. Once a missionary from India spoke to the author on the radical poverty of the sisters of Mother Teresa which has become a matter of evangelical witness: "The Sisters of Mother Teresa whom I saw at work in Ranchi and Calcutta are extremely conscientious religious. The poor way in which they live is simply staggering" (*Ibid.*).

She was convinced that more than preaching the Word of God, the aspect of witnessing the Word of God has to be given priority in carrying out the mission of Christ. Therefore her teaching and practice on evangelisation was centred on this thought. According to her, God has to be made present in the world of today by our life and witness.[113] She taught that the most appealing invitation to embrace the religious life is the witness of our own lives, the spirit in which we react to our divine calling. It is the apostolic zeal with which we give witness to Christ's love for the poorest of the poor.[114] Emphasising the importance of life witness in the mission, she mentioned the words of Mahatma Gandhi and gave us a lesson that we Christians have to live our Christianity fully in order to achieve success in our mission.[115] Once she expressed how the MCs fulfil the missionary command of Jesus:

> Every day we try to live out Christ's love in a very tangible way in every one of our deeds. If we do any preaching, it is done with deeds, not with words. That is our witness to the Gospels.[116]

---

[113] Cf. L. Gjergji, *Mother Teresa: To Live, to Love, to Witness – Her Spiritual Way*, translated by J. Aumann, p. 97; cf. Mother Teresa, *Essential Writings*, selected with an introduction by J. Maalouf, p. 32.

[114] Cf. Mother Teresa, *Thirsting for God: A Year Book of Prayers, Meditations and Anecdotes*, compiled by A. D. Scolozzi, p. 142.

[115] "Gandhi once said that if Christians were really Christians, there would be no Hindus in India. People expect us to fully live our Christian life." (Mother Teresa, *Heart of Joy: The Transforming Power of Self-Giving*, ed. J. L. Gonzalez-Balado, p.134).

[116] Mother Teresa, *Loving Jesus*, ed. J. L. González – Balado, p. 132; Mother Teresa, *No Greater Love*, ed. B. Benenate and J. Durepos, p. 179.

More than money, the people need our heart, she continued; a heart that contains the love of Christ. Giving to Christ is our mission, and then we have to concentrate on giving the poor the love of Christ through our concrete presence in their midst, sharing their sufferings. She affirmed that the MCs strive to live out concretely the love of Christ in each of their actions every day, despite their weaknesses and miseries. Every day they are in touch with the most marginal of society.[117] She emphasised the concrete and direct personal service of love to the needy rather than financial assistance:

> Money is not enough. I do not want anyone to offer me money which I can get if I ask for it. My poor need to be loved with the heart and to be served with the hands.[118]

Mother Teresa taught the importance of life-witness in carrying out the mission of Christ through various concrete examples, prove with good effect. Once she narrated an incident whereby an atheist became a believer in God through the life-witness of a sister. As he exclaimed at his departure: "I came here today, not believing in God . . . but now I am leaving here believing in God."[119] In another occasion, one of her sisters was washing a leper covered with sores. A Muslim holy man was present, standing close to her. He said, "All these years I have believed that Jesus Christ is a prophet. Today I believe that Jesus Christ is God since he has been able to give such joy to this sister, so that she can do her work with so much love."[120] In the words of a

---

[117] Cf. Mother Teresa, *Heart of Joy: The Transforming Power of Self-Giving*, ed. J. L. González – Balado, p. 113.

[118] *Ibid.*, p. 116.

[119] Mother Teresa, *One Heart Full of Love*, ed. J. L. González – Balado, p. 65.

[120] *Ibid.*, p. 27; cf. Mother Teresa, *Total Surrender*, ed. A. D. Scolozzi, p. 147.

distinguished person in India: "When I see the sisters in the streets of Calcutta, I always have the impression that Jesus Christ has come again into the world."[121]

Pope John Paul II appraised Mother Teresa's life witness for the mission of Christ in preaching the good news to the poor and the effort for the conversion of sinners.[122] Once, Mother Teresa expressed her gratitude towards the Church for allowing her congregation to lead a life of strict poverty and become the presence of Jesus among the poorest of the poor, enabling them to be God's love and compassion for the poor.[123] She received praise from all corners of the world for her life-witness. In the words of J. Moniz: "To the world of today, which prefers life more than words, witness more than teaching and action more than theory, Mother Teresa speaks through her life and concrete deeds. At a time when

---

[121] Mother Teresa, *One Heart Full of Love*, ed. J. L. González – Balado, p. 68.

[122] "It is a witness which the whole world watches, a testimony which smites the conscience of the world. I am speaking of the witness of the life and work of one, who although she was not born in India now known as Mother Teresa of Calcutta. . . . Such charity and self- service, done out of love for Christ challenges the world, a world which is all too familiar with selfishness and hedonism, with greed for money, prestige and power. In the face of the evils of our modern age, this testimony proclaims not with words, but by deeds and sacrifice, the pre-eminent value of love, the love of Christ our redeemer. It calls the sinner to conversion and invites him to follow the example of Christ to preach Good News to the poor" (John Paul II, "Homily during the concelebration in West Bengal, India)", 4 February 1986, in *Insegnamenti di Giovanni Paolo II*, 9/1, Libreria Editrice Vaticana, Roma 1986, pp. 316-317).

[123] Cf. Mother Teresa, *One Heart Full of Love*, ed. J. L. González – Balado, p. 20.

preaching has become a fashion, witness through life is preaching."[124]

4.3. Deliberate Choice of Simple and Lowly Means

Mother Teresa taught us to understand how, through lowly and humble means, we are in the hands of God in carrying out His mission. She was of the opinion that the contemplative and apostolic fruitfulness of our way of life depends on our being rooted in Christ Jesus. This state of deep rootedness in Christ can be achieved through one's deliberate choice of small and simple means for the fulfilment of one's mission and fidelity to humble works of love among the poorest.[125] In the MCs constitution this idea is seen:

> The spiritual and apostolic fruitfulness of our Society will depend on our deliberate choice of simple and lowly means in the fulfilment of our mission.[126]

Mother Teresa insisted that mission among the poor for the salvation and sanctification of souls has to be carried out by a life marked by the simplicity and humility of the Gospel.[127] She taught her sisters to be convinced of the freedom of poverty and keep to the most humble means. She gave them some practical tips for remaining in the simple path of poverty and gave awareness that they have an opportunity

---

[124] J. Moniz, *No Greater Service: Mother and the Mahatma,* p.180.

[125] Cf. Mother Teresa, *Jesus, the Word to Be Spoken,* compiled by A. D. Scolozzi, p. 39.

[126] *MCs Constitutions,* Art. 6. Constitution instructs the sisters about the usage of humble means in their apostolate: "In our apostolate we shall use humble and simple means charged with the power of God Himself." (*Ibid.,* Art. 111).

[127] Cf. Mother Teresa, *Total Surrender*, ed. A. D. Scolozzi, p. 16.

to practice marvellous poverty.[128] She also instructed them to choose poor conveyance in their mission of searching for souls through walking and cycling. They must be grateful to God for these burdensome trips, for the joy they have tried to spread in the world.[129] She inspired them and encouraged them to have a sense of humility in the deliberate choice of humble means in carrying out one's mission by accepting each one as a small instrument: "Each one of us is merely a small instrument; all of us, after accomplishing our mission, will disappear."[130]

---

128 Cf. Mother Teresa, *Heart of Joy: The Transforming Power of Self-Giving*, ed. J. L. González – Balado, p. 129. Once she spoke to her sisters: "Keep simple ways of poverty, of repairing your own shoes, and so forth, in short, of loving poverty as you love your mother." (Mother teresa, *Jesus, The word to be Spoken*, compiled by A. D. Scolozzi, p. 105; Mother Teresa, *The Love of Christ: Spiritual Counsels*, eds. G. Goree and J. Barbier, p. 107).

129 Cf. *Ibid*., p. 139.

130 *Ibid*., p. 115.

CHAPTER 3

The Vow of Poverty and its Relation with Other Religious Vows

Many are poor by birth or due to a certain forced situation, but many are poor by one's own choice for a greater purpose. In the religious life, poverty by choice for spiritual glory is made a promise after due understanding about its importance through a period of formation. We call this promise a vow.[1] The value of a vow does not lie in the choosing of a good over a bad in life but in choosing a good of still higher value. For instance, to vow poverty is not to despise the goodness in the creation but to commit oneself to dependence on the Creator and experience a freedom to love him more through the detachment from

[1] "A vow is a deliberate and free promise made to God of a good that is possible and better, the fulfilment of which obliges from the virtue of religion" (J. F. Dede, "Vows: impediment to marriage", in *New Catholic Encyclopaedia,* The Catholic University of America, Gale, New York 2003, vol. 14, p. 758).

worldly goods.[2] In this chapter we will be dealing with the concept of poverty as a religious promise or vow by which religious are bound to live. A short description of the general meaning of the vow of poverty, a central teaching of Mother Teresa, and its relation to other common vows, namely chastity and obedience, will be shown. Mother Teresa has coined a fourth vow of charity called service to the poorest of the poor. This vow will be dealt with in the sixth chapter, as it particularly deals with the relation between charity and poverty. Thus there are four vows professed and practiced by religious communities founded by Mother Teresa.[3]

According to Mother Teresa there is an interrelationship between vows,[4] one supports the other, and also negligence of one vow affects the other. This fact was well expressed by

---

[2] Cf. J. Chittister, "Vows", in *The New Dictionary of Catholic Spirituality*, ed. M. Downey, The Liturgical Press, Minnesota 1993, p. 1011.

[3] "We profess the three vows of loving Christ with undivided love in chastity, through the freedom of poverty, in total commitment through obedience. We assume a fourth vow whereby we commit ourselves to offer from our hearts voluntary service to the poorest among the poor, that is to say, to Christ under the humble appearance of the poor" (Mother Teresa, *Heart of Joy: The Transforming Power of Self-Giving*, ed. J. L. González-Balado, p. 37).

[4] Mother Teresa explained the coherence of the four vows through a letter written to her sisters: "The vow of chastity makes us cleave to Christ, and the fruit of our union with Christ is the vow of charity (4th vow) . . . To enable the vow of charity to grow we make the vows of poverty and obedience; just as a lamp cannot live without oil, so the vow of charity cannot live without the vows poverty and obedience; and all three vows are because of chastity" (Mother Teresa, quoted in J. Neuner, "Mother Teresa's Charism", in *Review for Religious*, Vol. 60, no. 5 (2001), p. 489).

her: "If I neglect obedience, poverty will go. When poverty goes, chastity will go."[5] Thus, for her, poverty is the safeguard for chastity and obedience is the safeguard for poverty. If some one did not obey superiors in keeping the vow of poverty, then the vow of poverty is damaged. On another occasion she brought out that this interconnection between vows and their interdependence enables unity among the members in the religious community. She said:

> We are all one. To achieve this unity, the sisters profess the vow of chastity. That means loving Christ with an undivided love in the freedom to be poor and in total surrender through obedience.[6]

1. VOW OF POVERTY

In the religious life, voluntary poverty is actualized by the vow of poverty. The official definition of the vow of poverty by the Roman congregations in approving their constitutions is: "By the vow of poverty religious renounce the right of disposing licitly of any temporal thing of monetary value without the permission of their lawful superior. In solemn vow to be added - By law, the solemnly professed become incapable of retaining or acquiring temporal goods for themselves."[7] Two elements enter into the obligations of this vow: the renunciation of at least the independent use of material possessions and the practice of the community life. Further obligations concerning these two elements are determined by various canons of the Code of Canon Law,[8] and are then more particularly specified by the constitutions

---

[5] Mother Teresa, *Total Surrender*, ed. A. D. Scolozzi, p. 76.

[6] Mother Teresa, *One Heart Full of Love*, ed. J. L. González – Balado, p. 96.

[7] J. F. Gallen, "Religious Poverty Re-examined" in *Review for Religious*, Vol. 37, no. 5 (1978), p. 739.

[8] Cf. Canons, 600, 668, 669, 672, 706.

of each individual religious institute. By the solemn vow of poverty, of course, not only is the independent use of material possessions relinquished, but the actual ownership and the right to future ownership is renounced, thereby binding a person against the possession and free use of temporal goods. It also leads to a state of virtue with inordinate detachment towards worldly matters. Mother Teresa while explaining about the meaning and nature of vow poverty exhorted this view:

> By the vow of poverty we deprive ourselves of the possession and free use of temporal goods. Its virtue causes the destruction of inordinate attachment to the things of this world. The vow is the means and the virtue is the end.[9]

The various features of religious poverty reflected in the teaching of Mother Teresa are that it is freely chosen, yielding the experience of freedom, a state of joy, and is offered as a dowry to Jesus out of love of Christ and the poor.[10]

1.1. Poverty is Out of Free Choice

Evangelical poverty is to be freely chosen with one's own conviction and not out of compulsion. This poverty is different from the poverty someone experiences because he happened to be born in such a situation or from the poverty that came into his life against his wishes. Mother Teresa repeatedly emphasised that her poverty and that of her

---

[9] Mother Teresa, *Jesus, the Word to be Spoken*, compiled by A. D. Scolozzi, p. 97.

[10] "Our poverty is the result of a choice. That is why I speak of the freedom of poverty. We have the freedom to love God, to love Jesus, and to the poor, all with an undivided heart" (Mother Teresa, *Heart of Joy: The Transforming Power of Self-Giving*, ed. J. L. González-Balado, p. 9).

sisters are freely chosen. She states the difference in the poverty of the poor and the poverty of MCs as that the poor are poor by birth and by force, while the MCs are poor by choice.[11] Thus the MCs willingly learn to enjoy and experience freedom while they are in want or suffering through poverty. They should refrain from demands which the poor themselves would not make with regard to goods, clothing, medical care, recreational facilities, and mode of travel or working equipment.[12] She also affirmed that the vow of poverty is not attached to any misconception about wrongness of having things; rather it is a free choice. Therefore she expressed:

> We vow poverty not because it is wrong to have things but we choose to do without these things.[13]

Mother Teresa considered that the motive for this choice is the deep conviction that Christ remains hidden in the face of the disowned of this world and without this conviction religious poverty is impossible.[14] According to her this choice to practice the life of poverty is also out of love for Jesus. She said:

---

[11] Cf. Mother Teresa, *No Greater Love,* ed. B. Benenate and J. Durepos, p. 97; Mother Teresa, *Heart of Joy: The Transforming Power of Self-Giving*, ed. J. L. González-Balado, p. 65; Mother Teresa, *Thirsting for God: A Year Book of Prayers, Meditations and Anecdotes,* compiled by A. D. Scolozzi, p. 75; J. L. González – Balado, *Always the Poor - Mother Teresa: Her life and Message*, p. 83; E. Le Joly, *We Do it for Jesus: Mother Teresa and the Missionaries of Charity*, p. 131.

[12] Cf. A. Savarimuthu, *Spirituality of Mother Teresa of Calcutta*, pp. 158-159; also cf. *MCs Constitutions*, Art. 52.

[13] Mother Teresa, *Total Surrender*, ed. A. D. Scolozzi, p. 67.

[14] Cf. J. L. González – Balado, *Always the Poor - Mother Teresa: Her Life and Message*, p. 83.

> We do not accept poverty because we are forced to be poor but because we choose to be poor for the love of Jesus; because he, being rich, became poor for love of us. Let us not deceive ourselves.[15]
>
> Our people are poor by force, but our poverty is of our own choice. We want to be poor like Christ who, being rich, chose to be born and live and work among the poor."[16]

Religious poverty is personal response to the initiative of God, Who offers His only Son to man and invites him to enter into communion with Christ. Christ took a life of poverty upon himself as a free choice. Therefore, religious, disciples of Christ, have to take poverty upon themselves in a similar way: freely chosen, accepted and embraced. In this way a religious life enables an intimate participation in the life of Christ. Mother Teresa was sure that she and her sisters' poverty comes under this category of poverty. She said:

> Of our own free will, we have chosen to be faithful to poverty. This is a sign of God, of the true poverty of Christ.[17]

Once a journalist of Time Magazine put before Mother Teresa a question with regard to the criticism people make about the severity of life that she imposes on herself and her Sisters.

---

[15] Mother Teresa, *Jesus, the Word to be Spoken,* compiled by A. D. Scolozzi, p. 97; Mother Teresa, *Thirsting for God: A Year Book of Prayers, Meditations and Anecdotes,* compiled by A. D. Scolozzi, p. 108.

[16] These are the words of Mother Teresa wrote to E. Le Joly about the reason for the poverty and he quoted in his book (E. Le Joly, *We Do it for Jesus: Mother Teresa and the Missionaries of Charity,* p. 131; cf. J. L. Gonzalez – Balado, *Always the Poor: Mother Teresa Her Life and Message,* p. 83).

[17] Mother Teresa, *Thirsting for God: A Year Book of Prayers, Meditations and Anecdotes,* compiled by A. D. Scolozzi, p. 167.

She answered very plainly that there is difference between the severe life of the poor and the severe life of MCs. She explained that MCs poverty is by free choice in order to be more effective in their mission as experiencing the difficulties of the poor and saving them from that situation;[18] in effect, an approach of Christ in incarnation and the experience of poverty in his public life. On another occasion she also explained how young people embrace poverty with love and chose freely,[19] and she made it clear that no one was forced to accept severe poverty to be a religious in her community.

While referring to evangelical poverty, recent Church documents also emphasise the voluntary nature of poverty.[20] To this extent Mother Teresa remained within the framework of Church's teaching in practising and teaching religious poverty.

1.2. Poverty is Freedom

Poverty enables the religious to experience more freedom in their life to love Jesus. As Jesus taught that no one can serve two masters at the same time, for either he/she will hate the one and love the other, or will be devoted to the one and despise the other. Therefore, religious cannot serve both God and Mammon at the same time (Cf. Lk.16:13). Life becomes freer when there are fewer matters to attend to, and it becomes joyful when one willingly accepts this

---

[18] Cf. F. ZamboninI, *Teresa of Calcutta: A Pencil in God's Hand*, p. 122.

[19] "Young people love renunciation. They desire to experience the freedom of poverty, freely chosen" (Mother Teresa, *Heart of Joy: The Transforming Power of Self-Giving*, ed. J. L. González-Balado, p. 9).

[20] Cf. PC 13; LG 42; PO 17.

situation with the conviction that this detachment is for a better cause.[21] Thus evangelical poverty for Mother Teresa is for a joyful freedom. The quintessence of the teaching on the joyful freedom inherent in the religious poverty is well understood from her following words:

> Poverty is freedom for us. Poverty is an offering that we make to God. It is something that brings us very close to Jesus. I don't mean that poverty consists of simply not having things. . . . It is a freedom so that what I possess doesn't own me, so that what I possess doesn't hold me down, so that my possessions don't keep me from sharing or giving of myself.[22]

The more one has material possessions, the more he is occupied with them; and the fewer material possessions, the less will he be occupied with them. When there are fewer materials to be engaged with, then the religious have more time to be with Jesus or to serve Jesus in whatever form of His presence be on earth. Religious poverty is a detachment in order to make one more freer for Jesus by denying material comfort voluntarily. And this freedom, which one gets from

---

[21] "Poverty makes us free. We need to experience the joy of poverty. . . We are free because nothing belongs to us. Our poverty means that we do not have the kind of shoes we may want or the house we may want. We cannot keep things or give anything away or lend anything of value. We have nothing. We own nothing. This is the experience of poverty" (Mother Teresa, *Thirsting for God: A Year Book of Prayers, Meditations and Anecdotes,* compiled by A. D. Scolozzi, p. 75).

[22] Mother Teresa spoke these words in her talk which was given at Brompton Oratory in London on June13, 1977 to the Co-workers of the Missionaries of Charity in England. This was collected by J. L. Gonzalez-Balado and published in his book (J. L. Gonzalez – Balado, *One Heart Full of Love: Mother Teresa,* p. 53).

exercising voluntary poverty, is a joyful freedom. Poverty is neither mortification nor penance; rather it is a freedom.[23]

She also exhorted once how true poverty gives detachment and freedom from various other affairs, so as to understand the poorest of the poor in a better way. And also, she continued to stress the importance of poverty in the life of MCs compared to other religious orders. She explained once that, more than any other religious order, MCs need poverty, true poverty. Poverty gives them the detachment and freedom that are necessary if they are to understand the very poorest with whom they work.[24]

When she spoke about the freedom in the practice of poverty, did not mean the ordinary sense of freedom to use the material objects. She meant another kind of freedom, liberation from material attachments and a freedom to love Jesus, derived from total detachment from the material objects in life. A religious has to arrive at such a level of detachment that even articles given for personal use should be considered as common property and not as one's own. There is nothing to be considered as one's own, and thus a person is fully free to give oneself to Jesus, a total offering and undivided love for Jesus. Mother Teresa expressed it very beautifully in the words:

> When you make the vow of poverty, you say 'I have nothing.' That is why you cannot destroy things or give them away without permission. By right, you can't say, 'This is my sari.' For us poverty is freedom. You are free to love God – free to love Jesus with an undivided heart.[25]

---

[23] Cf. F. Zambonini, *Teresa of Calcutta: A Pencil in God's Hand*, pp. 121-122.

[24] Cf. *Ibid.*, p. 160.

[25] Mother Teresa, *Total Surrender*, ed. A. D. Scolozzi, pp. 59-60; "If I could have only one sari, it would be mine. Yet if I become

Sometimes this understanding of poverty as joyful freedom becomes a contradiction. There are people who wish to be poor according to their personal wishes, a kind of freedom to dispose of things according to their own interest. According to Mother Teresa this is another kind of contradiction. If any one uses this kind of personal liberty, in possessing and disposing, then he ceases to be poor. For her poverty would mean a kind of giving up of one's freedom to possess and dispose of things. In other words, to be free from the freedom to possess and detach in accordance with one's own wish.[26] She went on to say that the misunderstanding of this freedom causes the suffering of the Church:

> The suffering of the church is caused by a misunderstanding of freedom and renewal. We cannot be free unless we are able to renounce our own will for Christ's.[27]

1.3. Poverty is Joy

Mother Teresa instructed her sisters to be cheerful and emphasised specially to radiate the joy of being poor. Poverty must be practised with happiness. The religious vow of poverty is freely and willingly taken, so they must be happy in their life of poverty.[28] The less the attachments to

---

a Missionary of Charity, I am given a sari to use, not to keep. This is the difference between having your own sari and receiving one to use. That difference has been our strength and our joy"(Mother Teresa, *One Heart Full of Love*, ed. J. L. González – Balado, p. 52).

[26] Cf. Mother Teresa, *Total Surrender*, ed. A. D. Scolozzi, pp. 57-58; Mother Teresa, *Essential Writings*, selected with an introduction by J. Maalouf, p. 108.

[27] Mother Teresa, *Heart of Joy: The Transforming Power of Self-Giving*, ed. J. L. Gonzalez-Balado, p. 128.

[28] Cf. *Ibid.*, pp. 74, 95.

material things, the more the religious are able to give themselves to Jesus. Certainly it is a state of happiness that, since they have nothing of their own and they are able to give more of themselves to Jesus, He in turn gives His peace and joy to them.[29] Therefore poverty is not only renunciation but also an experience of joy. This joy can be achieved only through the practice of poverty in the way she proposed. And she claimed it is difficult to understand unless a person experiences personally the joy of poverty.[30] The reason for this great joy is clear from her words:

> Poverty is joy. We must be happy with what we have and be happy with what we don't have. Poverty for us is a choice and therefore a joy. The less we have the more we can give.[31]

Mother Teresa taught her sisters to accept suffering with joy. They have to live a life of poverty with cheerful trust and to

---

[29] "Poverty makes us free. That is why we can joke and smile and have a happy heart for Jesus" (Mother Teresa, *Thirsting for God: A Year Book of Prayers, Meditations and Anecdotes,* compiled by A. D. Scolozzi, p. 127; Mother Teresa, *Total Surrender,* ed. A. D. Scolozzi, p. 56; Mother Teresa, *Essential Writings,* selected with an introduction by J. Maalouf, p. 107; Mother Teresa, *Love: A Fruit Always in Season – Daily Meditations,* ed. D. S. Hunt, p. 160; Mother Teresa, *The Love of Christ: Spiritual Counsels,* eds. G. Goree and J. Barbier, p. 106).

[30] Cf. Mother Teresa, *Total Surrender*, ed. A. D. Scolozzi, p. 60; Mother Teresa, *Essential Writings,* selected with an introduction by J. Maalouf, pp. 113-114; cf. *The Mother Teresa Reader: A Life for God,* compiled by L. V. NEFF, p. 219.

[31] Mother Teresa, *Thirsting for God: A Year Book of Prayers, Meditations and Anecdotes*, compiled by A. D. Scolozzi, p. 178. A rich man of Delhi, in speaking of MCs, said, "How wonderful it is to see Sisters so free from the world – in the twentieth century when one thinks everything is old-fashioned but the present day" (Mother Teresa, *Jesus, The Word to be Spoken,* compiled by A. D. Scolozzi, p. 105).

minister to Jesus in the poorest of the poor with cheerfulness. God loves a cheerful giver. She or he gives best who gives with a smile. If they are always ready to say 'Yes' to God, they will naturally have a smile for all and be able, with God's blessing, to give until it hurts.[32] She further emphasised:

> Cheerfulness is often a cloak which hides a life of sacrifice, continual union with God, fervour, and generosity.[33]

In the midst of inconveniences and lack of comforts one can be happy only when he/she has a right attitude toward poverty, as it is out of a personal choice for the better spiritual experience. Mother Teresa and her sisters were happy even in the midst of radical poverty in their house.[34] She advised her sisters not to complain about the hardship in life while practicing poverty and also to avoid telling the people about the hardship they have to undergo in the house. Instead, she urged, be cheerful and radiate the joy of being poor for Christ's sake. In this regard she wrote to her sisters:

> Radiate the joy of being poor, not telling the people of our hard life but just being happy to be poor with Christ.[35]

---

[32] Cf. Mother Teresa, *A Simple Path,* compiled by L. Vardey, p. 105. "The joy of the Lord is our strength. Therefore, each of us will accept the life of poverty in the cheerful trust" (*MCs Constitutions,* 25).

[33] Mother Teresa, *Total Surrender,* ed. A. D. Scolozzi, p. 44.

[34] "Look, there is no television here; there is neither this nor that. Although it gets very hot here, in the whole house there is only one fan, and that is not for us but for the guests. Nevertheless, we are perfectly happy." Mother Teresa spoke these words to E. W. Desmond, a journalist of Time Magazine, in an interview. Later F. Zambonini quoted this in his book (F. Zambonini, *Teresa of Calcutta: A Pencil in God's Hand,* pp. 121-122).

[35] Mother Teresa, *Thirsting for God: A Year Book of Prayers, Meditations and Anecdotes,* compiled by A. D. Scolozzi, p. 167.

While starting a new house, she never failed to instruct the local people to help the sisters not to lose the joy of poverty, rather help them to treasure the joy of poverty.[36] This instruction became necessary, because people of the locality out of respect and concern generously brought modern household articles and equipment to the sisters. Mother Teresa had to watch over the spirit of poverty in her convents and control it, when there was a chance of losing the genuine spirit of poverty due to the generosity of the people for the sisters.[37]

1.4. Poverty is Dowry

The property that a woman brings to her husband in marriage is dowry. Mother Teresa compares religious poverty as dowry to Jesus, the Spouse of the religious. Religious are married to Jesus from the time of their profession. There is a difference between the ordinary meaning of dowry and the dowry which she speaks about. In the ordinary sense of marriage, a bride brings to her husband wealth; whereas the religious brings to her husband no material riches, but a heart enriched with love; a heart full of love. This is to love him more and more without any distraction and not to share her love with anything else but Jesus. The less the material aspect of wealth one has the more one can give one's wealth of love, of oneself, to Jesus. In this regard she spoke:

> Poverty is our dowry. The less we have, the more we can give. The more we have, the less we give. There are no

---

[36] Cf. Mother Teresa, *One Heart Full of Love*, ed. J. L. González – Balado, p. 102.

[37] Cf. F. Zambonini, *Teresa of Calcutta: A Pencil in God's Hand*, pp. 120-121.

> complications and yet we complicate our lives so much, by so many additions.[38]

According to Mother Teresa, poverty is indeed a total gift of the self to Jesus. Religious need a pure heart, purified by the freedom of poverty, in order to become all for Jesus and to love Him with undivided love. Poverty is not primarily economic want but an attitude of sharing, self-giving.[39] By offering oneself totally to Jesus, the religious enters into a union with Him. Moreover, religious poverty for Mother Teresa is the outcome of being the handmaid of the Lord: union and identification with Jesus. So with deep awareness of God's presence and experience of union with Jesus, Mother Teresa with profound sentiments exclaimed:

> What is our spiritual life? A love union with Jesus. The Divine and the human give themselves completely to one another. All that Jesus asks of me is to give myself to Him in all poverty.[40]

Mother remained focused on what she was called to do, strong in her convictions and her spirit of poverty. She used to say that the religious must cling to Jesus, and nothing else. Nothing and nobody must come between Jesus and the religious. Poverty gave the freedom for her to love her crucified Spouse and to serve Him in the distressing disguise of the poorest of the poor. She emptied herself in order to become the abode of the Blessed Trinity. She understood

---

[38] Mother Teresa, *Thirsting for God: A Year Book of Prayers, Meditations and Anecdotes,* compiled by A. D. Scolozzi, p. 90; cf. J. Neuner, "Mother Teresa's Charism", in *Review for Religious,* Vol. 60, no. 5 (2001), p. 489.

[39] Cf. J. Neuner, "Mother Teresa's Charism", in *Vidyajyoti: Journal of Theological Reflection,* Vol. 65 (2001), p. 188.

[40] *Mother's Letter,* 31 October 1966; Mother Teresa, *No Greater Love,* ed. B. Benenate and J. Durepos, p. 85.

that the life she lived was no longer of her own, but that of Christ, who lived in her (Cf. Gal.2:20). The poorer she was, the more closely she resembled Jesus.[41]

The idea of religious poverty as dowry to Jesus, the bridegroom, can be understood only from the acceptance of one's own nothingness and sinfulness. A religious at the time of profession, the moment of spiritual marriage between a religious and Jesus, brings an unworthy heart compared to that of Jesus. This is all the property that a religious has to offer to enter into spousal union with Jesus. Mother Teresa enlightened us all concerning this understanding of religious poverty through the following words:

> Our poverty is our dowry. With regard to God, our poverty is our humble recognition and acceptance of our sinfulness, helplessness, and utter nothingness, and the acknowledgement of our neediness before Him, which expresses itself as a hope in Him, as an openness to receive all things from Him as from our Father.[42]

1.5. Poverty for the Love of Christ and the Poor

The basic source of motivation for voluntary poverty is love. The demand of Jesus to be his disciple is renunciation: "None of you can be my disciple, unless he gives up all his possessions" (Lk. 14:33). This renunciation will be fruitful only when it is done out of love for Christ and other fellow brethren.[43] St. Paul makes it very clear; "If I give away all that I possess . . . but am without love, it will do me no good

---

[41] Cf. S. Vazhakala, *Life with Mother Teresa*, p. 110.

[42] Mother Teresa, *Total Surrender*, ed. A. D. Scolozzi, p. 54.

[43] Cf. Mother Teresa wrote to her sisters: "We too must become poor for love of Jesus and the poor we serve" (*Mother's Letter*, 23 January, 1982).

whatever" (1 Cor. 13:3). This sense of Gospel poverty can be seen in the MCs constitution and instructions of Mother Teresa:

> Our poverty should be true Gospel poverty: gentle, tender glad and open hearted, always ready to give an expression of love.[44]

Mother Teresa while teaching about the meaning of renunciation, made it clear that it has a dimension of love. The more a person renounces, the more he can love God and man.[45] She was convinced that God used poverty to prove his love to the world. His glory and greatness always radiates from His humility. He used humility, smallness, helplessness in the process of loving the world. Religious too must become humble, small and helpless in order to prove their love for God.[46] She revealed that the reason for her to remain detached from material things and to practice the virtue of poverty is love of Jesus. She also declared that nothing and nobody can separate her from the love of Christ.[47] Therefore, she could say with full conviction:

---

[44] *MCs Constitutions, Art. 51;* also cf. *Mother's Instructions: Let us Make Our society Something Beautiful for God,* Vol. 1, p. 56; J. Neuner, "Mother Teresa's Charism", in *Review for Religious,* Vol. 60, no. 5 (2001), p. 489.

[45] Cf. Mother Teresa, *No Greater Love,* ed. B. Benenate and J. Durepos, p. 81; Mother Teresa, *Heart of Joy: The Transforming Power of Self-Giving,* ed. J. L. González-Balado, p. 126.

[46] Cf. Mother Teresa, *Thirsting for God: A Year Book of Prayers, Meditations and Anecdotes,* compiled by A. D. Scolozzi, p. 121. "Jesus took the nature of man out of love and give joy to the humanity: To bring joy to us, Jesus became man" (Mother Teresa, *Thirsting for God: A Year Book of Prayers, Meditations and Anecdotes,* compiled by A. D. Scolozzi, p. 162).

[47] Cf. Mother Teresa, *Total Surrender,* ed. A. D. Scolozzi, p. 60; Mother Teresa, *Essential Writings,* selected with an introduction

> Poverty is love before it is renunciation. To love, it is necessary to give. To give, it is necessary to be free from selfishness.[48]

According to Mother Teresa, religious have to love Christ and the poor to the point of hurting through their sacrifices out of voluntary poverty. The knowledge about the sufferings of the poor gained through our own experience of poverty leads us to love the poor more and more. And if they do not love them, they cannot serve them. Knowledge leads to love, and love to service.[49]

Whenever Mother Teresa saw some elements of luxury insinuating themselves into this life of poverty, into her life or into her congregation's life style, she vehemently opposed them. The reason for the practice of voluntary poverty was for the love of Jesus and the poor. It is clear from her words:

> To be accepted by the poor, we must live like the poor. Poverty is our charism. I entrust my Sisters to you; do not spoil them. Help them to observe poverty. We do not simply endure poverty, but we choose it voluntarily for the love of Jesus and the poor.[50]

---

by J. Maalouf, pp. 113-114; Mother Teresa, *A Life for God*, compiled by L. V. Neff, p. 219.

[48] *MCs Constitutions*, Art. 51; also cf. *Mother's Instructions: Let Us Make Our Society Something Beautiful for God*, Vol. 1, p. 56; Mother Teresa, *No Greater Love*, ed. B. Benenate and J. Durepos, p. 98; Mother Teresa, *Total Surrender*, ed. A. D. Scolozzi, p. 54; Mother Teresa, *Essential Writings*, selected with an introduction by J. Maalouf, p. 110.

[49] Cf. Mother Teresa, *Heart of Joy: The Transforming Power of Self-Giving*, ed. J. L. González-Balado, p. 109.

[50] Mother Teresa spoke these words to Archbishop and the parishioners at the end of the inauguration Mass of a convent at San Francisco. An eye witness of the incident Gjon Sinishta narrated this to the writer F. Zambonini and he quoted it in his book (F. Zambonini, *Teresa of Calcutta: A Pencil in God's Hand*, p. 121).

Mother Teresa and the members of her congregation do not profess the poverty of beggars but the poverty of Christ in their love of Christ. The inner motive for the practice of poverty is love toward Christ. She always insisted that the members have this awareness. This strict life of poverty becomes possible with the conviction that Christ remains hidden in the face of this materialistic world.[51]

Mother Teresa's teaching on poverty for the love for Christ had a great impact on the members of her congregation. The sacrifice that they make, the inconvenience which they experience, is everything for the love of Christ. Sr. Agnes, formerly Subhashini Das, said that the love of Jesus toward us, through His sacrifice, and the beauty of sacrificing ourselves in turn for Him were through the words of Mother Teresa branded on the soul.[52]

This view is stressed by Mother Teresa herself, that the Sisters' hard life and radical poverty are possible only by the love for Christ. According to her, Sisters give themselves to the love of Christ with a heart protected by chastity, with the freedom of poverty, with wholehearted obedience, in total service to the poorest of the poor and therefore to Christ under the suffering aspect of the poor.[53]

---

[51] Cf. *Mother's Instructions: Let us Make Our Society Something Beautiful for God*, vol. 3, Supplement 1, p. 35; also cf. J. L. Gonzalez – Balado, *Always the Poor: Mother Teresa Her Life and Message*, p. 83.

[52] Cf. F. Zambonini, *Teresa of Calcutta: A Pencil in God's Hand*, p. 45.

[53] Cf. *Ibid.*, p. 78.

2. VOW OF CHASTITY AND POVERTY

"Chastity (Latin *castitas*) is the moral virtue referring to the adoption of ethical and moral norms that moderate and regulate the sexual appetite."[54] According to the Council of Trent chastity is also one of the three monastic vows, along with poverty and obedience.[55] Chastity is both a gift of the Holy Spirit and a task of self-discipline. The asceticism of chastity forms an important theme of Christian spirituality in all ages.[56]

In this section of my research, my attempt will be to present the meaning of vow of chastity according to the recent Church teachings and in the teaching of Mother Teresa of Calcutta. And also to highlight her views on its interrelationship with the religious vow of poverty.

2.1. Meaning of Chastity in the Recent Church Teachings

The meaning of chastity found in the recent teachings of the Church is taken from the Council of Vatican II to the present. Chastity is considered to be the best way for religious to lead a life in their specific calling. In the document *Perfectae Caritatis* its meaning is given as follows:

> Chastity is an outstanding token of heavenly riches, and also most suitable way for religious to spend themselves readily in God's service and in works of the apostolate.[57]

---

[54] M. S. Driscoll, "Chastity", in *The New Dictionary of Catholic Spirituality*, ed. M. Downey, The Liturgical Press, Minnesota 1993, p. 147.

[55] Cf. *ibid.*, p. 150.

[56] Cf. S. O'riordan, "Chastity: Asceticism of Chastity", in *New Catholic Encyclopaedia,* The Catholic University of America, Gale, New York 2003, vol. 3, p. 444.

[57] PC 12.

Chastity is a special symbol of heavenly benefits and is a most effective means for the religious in dedicating themselves wholeheartedly to the divine service and the works of the apostolate. Because religious profess chastity for the sake of the Kingdom of heaven (Mt. 19: 12), it is an exceptional gift of grace that uniquely frees the heart (cf. 1 Cor. 7: 32-35), enabling them to be more fervent in love for God and for all men.[58] A similar idea is contained in the definition stated in the Code of Canon Law:

> Evangelical counsel of chastity, embraced for the sake of the Kingdom of heaven, is a sign of the world to come, and a source of greater fruitfulness in an undivided heart. It involves the obligation of perfect continence observed in celibacy.[59]

Pope Paul VI, in his Apostolic Exhortation on the renewal of religious life, reiterated the positive role of the vow of chastity as a sign of God's love and the response to God's call. A demand for fraternal charity inspires the religious to live more profoundly with his contemporaries in the heart of Christ. Consecrated chastity is a gift self made to God and to others. It complements marital love and stands as an image and sharing of union of love joining Christ and the Church. It also demands from religious a life lived with uprightness and generosity as it witnesses preferential love for the Lord and union of the Mystical Body – the union of the Bride with her eternal Bridegroom.[60]

In the *Mulieris Dignitatem*[61] Pope John Paul II restates the classical view of the value of virginity and celibacy for

---

[58] Cf. *Ibid*.

[59] Can. 599.

[60] Cf. ET 13.

[61] John Paul II, Apostolic Letter, *Mulieris Dignitatem*, 15 August 1988, *AAS* 80 (1988) 513-586: English Edition Catholic Truth Society, London 1988 (here after MD with number).

the sake of the Kingdom. Basing this assertion on the Gospel, it underlines consecrated chastity as a means by which one dedicates oneself exclusively to God.[62] Therefore, consecrated chastity is a radical way to live according to the gospel values.

Pope John Paul II in his Apostolic Exhortation *Redemptionis Donum* gives an explanation on chastity in the light of the mystery of redemption. He mentioned that it is according to the measure of the economy of the redemption that religious must judge and practice the vow of chastity. In this reflection chastity or celibacy is an expression of spousal love for the Redeemer Himself.[63]

In the Apostolic Exhortation *Vita Consecrata,* Pope John Paul II brought out the reflection of Trinitarian life in the evangelical counsels. According to this reflection, the chastity of celibates and virgins is a manifestation of dedication to God with an undivided heart (cf. 1 Cor 7: 32-34). It is also a reflection of the infinite love which links the three divine Persons in the mysterious depths of the life of the Trinity. The specific love to which the Incarnate Word bears witness, even to the point of giving his life, evokes a response of total love for God and the brethren.[64]

2.2. Meaning of Chastity in the Teachings of Mother Teresa

The vow of chastity is a personal response to the call of Christ, embraced for the sake of the Kingdom of heaven. It is a sign of the world to come and a source of greater fruitfulness in an undivided heart – a heart fully given to Jesus. It involves

---

[62] Cf. *Ibid.,* 20.
[63] Cf. RD 11.
[64] Cf. VC 21.

the obligation of perfect continence observed in celibacy.[65] By this vow, MCs commit themselves to live a celibate life in the fervour of charity and the perfection of chastity. They are convinced that complete continence is neither impossible nor harmful to human development because, in the maturity and delicacy of their vocation as women, they love Christ with a deep and personal love, expressed in their love for their own community members, the poor, and the world in which they live.[66]

Along with the teachings of the Church, Mother Teresa asserts that, by profession, a religious enters into a spousal union with Jesus. Given within the Church, consecrated chastity gives witness to the reality of that wondrous marriage established by God on this earth, to be fully manifested in the world to come, in which the Church[67] has Christ for her only Spouse.[68] Faithfulness to the vow of chastity is an external sign of this union with Jesus. Chastity is also considered a gift from God. Her understanding of chastity is reflected in the Constitution:

> Consecrated chastity is Christ's precious gift of Himself to us by which He offers us His lifelong, faithful and personal friendship, espousing us to Himself in tenderness and love.[69]

---

[65] Cf. *MCs Constitutions,* Art. no. 45; cf. Can. 599.

[66] Cf. Mother Teresa, *Total Surrender,* ed. A. D. Scolozzi, p. 62; cf. LG 46.

[67] Cf. *MCs Constitutions,* Art. no. 44; Mother Teresa, "Women Religious and Mission", in *Consecrated Life at the Frontiers of Mission,* ed. M. Bianchi, Pontifical Missionary Union, Roma 1994, Lesson 5, p. 6.

[68] Cf. Can. 607, par. 1

[69] *MCs Constitutions,* Art. no. 44; Mother Teresa, "Women Religious and Mission", in *Consecrated Life at the Frontiers of Mission,* ed. M. Bianchi, Pontifical Missionary Union, Roma 1994, Lesson 5, p. 6.

Mother Teresa was strong in the conviction that she was wedded to Christ[70] and could not have spousal relation with anyone else in the world. This thought helped her to remain in the vow of chastity. She taught her sisters to have this sense of respect to their religious life and remain always faithful to Christ, to whom they are wedded at the time of their profession. She reminded her sisters that, by the very fact of their marriage with Christ, they are also bound to share his sufferings. In other words, they should be able to face any sufferings for the sake of Christ and to remain ever as his only bride. In the words of Mother Teresa:

> Remember that we are wedded to Christ and so as we belong to Him we must therefore, share His passion also.[71]

In the spousal union, bride and bridegroom have to become one with an undivided heart. Mother Teresa opined that, by the vow of chastity, one has to give one's heart to our Lord, to the crucified Christ, an offering of heart to Christ alone.[72] This idea of wholehearted dedication of one's heart to Christ

---

[70] "Why do I desire to be chaste? I want to be chaste because I am the spouse of Jesus Christ, the son of the Living God. I want to be chaste because of the work I have to do as the co-workers of Christ. My chastity must be so pure as to draw the most impure to the sacred Heart of Jesus" (*Little Book of Mother's Letters*, pp. 77-78; Mother Teresa, *Jesus, The Word to be Spoken,* compiled by A. D. Scolozzi, p. 107). "Remember I am espoused to Him whom the angels serve, at whose beauty the very sun and moon stand in awe" (*Little Book of Mother's Letters*, p. 77).

[71] *Little Book of Mother's Letters*, p. 21.

[72] Cf. Mother Teresa, *Jesus, The Word to be Spoken,* compiled by A. D. Scolozzi, p. 107; *Little Book of Mother's Letters*, p. 21. "We must be free to love – and love him with an undivided love. Nothing will separate us from the love of Christ – and that is our vow of chastity" (Mother Teresa, *Total Surrender*, ed. A. D. Scolozzi, p. 68).

through the vow of chastity is expressed by her in an interview:

> We take the vow of chastity, of giving our hearts complete and undivided to Christ – an entire dedication to Christ.[73]

It is not only that religious cannot have a family, they cannot get married. But it is something deeper, something living, and something real – it is to love Him with undivided, loving chastity through freedom of poverty. Thus the vow of chastity is to love Christ with undivided, loving chastity.[74] This undivided love for Christ developed through the vow of chastity keeps one away from having spousal relationship with others. The conviction that the deep union with Christ and the obligation to keep the promise made in the profession enable a religious not to engage with someone else in similar union:

> By the vow of chastity, I not only renounce the married state of life, but I also consecrate to God the free use of my internal and external acts – my affections. I cannot in conscience love a creature with the love of a woman for a man. I no longer have the right to give that affection to any other creature but only to God.[75]

The objectives of the vow of chastity, in the vision of Mother Teresa, are seen in the constitutions of MCs. Chastity liberates them totally for the contemplation of God and the wholehearted and free service of the poorest of the poor. Further, by chastity they cleave to Jesus with undivided love

---

[73] Mother Teresa spoke these words to M. Muggeridge in an interview while she was answering about the formation of the sisters, and the writer quoted her in his book (M. Muggeridge, *Something Beautiful for God: Mother Teresa of Calcutta*, p. 84).

[74] Cf. Mother Teresa, *Total Surrender*, ed. A. D. Scolozzi, pp. 67-68.

[75] *Ibid.*, p. 64.

with four motives. First of all, it is imperative to live in Him, for Him and with Him as their sole guide; secondly, to be invaded by His holiness and filled with His own spirit of love; thirdly, to show forth the luminous face of Jesus, radiant with purity and love for the Father and mankind. Finally, it is to make reparation to God for all the sins of the flesh committed in the world today.[76]

The vow of chastity plays a great role in fulfilling the mission of religious toward humanity, especially wholehearted free service to the poorest of the poor, which is a specific mission of Mother Teresa and her religious community. If the vow of chastity is shaken then it will affect their mission for the poorest of the poor. For her, wholehearted free service is the outcome of chastity. The service aspect comes from the love for Christ, in His visible form, and the control of affection only to Christ comes from the promise they have made to Christ to be the only bridegroom. This idea can be drawn from her following words:

> By my vow of chastity I free myself for the kingdom of God. I become his property and he binds himself to take care of me. I must then give wholehearted free service. What is this wholehearted free service? It is the outcome of chastity, of binding myself to Christ. Therefore, I bind myself to give not half-hearted but wholehearted service. When we neglect to do our work well, this vow suffers most – our service to the poor – because we become preoccupied with whatever we are giving our affection to.[77]

---

[76] Cf. *MCs Constitutions*, Art. no. 46; Mother Teresa, *Total Surrender*, ed. A. D. Scolozzi, pp. 62-63.

[77] Mother Teresa, *Total Surrender*, ed. A. D. Scolozzi, p. 66.

With the right attitude and the proper practice, the vow of chastity enriches the religious rather than mere taking away something. The virtue of chastity is rewarded with great splendour: reward for the victory over temptation. The religious person sacrifices conjugal love with human beings and instead enters a deep union of love with God. The entire love of that person is offered to God and in turn, a good measure of love from God is received. Therefore, the giving and receiving of love remains even in the life of the religious. By the vow of chastity, that person does not lose this love in life; rather she becomes richer in this aspect of love. Through the vow of chastity, the transaction of love is something mystical and provides mystical joy and peace to a person. Based on this theological principle Mother Teresa stated:

> The vow of chastity does not diminish us; it makes us live to the full if it is kept properly. The vow of chastity is not simply a list of don'ts – it is love. I give myself to God and I receive God. God becomes my own and I become his own. That is why I become completely dedicated to him by the vow of chastity.[78]

The glory of chastity is in the victory over temptation and not just the avoidance of temptation. The virtue of chastity is rewarded with great splendour; reward for the victory over temptation.[79] This vow of chastity is to be seen as something positive that takes a person to a higher realm.

---

[78] *Ibid.*, p. 65.

[79] "We must be convinced that nothing adorns a human soul with greater splendour than the virtue of chastity and nothing defiles a human soul more than the opposite vice. Yet there must be no mistake that the glory of chastity is not in immunity from temptation but in victory over these temptations" (Mother Teresa, *Jesus, The Word to be Spoken*, compiled by A. D. Scolozzi, p. 108).

2.3. Interrelation between Chastity and Poverty

It is generally accepted that the vow of chastity is based on renunciation. Mother Teresa, focusing on the aspect of renunciation in the vow of chastity, explained the relationship between the vow of poverty and chastity. She envisaged that by the vow of chastity one renounces marriage and family life. By this vow, a religious not only has to renounce marriage but also should avoid every external or internal offence against chastity. In this vow a religious has to renounce God's natural gift to women to become mothers, in order to enter into a spousal union with Christ – a greater gift as the virgin of Christ, a beautiful motherhood.[80] She proclaimed this greater value which a religious gets through the spirit of renunciation in the vow of chastity through the following words:

> By our vow (chastity) we consecrate our heart to God and renounce the joys of family life. Yes, we do renounce the natural gift of God to women to become mothers for the greater gift that of virgins of Christ, of becoming mothers of souls.[81]

Mother Teresa, while explaining the interconnection between poverty and chastity, says that if the sisters are not very careful about receiving and giving things, then the desire to possess that person or that thing will grow. The undivided love for Christ will be lost. Poverty is the protector of chastity.[82] She came to this conviction from her many years of experience in religious life. Jesus said: "No one can serve two masters;

---

[80] Cf. Mother Teresa, *Total Surrender*, ed. A. D. Scolozzi, pp. 62-63.

[81] Mother Teresa, *Jesus, The Word to be Spoken*, compiled by A. D. Scolozzi, p. 107.

[82] Cf. *Mother's Instructions: Let Us Make Our Society Something Beautiful for God*, Vol. 1, p. 65.

for either he will hate the one and love the other, or he will be devoted to the one and despise the other. You cannot serve God and Mammon" (Mt. 6:24). Therefore she emphatically instructed:

> Money is a danger and it can cause great harm and it can be the cause of suffering. Moreover it is a dangerous weapon in the hand of the devil. I have seen from my experience of many years, when we touch poverty, we always lose chastity. It is like fire, we cannot play with it. The devil will never try to tempt us with something big, but with a small thing.[83]

Love of Christ with an undivided love is an outcome of the vow of chastity. At the time of profession, especially through the vow of chastity, Christ becomes the only person with whom a religious enters into a spousal union and the faithfulness to the vow undivided love for Christ is thereby maintained. And this love again is facilitated by detachment from material possessions in maintaining the vow of poverty. Thus undivided love for Christ is pivotal for the unification of the vow of chastity and the vow of poverty. The vow of chastity helps a religious to love Christ with an undivided love. Similarly the vow of poverty gives freedom from all material worries, from the possession of every material good; this freedom enables the religious to love Christ with an undivided love.[84]

According to Mother Teresa when the vow of poverty is affected to a certain extent it affects the vow of chastity too. Because for her chastity would mean not only keeping away from sexual relationships and personal attachments, but even

---

[83] *Mother's Instructions: Let Us Make Our Society Something Beautiful for God*, Vol. 3, Supplement 1, p. 14.

[84] Cf. Mother Teresa, *Heart of Joy: The Transforming Power of Self-Giving*, ed. J. L. Gonzalez-Balado, p. 103.

the attachment to the material things can reduce the love for Christ and become a violation of the vow of chastity. She maintains that the religious should have a total detachment from things and persons. They should not have attachments even to small things.[85] From her long experience in the religious life she was convinced that damage to the vow of poverty creates damage to the vow of chastity too. Therefore she once said: "When poverty goes, chastity will go."[86] How the destruction of poverty affects the existence of chastity and the whole religious life of a person can be well understood from her following expression:

> To be able to understand chastity we must know what poverty and obedience are. They are like pillars. If we remove the pillars, the whole building will tip to one side and fall.[87]

3. VOW OF OBEDIENCE AND POVERTY

The common-sense understanding of obedience is in compliance with the bidding of another, generally of superior status. From the Latin *ob+ audire*, meaning "to hear," obedience in the spiritual life is a matter of receiving and responding appropriately to a message or Word from God. Along with the evangelical counsels of poverty and chastity, faithful adherence to a vow of obedience became the primary test of Christian commitment in monastic life. In monasticism obedience to a spiritual father or mother is a form of spiritual

[85] Mother Teresa explained this through a story: Once there was rich man who joined a monastery. He gave up everything but he had great attachment to a small penknife that they found when he died. During the funeral service the abbot of the monastery said: "It was with you on earth, let it go with you in death" (*Mother's Instructions*, Vol. 3, Supplement 2, p. 54).

[86] Mother Teresa, *Total Surrender*, ed. A. D. Scolozzi, p. 76.

[87] *Ibid.*, p. 69.

discipline, just as prayer and fasting are, and it is humble submissiveness to authority.[88] According to E. Le Joly, "Religious bind themselves by vow to obey, in imitation of Jesus who came into the world to do not His own will, but His Father's will. . . . Obedience makes the religious available, puts him at the disposal of his superior for any task within the ambit of his institute's constitutions."[89]

In this section of research, my attempt is to present the meaning of obedience as a religious vow according to recent Church teachings and the teaching of Mother Teresa of Calcutta, and also to highlight her views on its interrelation with the religious vow of poverty.

3.1. Meaning of Obedience in the Recent Church Teachings

The theological basis of the vow of obedience is the imitation of Christ, Who was obedient even unto death. Religious, as close followers of Christ through a specific way of life, are to practice, Christ-like obedience. This is well reflected in the meaning of obedience given by the Canon Law:

> The evangelical counsel of obedience, undertaken in the spirit of faith and love in the following of Christ, Who was obedient even unto death, obliges submission of one's will to lawful Superiors, who act in the place of God when they give commands that are in accordance with each institute's own constitutions.[90]

In the light of faith and in accordance with the dynamism of the charity of Christ, a religious receives inspiration to remain faithful to the vow of obedience. Through the

---

[88] Cf. R. Mass, "Obedience" in *The New Dictionary of Catholic Spirituality*, ed. M. Downey, pp. 709-710.

[89] E. Le Joly, *Mother Teresa: Messenger of God's Love*, p. 50.

[90] Can. 601.

profession, a religious makes a total offering of one's will and enters more decisively and more surely into Christ's plan of salvation. Further, the obedience of Christ, who came to do the will of His Father, becomes a model and strength for the commitment of the religious towards the ministry of the Church and of fellow brethren.[91] The vow of obedience is said to be a commitment to live according to a given Rule of life, and an efficacious means to attain the goal of religious life. Vatican Council II defines obedience as follows:

> By their profession of obedience, religious offer the full dedication of their own wills as a sacrifice of themselves to God . . . moved by the Holy Spirit (they) subject themselves in faith to those who hold God's place, their superiors. Through them they are led to serve all their brothers (and sisters) in Christ. . . .[92]

The document also gives the necessary qualification of the superior in making his inferiors obedient to him. The superior must be humble, pliant, and must himself be tested in the fiery kiln of obedience. He should use his authority in a spirit of service for brethren, and manifest thereby the charity with which God loves them. In executing authority, the superior should take into consideration that his inferiors are God's own children. He should duly respect their human personality to make them to obey gladly. He must give his subjects due freedom with respect to the sacrament of penance and direction of conscience.[93]

The vow of obedience is also explained in the light of the mystery of redemption by John Paul II through his Apostolic Exhortation *Redemptionis Donum*. St. Paul in his letter to Philippians gives us a beautiful picture of obedience

---

[91] Cf. ET 23.
[92] PC 14.
[93] Cf. *Ibid*.

of Christ as He was in the form of God become man, obedient unto death, even death on a cross (Cf. Phil. 2: 6-11). The vow of obedience is the call which derives from this obedience of Christ. Through the life of obedience, religious can reach the deep essence of the entire economy of Redemption. By faithfulness to the vow of obedience, religious can work on their own redemption and that of their brethren.[94]

The origin of the consecrated life is in the mystery of Christ and of the Trinity. Evangelical counsels are the gift of the Holy Trinity. A reflection of Trinitarian life in the evangelical counsel of obedience according to John Paul II is as follows:

> Obedience, practiced in imitation of Christ, whose food was to do the Father's will (cf. Jn. 4:34), shows the liberating beauty of a dependence which is not servile but filial, marked by a deep sense of responsibility and animated by mutual trust, which is a reflection in history of the loving harmony between the three Divine Persons.[95]

3.2. Meaning of Obedience in the Teachings of Mother Teresa

The vow of obedience is a response to the call of Christ. This is also an evangelical counsel, undertaken in the spirit of faith and love in the following of Christ, Who was obedient even unto death. This vow obliges submission of one's will to lawful Superiors, who act in place of God when they give commands that are in accordance with the Constitutions, in all things which are of the life and work of the society.[96]

---

[94] Cf. RD 13.

[95] VC 21.]

[96] Cf. *MCs Constitutions,* Art. no. 59; cf. Can. 601. "Through consecrated obedience Christ calls us to unite our will to His by an unconditional surrender in faith, and thus to penetrate deep into the mystery of His Father's saving will for mankind" (*MC's Constitutions,* Art. no. 58).

Mother Teresa spoke clearly about the submission of one's will to God's will in obedience and how all other vows are based on the vow of obedience:

> We have also the vow of obedience and we take all the vows according to obedience. We have to do God's will in everything.[97]

In the imitation of the obedience of Christ, Mother Teresa taught that religious have to go down with Christ and be subject to those who have authority from above and who therefore declare Christ's obedience unto death. Religious must obey as Christ obeyed – obeyed unto death, even death on the cross. He saw the will of His Father in everything and everybody. He obeyed Caiaphas and Pilate because their authority was given 'from above'. He submitted to them with obedience and dignity. He did not look at the human limitations of Caiaphas and Pilate; instead He looked at his Father, for whose love He submitted himself to them. Christ-like obedience of religious would be pleasing to God and it will enable them to get the title of His beloved children.[98] How Jesus can teach the religious about obedience was expressed by her in the following words:

> Only Jesus in the Blessed Sacrament, Jesus on the cross, can teach us obedience, and that is by the reality of His own example.[99]

Mother Teresa believed that obedience is the most beautiful offering religious can give to God, because one's will is the

---

[97] Mother Teresa spoke these words to M. Muggeridge in an interview while she was answering about the formation of the sisters, and the writer quoted her in his book (M. Muggeridge, *Something Beautiful for God: Mother Teresa of Calcutta*, p. 84).

[98] Cf. Mother Teresa, *Jesus, The Word to be Spoken*, compiled by A. D. Scolozzi, pp. 118-119.

[99] *Ibid.*, p. 120.

only gift of God which is of one's own and which God will never take by force. He will accept it only when a person surrenders it.[100] It is also a total surrender. This complete surrender of self to God must secure for religious perseverance in God's service, since by obedience they always do his most holy will and consequently obtain freedom from doubts, anxieties, and scruples.[101]

By surrendering themselves to Jesus religious are placing themselves at His disposal, so that He may use them freely through their superiors, whenever and for whatever need. Thus through the vow of obedience they fully belong to Jesus; with full right to be used by Him.[102] It is not courtesy once a person offers a gift to someone and then takes it back. Similarly, if religious have taken the vow of obedience by their own free choice then they are obliged to keep it, especially when it is a solemn promise.

The best demonstration of a person's faith is considered to be his/her prompt, simple and joyous obedience. The vow of obedience has to be nurtured on the level of faith, because by obeying one's superiors a person is obeying God, Who gave authority to them. Superiors have their own human

---

[100] Cf. Mother Teresa, *Total Surrender*, ed. A. D. Scolozzi, p. 72; J. Neuner, "Mother Teresa's Charism", in *Review for Religious*, vol. 60, no. 5 (2001), pp. 489-490. "Nothing pleases God more than when we obey. Let us love God not for what he gives but for what he deigns to take from us. Our little acts of obedience give us the occasion of proving our love for him" (Mother Teresa, *Jesus, The Word to be Spoken*, compiled by A. D. Scolozzi, p. 120).

[101] Cf. Mother Teresa, *Jesus, The Word to be Spoken*, compiled by A. D. Scolozzi, p. 119.

[102] Cf. J. Neuner, "Mother Teresa's Charism", in *Review for Religious*, vol. 60, no. 5 (2001), p. 489.

limitations; in spite of this they stand to execute the will of God and if we are not able to accept it then it is the sign that we lack faith.[103] In the spirit of faith one should obey superiors, and even if superiors make mistakes in their orders, the inferior who obeys is not culpable before God. In this respect Mother Teresa said:

> We should obey the known wish of our superiors as well as their commands in a spirit of faith. They may make a mistake in commanding, but we are infallible in obeying.[104]

According to Mother Teresa, the superior is in the place of God. The position given to her is like a chair. The chair remains, but the person can change. Today one may sit in the chair; tomorrow somebody else might be sitting there, but the chair is the same. The chair may not fit some as well as others. Some are too short for it and others too tall, while yet others fit it perfectly. The chair is in the place of God who gave the superior this position. Whoever wishes to lead

---

[103] Cf. Mother Teresa, *Heart of Joy: The Transforming Power of Self-Giving*, ed. J. L. González-Balado, p. 81. "Our obedience, by being prompt, simple, blind, and cheerful, is the proof of our faith" (Mother Teresa, *Jesus, The Word to be Spoken,* compiled by A. D. Scolozzi, p. 118).

[104] Mother Teresa, *Total Surrender*, ed. A. D. Scolozzi, p. 70. The infallible nature in carrying out the order of superiors for an inferior is clear in the following words of Mother Teresa: "Right from the very beginning, learn to obey, it will lead you straight to God. . . . The superior who tells you to do this or do that may make mistake. I may make a mistake and tell the Sisters do this and go her and go there. But that Sister who does what I tell her is infallible" (Mother Teresa, *Jesus, The Word to be Spoken,* compiled by A. D. Scolozzi, p. 41). "We are infallible when obey. Ask the Holy Spirit to give us that one grace" (Mother Teresa, *Jesus, The Word to be Spoken,* compiled by A. D. Scolozzi, p. 120).

a life of peace has to obey the superior.[105] She made it clear to her sisters that in heaven the main question they are going to face from the Lord will be whether they have obeyed their superior who is in place of God, rather than a request to highlight the capability of their superior:

> In heaven our Lord will not ask you, 'Was your superior intelligent, understanding, cheerful?' He will simply ask you, 'Have you obeyed me?'[106]

Religious have to be convinced that it is Jesus whom they obey through the obedience to their superiors. This conviction enables them to be cheerful and prompt while obeying their superiors. They can reach to this conviction by the practice of the heroic virtue of obedience – love for love. It depends on each person that he or she can become a saint or a sinner, a choice made out of free will. From this we can understand the importance of obedience in the religious life. Sanctity, after the grace of God, depends upon one's own will. Therefore, religious need not waste time for big things to do for God. Unless they train themselves to say yes to the thousand-and-one occasions of obedience that come their way throughout the day, they will not have the readiness to say yes to the great things.[107] Once she pronounced the greatness of obedience as a prerequisite to becoming a saint: "It is impossible that a sister who is obedient will not become a saint."[108]

---

[105] Cf. Mother Teresa, *Total Surrender*, ed. A. D. Scolozzi, p. 71.

[106] Mother Teresa, *Heart of Joy: The Transforming Power of Self-Giving*, ed. J. L. González-Balado, p. 81.

[107] Cf. Mother Teresa, *Total Surrender*, ed. A. D. Scolozzi, pp. 71-72.

[108] *Ibid.*, p. 71. Mother Teresa requested the religious to follow the example of Blessed Virgin Mary in obedience for to grow in holiness: "If we really want to grow in holiness through obedience let us turn constantly to our Lady to teach us how to

Obedience is to know the will of God and a means to grow in holiness. Mother Teresa considered the aims of religious life are the knowledge of God, love of God and service of God. And obedience is the key to them all.[109] She was also of the opinion that religious can carry out their work in a better way only by knowing the will of God; how God wants them to carry it out. And this knowledge is transmitted through the superior. Thus there is no other way to know what God really wants them to do other than by obedience. Therefore religious have to submit themselves to their superior just like ivy to a wall. Ivy cannot live if it does not hold fast to something; religious will not grow or live in holiness unless they hold fast to obedience.[110] In her opinion, obedience gives a person inward joy and peace. Obedience well lived frees religious from selfishness and pride, and so it helps them to find God and in Him the whole world. Above all obedience is the only condition for close union with God. Therefore, if a religious wants to become holy then he or she has to be obedient.[111] She also spoke about the potentiality

---

obey, to Jesus who was obedient unto death" (Mother Teresa, *Jesus, The Word to be Spoken,* compiled by A. D. Scolozzi, p. 119).

[109] Cf. Mother Teresa, *Total Surrender*, ed. A. D. Scolozzi, p. 72.

[110] Cf. Mother Teresa, *Heart of Joy: The Transforming Power of Self-Giving*, ed., J. L. González-Balado, p. 83. "Whenever our superior think it desirable for the greater glory of God to give us change of residence, work, or companions, we should welcome this change as the very will of God and show a humble and joyful obedience" (Mother Teresa, *Total Surrender*, ed. A. D. Scolozzi, p. 70).

[111] Cf. Mother Teresa, *Jesus, The Word to be Spoken,* compiled by A. D. Scolozzi, p. 119. "It is much easier to conquer a country than to conquer ourselves. Every act of disobedience weakens my spiritual life. It is like a wound letting out every drop of one's blood. Nothing can cause this havoc in our spiritual life as quickly as disobedience" (Mother Teresa, *Total Surrender*, ed. A. D. Scolozzi, p. 73).

of obedience in leading the religious to the other virtues and its significance in the level of martyrdom:

> Obedience makes us practice the other virtues. It likens us to martyrs, for it is a much greater martyrdom to persevere in obedience all through life than to die in a moment by a stroke of the sword.[112]

Mother Teresa taught also the apostolic dimension of obedience and its consequent reward from God. While sending out the disciples for missionary journey, she pointed out, Jesus promised a reward for whoever is kind to them during their mission (Cf. Mt. 10: 42). She was of the opinion that if God loves him who gives joyfully, how much more he will love him who gives with obedience, who obeys as Christ obeyed![113] She invited her community members to become the apostles of obedience and be ready to receive the reward from Our Lord, Who promised rewards even for a glass of water.[114]

Obedience transforms small, commonplace things and occupations into acts of living faith, and faith in action into love, and love in action into service of the loving God. Obedience lived with joy creates a living awareness of the presence of God, so that fidelity to acts of obedience become like drops of oil that keep the light of Jesus aflame in the life of religious. For example, the bell, the timetable, the eating of food, that are the fruit of constant, prompt, cheerful, undivided obedience, become like drops of oil that keep the

---

[112] Mother Teresa, *Total Surrender*, ed. A. D. Scolozzi, pp. 70-71.

[113] Cf. Mother Teresa, *Heart of Joy: The Transforming Power of Self-Giving*, ed. J. L. González-Balado, p. 81; Mother Teresa, *Jesus, the Word to be Spoken*, compiled by A. D. Scolozzi, p. 118.

[114] Cf. Mother Teresa, *Heart of Joy: The Transforming Power of Self-Giving*, ed. J. L. González-Balado, p. 80.

light of Jesus living in their life.[115] To teach the importance of obedience in our life and how criticism affects the vow of obedience, Mother Teresa said:

> To strengthen ourselves to remain obedient, we must refrain from criticism. Anything that weakens my obedience, however small, I must keep away from. If we don't obey, we are like a building without cement. For us, obedience is like cement. Obedience is unreasonable for a proud soul, but there is no unreasonableness in obedience for a humble soul.[116]

3.3. Interrelation between Obedience and Poverty

The vow of poverty and obedience are related in so far as the vow of poverty is bound by the constitution. In the constitution there are certain ways explained by which each member has to practice poverty. To practice poverty in the exact manner prescribed by the constitution one must observe the rule of obedience. The corrections and instructions with regard to the practice of poverty may come in part from superiors and in part from the way the person accepts and executes obedience in one's life.

For Mother Teresa, trust in divine providence is one of the features of religious poverty, and this trust extends necessarily toward superiors. Each and every one has to obey superiors promptly and cheerfully. The corrections of superiors have to be taken with a childlike confidence and trust, as the will of God comes through the superiors.[117] In place of attachment to material possessions, the vow of

---

[115] Mother Teresa, *Jesus, the Word to be Spoken*, compiled by. A. D. Scolozzi, p. 119; Mother Teresa, *Total Surrender*, ed. A. D. Scolozzi, p. 80.

[116] Mother Teresa, *Total Surrender*, ed. A. D. Scolozzi, p. 74.

[117] Cf. *The Little Book of Mother's Letters*, p. 64.

poverty enables a person to be attached only to Christ with an undivided love. This undivided love is realised when religious commit themselves completely through the person who occupies Christ's position – hence their vow of obedience facilitates faithfulness to the vow of poverty.[118]

Mother Teresa emphasised the importance of obedience in the practice of poverty: "If we neglect obedience, poverty will go."[119] She was very strict regarding the vow of poverty and obedience. This is very evident from her instructions:

> I am going to be strict on poverty and obedience. If poverty and obedience are not kept, chastity goes. You run away. If you do not do what a MC should do, you must go home. If you are careful about silence and poverty, obedience will be all right. If you want to be pure, keep poverty and obedience.[120]

She also taught that poverty and obedience are united in such a way that they are complementary in nature. One can not exist without the other. Jesus became poor, materially and spiritually, to obey his Father. Similarly, we have to empty ourselves in order to practice obedience. Thus the real obedience demands that we forgo pride and uncharitableness.[121] Once she said:

> He, being rich, became poor. It is difficult for a proud person to obey. We do not like to bend, to be humble. . . Nothingness cannot disobey.[122]

---

[118] Cf. Mother Teresa, *Heart of Joy: The Transforming Power of Self-Giving*, ed. J. L. González-Balado, p. 103.

[119] Mother Teresa, *Total Surrender*, ed. A. D. Scolozzi, p. 76.

[120] *Mother's Instructions: Let Us Make Our Society Something Beautiful for God*, vol. 1, p. 200.

[121] Cf. Mother Teresa, *Total Surrender*, ed. A. D. Scolozzi, p. 75.

[122] *Ibid.*, pp. 76-77.

Taking the example of Jesus' obedience and poverty in incarnation Mother Teresa taught that religious must go down in the depths of their hearts and see how to bring holiness into their society. In order to obey one must be free of material things; that is the reason religious have to take a vow of poverty. A state of nothingness helps a person to obey freely.[123] Regarding the line of detachment of one's own will and coming down to the deeper level under obedience, she once stated that "Obedience is of our true spirit of poverty."[124] When a person is totally detached, he is free to obey the will of God. At times this will of God comes through the superiors. Thus poverty helps the vow of obedience. Hence the vow of poverty and the vow of obedience are intimately related to each other.

Poverty and obedience are twins. Poverty is considered to be the sister and obedience the brother. The practice of voluntary poverty must be something joyful and that of obedience must issue out of total surrender. Thus they are interrelated. If we know poverty and obedience then we will love them. If we love them we will keep them.[125]

4. RELEVANCE OF RELIGIOUS POVERTY AND ITS PRACTICAL ASPECTS

We have seen in detail the importance of renunciation in the call of Christ. Religious are called by Christ for a specific way of life, being faithful to the vows they make during the profession, to work for one's own salvation and the salvation of others. The vow of poverty is one of the vows they are

---

[123] Cf. *Ibid.*, p. 78.

[124] Mother Teresa, "Women Religious and Mission", in *Consecrated Life at the Frontiers of Mission*, ed. M. Bianchi, Pontifical Missionary Union, Roma 1994, Lesson 5, p. 7.

[125] Cf. Mother Teresa, *Total Surrender*, ed. A. D. Scolozzi, p. 79.

bound to keep in life in accordance with their religious profession. How Mother Teresa was meticulously practising this vow and also her views of it have been shown in the above pages of this book. The vow of poverty was very important for her to remain faithful in the consecrated life, and it is reflected in her special attention to the poverty maintained in different houses of her congregation. Once in an interview she answered a question about what she used to insist upon when she visited her houses:

> I insist mainly on poverty. I check whether poverty is kept according to the spirit and word of our Constitutions, especially as regards the superiors of the houses. They can so easily become lax in the matter of poverty.[126]

In this section we are going to see the importance of religious poverty in the vision of Mother Teresa and her suggestions with regard to its practical applications in life. This theme will be dealt with under three subtitles: poverty is the strength and protection of religious life, the strict observances of religious poverty, and practical aspects.

4.1. Poverty is the Strength and Protection of Religious Life

Mother Teresa considered that the practice of poverty serves as the strength and protection of religious life. She started the congregation with the main charism of serving the poorest of the poor. And for this it is essential for whoever wishes to serve the poorest of the poor to have the experience of the difficulties of the poorest of the poor in one's religious life. As Jesus being rich became poor in the incarnational approach of salvation economy, so anyone who wishes to serve the poorest of the poor needs to experience the

[126] E. Le Joly, *Mother Teresa: Messenger of God's Love*, p. 50.

hardships and become one with them in their sufferings. She was so convinced of this matter that for her, if the members of her congregation loosen the ties of poverty, then it is the beginning of the death of the congregation. It would mean that the growth of the congregation will be blocked, followed by a gradual death. Once she emphatically instructed the members of her congregation: "Let poverty die and you let the Congregation die."[127] For her the existence of her religious congregation depends on the sincere practice of vow of poverty by the members of her community. She reminded her religious colleagues on this matter:

> Our congregation will live as long as this real poverty continues. Institutions where poverty is faithfully practiced have no reason to fear decadence.[128]

When the life of religious is centred on money and property ownership, they go the way of the material world, of the big, of up and more. It may become their agenda, and then faith can fly out of the window.[129] Mother Teresa was not in favour of having rich buildings and infrastructures for her religious community to live in. Instead she always preferred to have simple residences. She again and again reminded her religious colleagues, the day MCs possess rich buildings, from that day onward its ruin is certain; the decay through worldliness will kill its very life.[130]

---

[127] *Mothers Instructions: Let Us make Our Society Something Beautiful for God*, vol. 1, p. 53.

[128] Mother Teresa, *Heart of Joy: The Transforming Power of Self-Giving*, ed. J. L. González-Balado, p. 129; Mother Teresa, *Love: A Fruit Always in Season – Daily Meditations*, ed. D. S. Hunt, p. 160; Mother Teresa, *The Love of Christ: Spiritual Counsels*, eds. G. Goree and J. Barbier, p. 107.

[129] Cf. L. Vardey, *Mother Teresa: A Simple Path*, p. 46.

[130] Cf. *Missionaries of Charity: Explanation of Original Constitution*, p. 44.

Mother Teresa was firmly convinced that rigorous poverty is the safeguard of her religious order. She lived according to this conviction.[131] Later she cautioned her sisters about it, and said that when they are out of step with the rhythm of Christ's suffering and poverty, it was the beginning of the destruction of the religious order.[132] She believed that if her sisters are strict in poverty then they can remain so without losing the charism and original spirit of their religious order. Thus for her rigorous poverty is the safeguard of her religious order.[133] This conviction of poverty as the safeguard of her congregation is expressed on another occasion by Mother Teresa as the unique quality found in her congregation, that which singles out the specific feature of the congregation. She expressed vehemently:

> Our rigorous poverty is our safeguard. We do not want, as has been the case with other religious orders throughout the history, to begin serving the poor and then gradually move toward serving the rich. In order to understand and help those who have nothing, we must live like them.[134]

---

[131] "Mother Teresa lives her own philosophy: 'Our best protection is in our poverty'" (J. L. González – Balado, *Always the Poor - Mother Teresa: Her Life and Message*, p. 82).

[132] Cf. Mother Teresa, *Heart of Joy: The Transforming Power of Self-Giving*, ed. J. L. González – Balado, p. 64; cf. R. Allegri, *Teresa of the Poor: The Story of Her Life*, p. 116.

[133] Cf. G. Goree and J. Barbier, *Love Without Boundaries*, translated by P. Speakman, Our Sunday visitor, Huntington, Indiana 1976, p. 62; K. Spink, *Mother Teresa: An Authorised Biography*, p. 44; cf. J. L. González – Balado, *Always the Poor - Mother Teresa: Her Life and Message*, p. 31; cf. R. Allegri, *Teresa of the Poor: The Story of Her Life*, pp. 116 – 117.

[134] Mother Teresa, *Heart of Joy: The Transforming Power of Self-Giving*, ed. J. L. González – Balado, pp. 64-65; Mother Teresa, *No Greater Love*, ed. B. Benenate and J. Durepos, p. 97.

According to Mother Teresa poverty is the wall of defence to protect the religious life. Following this assertion, she advised her community members to aim at a most perfect poverty. She explained how poverty becomes a wall of defence to their religious life with its two effects. Primarily, poverty excludes the enemy. As we know from the Spiritual Exercises, the first trick of the devil is to lead men to the love of wealth. The true love of evangelical poverty closes this avenue of our soul to the evil spirit. Secondly, the practice of voluntary poverty secures peace and protection for those who dwell within the wall.[135]

The undivided love for Christ under a total detachment in the spirit of poverty remains a strong protection for the religious. Religious, especially those who are involved in bringing souls to God, have to face the tricks the devil employs to destroy the bond of personal union with Jesus. The devil always tries to spoil the work which aims to bring souls to God. Therefore, he attacks the persons who are involved in it and even attempts to destroy the state of religious life, seeking their loss of vocation. A religious who is very strong in the genuine spirit of poverty cannot be affected by the tricks of the devil and will remain strong in the promises made to Jesus. Mother Teresa further called this virtue of poverty as a freedom to love Christ and claimed that nothing and nobody could separate her from this undivided love of Christ.[136]

She requested the members of her congregation to approach the Blessed Virgin Mary in order to keep up poverty, always with the attitude of strength and for the

---

[135] Cf. Mother Teresa, *Total Surrender*, ed. A. D. Scolozzi, pp. 55-56.

[136] Cf. *Ibid.*, p. 60.

protection of the congregation. She expressed it in these words:

> Poverty is for us Missionaries of Charity our strength and protection. Love and poverty made our Lady so Christ-like. Let us ask her to obtain love and poverty from the heart of her son.[137]

The simple and modest habit chosen for her and her sisters not only projects their religious poverty but also contains rich meaning in the protection of religious life. The white cotton sari with blue border and a cincture made of rope signifies renunciation of the world and the purity each religious who wears it is supposed to maintain. She considered this habit as a means of both bodily and spiritual protection. Thus in her opinion, for a religious who wears such poor religious habit with the awareness of its real meaning, it becomes a protection of religious life:

> The white habit and a sari with blue border is the sign of my separation from the world and its vanities, of my baptismal robe and how pure I must keep my heart. The girdle made of rope is the sign of Mary's angelic purity. It should remind me that I should aim at the same purity helped by the strong guardian, Holy Poverty.[138]

4.2. The Strict Observances of Religious Poverty

The strictness in practicing the vow of poverty is worth noting in the life of Mother Teresa and her sisters. She taught them the vow of poverty by her exemplary life and timely instructions. A total poverty is visible in her life and teachings. The essential reasons for this poverty Mother Teresa explains as a free choice made for the love of Jesus

---

[137] *Mother's Letter*, 12 October 1979.

[138] Mother Teresa, *Total Surrender*, ed. A. D. Scolozzi, pp. 89-90.

and the poor people. And it is different from the poverty of the poor people who are poor against their will.[139] She herself agrees about the strictness of the vow of poverty in her congregation, and its intention is expressed in these words:

> The vow of poverty is very, very strict in our congregation because to be able to love the poor and to know the poor we must be poor ourselves.[140]

Mother Teresa left a great impact on others about the strict nature of the vow of poverty and its sincere practice by her and her sisters. One of her biographers who had close relations with MCs mentioned this in his book: "It is worth noting that the vow of poverty Mother Teresa and her sisters profess is a vow of total poverty, a poverty that seems unthinkable in our times. Mother Teresa and her sisters do not possess anything. They live like the people they serve, the poorest of the poor. The rule they scrupulously observe is very strict on this point. The sisters must be poor as individuals and as a community."[141]

The vow of poverty designed by Mother Teresa for her and her sisters does not allow them to posses anything as individuals and as a community. There is a difference between the vow of poverty in the other religious orders and the vow practiced and taught by Mother Teresa. In spite of its hard nature on individual persons, even in the name of community they are forbidden to have any possessions or regular income. Normally, in other religious orders,

---

[139] Cf. R. Allegri, *Teresa of the Poor: The Story of Her Life*, p. 121.

[140] Mother Teresa spoke these words to M. Muggeridge in an interview while she was answering about the formation of the sisters, and the writer quoted her in his book (M. Muggeridge, *Something Beautiful for God: Mother Teresa of Calcutta*, p. 84).

[141] R. Allegri, *Teresa of the Poor: The Story of Her Life*, p. 121.

poverty is binding on the individuals of the order, but in the name of the community they can have properties and regular income. For MCs even as an entity, they neither possess anything nor have any revenue of fixed income nor receive any stipends for the work they do. They live on charity. The reason she instructed them not to earn anything from their work is that MCs have taken a special vow to offer free service to the poorest of the poor.[142] She emphasised the strict observances of community life as the principal means to practice the vow of poverty:

> The principal means of observing the essential of poverty is the strict observance of the common life; that is, everyone, including the superior, should be satisfied with the food, clothing, and outfit given to all alike without the least privilege for any expense but what is truly necessary.[143]

4.3. Practical Aspects

Mother Teresa did not teach a few vague ideas on voluntary poverty which cannot be practiced at all; she rather taught some practical and concrete measures with regard to the practice of her teachings. Some of the practical aspects for

---

[142] Cf. *Ibid.*, p. 122. Mother Teresa always responded the same way whenever her biographer Renzo Allegri asked her about this: "My work is administered by Divine providence. It is written in our constitution. 'We and our poor will rely completely on Divine Providence. As members of the Body of Christ who lived of charity during his public life and who served the sick and the poor, we will not be ashamed of begging from door to door.' We posses nothing...we make a special vow to freely serve the poorest of the poor. This vow prohibits us from earning anything from our work" (R. Allegri, *Teresa of the Poor: The Story of Her Life*, p. 122).

[143] Mother Teresa, *Jesus, The Word to be Spoken*, compiled by A. D. Scolozzi, p. 97.

the maintenance of religious poverty in her community are as follows:

- Have everything in common and share with one another in the community.
- Accept nothing for personal use and if at all anything is given by parents or well wishers hand it over to the superior for common use.
- Eat the food of the local people using what is cheapest, but sufficient to maintain good health.
- Houses should be simple and modest, where the poor feel at home.
- Walk whenever opportunity offers, in order to take the cheapest means of transport available.
- Sleep in common dormitories without privacy like the poor.
- Depend on Divine Providence both for material and spiritual needs.[144]

In order to reduce the travelling expenses, she instructed her community members to take minimum luggage when travelling. Besides one's own clothes, each one is allowed to carry only certain articles fixed by common understanding: one pillow, pillow case, two sheets, one blanket, a glass, a cup, and one dinner plate.[145] Each member is given things of daily use with a specific number written on the articles, awakening one's sense of responsibility in taking care of them and also to reduce the number of articles in a house.[146]

---

[144] Mother Teresa, *Total Surrender*, ed. A. D. Scolozzi, pp. 54-55.

[145] Cf. *Ibid.*, p. 91. "Our sisters must travel as poor people and not have a whole compartment of luggage. If we keep strictly to what obedience and poverty combined give us we shall travel with a very light heart"(*Little Book of Mothers Letters*, p. 90).

[146] "Things should be numbered one, two, three, etc. – everything numbered; number one will go to one sister; number

Mother Teresa instructed her sisters that, when a building is constructed for the use of sisters, it must consist of a dormitory for sisters instead of single rooms. The common dormitory is a means of practicing the virtue of poverty.[147]

Mother Teresa invited her sisters to be aware of the hardship of the poor growing day by day due to the rise in the cost of basic materials for livelihood. The poor find it very hard to fulfil the basic needs in their houses. In this situation, in the light of moral responsibility, religious houses have to be more careful in the use of daily things. Thus they may be able to share the hardship of the poor in obtaining the basic necessities of daily life. She mentioned the control of certain basic materials of livelihood, such as food, clothing, water, electricity, soap. These are the things the poor often go without. Since religious get these things very easily, it does not mean that they have to use them in abundance, but that they have to control their use according to the spirit of voluntary poverty.[148] In this context she insisted that her sisters give up food that is not absolutely necessary to their health and nutrition. Similarly, she urged them not to eat outside of regular meals except in times of sickness. She also emphasised the careful use of water and electricity, turning off the taps and putting out any unnecessary lights.[149] Some of the

---

two will go to the next sister; and so on. This means that each house should have things according to the number of the members in the house" (Mother Teresa, *Total Surrender*, ed. A. D. Scolozzi, pp. 91-92).

[147] Cf. *Little Book of Mother's Letters*, pp. 86, 89.

[148] Cf. Mother Teresa, *Total Surrender*, ed. A. D. Scolozzi, p. 61; cf. Mother Teresa, *Thirsting for God: A Year Book of Prayers, Meditations and Anecdotes*, compiled by A. D. Scolozzi, pp. 36, 165.

[149] Cf. Mother Tersa, *Thirsting for God: A Year Book of Prayers, Meditations and Anecdotes*, compiled by A. D. Scolozzi, p. 36.

concrete but ordinary situations in the life whereby one has to be attentive in practicing poverty are explained by her in a simple way:

> We may carry water upstairs for a bath and find three buckets already full in our bathing room. Then the temptation comes to use all the water. If you have to sleep in a corner where there is no breeze, do not gasp and pant to show how much you feel it. In these little things, you can practice poverty. [150]

In the practice of religious poverty, she made it clear that wearing torn clothes is not the sign of the virtue of poverty. Instead she advised her sisters to mend their clothes quickly as beautifully as they can, because they need not practice the poverty of beggars, but of Christ. She also made the arguments that our body is the temple of Holy Spirit - a tabernacle. Normally no one likes to cover the door of a tabernacle, the dwelling place of God, with dirty and torn cloth. Similarly one's own body, the temple of God, should be covered neatly and tidily.[151]

---

[150] Mother Teresa, *Love: A Fruit Always in Season – Daily Meditations*, ed. D. S. Hunt, p. 160; Mother Teresa, *Thirsting for God: A Year Book of Prayers, Meditations and Anecdotes*, compiled by A. D. Scolozzi, p. 127; Mother Teresa, *The Love of Christ: Spiritual Counsels*, eds. G. Goree and J. Barbier, p. 106.

[151] Cf. Mother Teresa, *Total Surrender*, ed. A. D. Scolozzi, p. 58.

CHAPTER 4

Religious Poverty in Relation with Charity

There is an intrinsic link between religious poverty and the virtue of charity. Religious poverty is based on participation in the economy of salvation through the incarnational approach, as showed by our master Jesus Christ. Condescending to the level of the poor in participation with their material misery, religious poverty effects a rapport with the poor. This relation leads to a real knowledge of their pitiful situation, inspiring compassion and charity towards the poor and needy. Religious poverty is strengthened by charity in many aspects and, similarly, charity is better facilitated by assuming religious poverty. The meaning of religious poverty is treated in the above chapters in detail. Therefore here in this chapter the meaning of religious poverty is not dealt with. This chapter is divided into five parts: The meaning and scope of charity, charity in its theological aspects, charity in the dimension of a religious vow, and how religious poverty strengthens the role of charity and how charity strengthens religious poverty. Charity is a theme reflected upon and interpreted by many great men and women throughout Christian history, but here in this book concentration is given only to the teachings of Blessed Mother Teresa on the theme.

1. MEANING AND SCOPE OF CHARITY

The central aim of the religious congregation founded by Mother Teresa is to offer wholehearted free service to the poorest of the poor. And the name of the congregation, the Missionaries of Charity, reflects well this aim; an aim which is pronounced to the world by their powerful witness and dedicated life of charity. It is the essential element and fundamental point of their constitution. They have developed a certain character from the spirit of their charism; a character distinct from all other religious orders. The spirit of the Foundress is found in this particular identity of life in perfect unity of spirit.[1] Mother Teresa once exhorted the aim of her congregation in the words:

> The particular aim of our congregation is to offer wholehearted free service to the poorest of the poor, to Christ in the semblance of those who suffer.[2]

The meaning of charity was defined and explained by Mother Teresa on many occasions to her sisters and other members in her congregations. Similarly, the different kinds of poverty that human beings face were also elaborated by her on various occasions, with the insistence to respond with charitable services to all these different kinds of poverty. We consider these different levels of poverty as the scope of charity.

---

[1] Cf. E. Le Joly, *Mother Teresa: Messenger of God's Love*, pp. 152, 157.

[2] Mother Teresa, *Heart of Joy: The Transforming Power of Self-Giving*, ed. J. L. Gonzalez-Balado, p. 127.

1.1. Meaning of Charity

The commandment to love is given from God and He cannot command something that is impossible for mankind to practice. It is acquirable for everyone who aspires after it and makes an attempt for it. And it is not something that is impossible but is available always within the reach of every hand in an unlimited measure.[3] The commandment of God, to love God and to love one's own neighbour (Lev. 19:18; Mk. 12:29-31), is the foundation for charity. Whoever practices it, is able to achieve various virtues, peace and joy in his or her life. There is a wonderful reflection by Mother Teresa on the spiritual value of charity:

> Charity is patient; it is kind; it is not jealous, it is not malicious, arrogant, or insolent. It is not self-seeking and never aims at evil. It is not pleased with the suffering of others; it rejoices in the victories of good; it has faith and hope and stands until the end (Cf. 1 Cor. 13: 4-7). The hem of love's garment touches the dust. It sweeps the stains in streets and alleys; it does so because it must.[4]

Charity which remains unexpressed in the heart of a person may become rusty and will do good to no one. As long as charity remains closed in one's own heart and is never acted out for the service of others, it is useless, for 'no man lights a candle and puts it under a bushel but upon a candlestick, that it may shine for all that are in the house (Mt. 5:15).'[5] Mother Teresa made it very clear that the poor need neither our condescending attitude nor our pity. They need our love and kindness through charitable service.[6]

---

[3] Cf. *Little Book of Mother's Letters*, p. 4.

[4] Mother Teresa, *Heart of Joy: The Transforming Power of Self-Giving*, ed. J. L. Gonzalez-Balado, p. 99; *Little Book of Mother's Letters*, p. 62.

[5] Cf. *Little Book of Mother's Letters*, p. 61.

[6] Cf. *Mother Teresa in Her Own Words*, compiled by J. L. González - Balado, p. 31.

Whatever we have is a gift from God. He does not give us things to hold but to share with others. The more we learn to share the more we come to know each other, we will love one another, and if we love one another we will be able to share the joy of what we have. Then we become a people of givers, which is a sign of having much; wealthy people, in a positive sense. Thus the criterion for riches does not lie in the amount of money or wealth one has, but rather in one's attachment toward what one has.[7] It can happen in the midst of much wealth that some are really poor according to their lack of peace and joy. Who is a really rich person can be understood from the following words of Mother Teresa:

> Whoever is dependent on his or her money or worries about it, is truly a poor person. If that person places his or her money at the service of others, then that person becomes rich, very rich indeed.[8]

Understanding of the greatness of the poor is an essential element for the virtue of charity. The proper understanding about the inner worth of the poor creates a love leading to serve them. Mother Teresa was sure that whoever commits oneself to knowing the poor soon realizes that the poor are our brothers, no matter what their race, nationality, or religion is.[9] The mission of charity requires the conviction that the people of less fortune are one's own brothers and sisters. This is possible only when we are able to accept God as our Father and human beings are created in the image and likeness of God our heavenly Father, to that extent all

---

[7] Cf. Mother Teresa, *The Joy in Loving*, compiled by J. Chalika and E. Le Joly, p. 336.

[8] *Mother Teresa in Her Own Words*, compiled by J. L. González - Balado, p. 89.

[9] Cf. Mother Teresa, *Heart of Joy: The Transforming Power of Self-Giving*, ed. J. L. González-Balado, p. 119.

are brothers and sisters of one family. The indifference toward the role of charity is due to the lack of this conviction. Mother Teresa expressed:

> The indifference of people who walk by without picking up those whom we pick up is confirmation of their ignorance and lack of faith. If they are convinced that the one who is lying on the ground is their brother or their sister, I think they would undoubtedly do some thing. Unfortunately, they do not know what compassion is and they do not know those beings.[10]

Money cannot be the remedy for everything. In certain cases love is the only remedy. Material things like food, clothing and shelter can be bought by money but certain evils can't be remedied with money instead those evils can be remedied with love.[11] Therefore we should not be satisfied with just giving money which one can get even otherwise. The most important needs of the poor are the work of our hands to serve them and our hearts to love them. These services of love touching the hearts of both the giver and the poor cannot be replaced by just giving money to the poor.[12] Money can be a means of charity but considered alone it cannot serve the real purposes of charity. But if we are able to utilise our money together with other elements of love from the depths of our heart towards the poor then our financial assistance

---

[10] *Ibid.*

[11] Cf. Mother Teresa, *Love: A Fruit Always in Season – Daily Meditations,* ed. D. S. Hunt, p. 182; cf. E. Le Joly, *Mother Teresa of Calcutta: A Biography,* pp. 19-20.

[12] Cf. Mother Teresa, *Life in the Spirit: Reflections, Meditations, Prayers,* ed. K. Spink, p. 53; cf. Mother Teresa, *Love: A Fruit Always in Season – Daily Meditations,* ed. D. S. Hunt, p. 223; cf. Mother Teresa Of Calcutta, *A Gift for God: Prayers and Meditations,* compiled by M. Muggeridge, p. 51; cf. *Mother Teresa in Her Own Words,* compiled by J. L. González - Balado, p. 90.

is worth more. How money can serve the needs of the poor and what else we should add with it to satisfy the hunger of the poor in a complete sense was explained by her in the following words:

> Money is useful only if it serves to spread Christ's love. It can serve to feed the hungry Christ. But he is hungry not just for bread, but for love, for your presence, for your human contact.[13]

We should respect the poor with dignity while doing charitable services to them. Let us not make use of them to empty our waste materials from our house by doing charity. If we give to the poor the things that are of no more use to us, we show that we consider them to be less important beings than us. For instance, giving to the poor the old food which we do not want to use because we know it may affect our health, the torn and unfashionable clothes, out-dated medicines etc. Our charity will become meritorious only when we are able to give the poor that which we use for ourselves and consider them as equals.[14] We should give in

---

[13] Mother Teresa, *Love: A Fruit Always in Season – Daily Meditations*, ed. D. S. Hunt, p. 182; J. L. González – Balado, *Stories of Mother Teresa: Her Smile and Her Words*, p. 61.

[14] "Do you not believe that it can happen, on the other hand, that we treat the poor like they are a garbage bag in which we throw everything we have no use for? Food we do not like or that is going bad – we throw it there. Perishable goods past their expiration date, and which might harm us, go in the garbage bag: in other words, go to the poor. An article of clothing that is not in style anymore, that we do not want to wear again, goes to the poor. This does not show any respect for the dignity of the poor; this is not to consider them our masters, like St. Vincent de Paul taught his religious, but to consider them less than our equals" (*Mother Teresa in Her Own Words,* compiled by J. L. González - Balado, p. 27).

such a way that our giving of an article should create some sort of inconvenience in our life. An experience that something has given out which was useful to us. And when we give an article it should be able to create its absence in our life; making ourselves poor. We also should see that not to give from our abundance.[15] In this line of charity Mother Teresa always instructed her listeners: "Do not give your leftovers."[16] What and how we should give is well explicated in her following words:

> We need to give from the resources we would like to keep for ourselves. We need to give to the point of sacrificing. We must give something that we find hard to give up.[17]

The felt need of the poor has to be considered in the act of charity. For Mother Teresa it was important to consider what the other person wants, and not what we want, or merely the good feelings we have in being the cause of an act of charity.[18] Charity sometimes become a way for self satisfaction in the line of one's own spiritual life and totally ignores the disposition of the receiver. With over enthusiasm to do charity very often people forget to see the felt need and receptiveness of the poor. Apparently they may be helping others but the main motive is one's own satisfaction

---

[15] Cf. Mother Teresa, *Life in the Spirit: Reflections, Meditations, Prayers*, ed. K. Spink, p. 53; cf. Mother Teresa, *Love: A Fruit Always in Season – Daily Meditations*, ed. D. S. Hunt, p. 223; cf. Mother Teresa, *A Gift for God: Prayers and Meditations*, compiled by M. Muggeridge, p. 51.

[16] *Mother Teresa in Her Own Words*, compiled by J. L. González - Balado, p. 29.

[17] Mother Teresa, *One Heart Full of Love*, ed. J. L. González – Balado, p. 73.

[18] Cf. J. Mcgovern, *To Give The Love of Christ: A Portrait of Mother Teresa and the Missionaries of Charity*, Paulist Press, New York 1978, p. 108.

without bothering the effect of charity in the receiver. If the poor rejects our offer due to his ignorance of the utility of our item, then we have to first convince them about its benefit and preparing their mind we have to offer our help.

1.2. Scope of Charity

Deprivation of food, shelter and clothing is generally considered to be the state of poverty. But according to Mother Teresa there are far greater kinds than this material poverty; there are other kinds of poverty which exist in the world and to which we have to give our attention.[19] Spiritual poverty and poverty of the heart, seen in the west, are much more severe than the material poverty in India and other third world countries.[20] Thus the field of charity varies from place to place. In some countries material poverty is very severe whereas in other countries in place of material poverty, some other levels of poverty are very severe. Mother Teresa compares these different situations and considered all these situations to come under the scope of charity. We can divide these different levels of poverty into two kinds; material poverty and spiritual poverty. The different levels of poverty found from place to place she expressed in these words:

> In India some people live and die in hunger. There, even a handful of rice is precious. In the countries of the West

---

[19] Cf. Mother Teresa, *One Heart Full of Love*, ed. J. L. González - Balado, p. 71.

[20] "The spiritual poverty of the Western world is much greater than the physical poverty of our people. You in the West have millions of people who suffer such terrible loneliness and emptiness. They feel unloved and unwanted" (Mother Teresa, *Love: A Fruit Always in Season – Daily Meditations*, ed. D. S. Hunt, p. 226; Mother Teresa, *Life in the Spirit: Reflections, Meditations, Prayers*, ed. K. Spink, p. 13).

> there is no material poverty in the sense in which we speak of poverty. There no one dies of hunger; no one even is hungry in the way we know it in India and some other countries.[21]

1.2.1. Material Poverty

Material poverty is a common phenomena and it is very easy to understand its existence. Whenever a person lacks the necessary materials for the existence of his life is generally known as material poverty. It is something tangible and visible for others. With this reason it is considered more important on the level of charity. Mother Teresa was not of the opinion just to satisfy the material needs of the person but together with satisfying the material needs of the person we have to give some values to the poor. In regard for material needs she suggested certain other helps that we have to add. She said:

> - feeding the hungry: not only with food but also with the Word of God,
> - giving drink to the thirsty: not only for water, but for knowledge, peace, truth, justice, and love,
> - clothing the naked: not only with clothes, but also with human dignity,
> - giving shelter to the homeless: not only a shelter made of bricks, but a heart that understands, that covers, that loves,
> - nursing the sick and the dying: not only the body, but also the mind and spirit.[22]

---

[21] Mother Teresa, *Love: A Fruit Always in Season – Daily Meditations*, ed. D. S. Hunt, p. 228; E. Le Joly, *Mother Teresa of Calcutta: A Biography*, p. 227.

[22] Mother Teresa, *Total Surrender*, ed. A. D. Scolozzi, pp. 81-82; *MCs Constitutions*, Art. 69; Mother Teresa, *Love: A Fruit Always in Season – Daily Meditations*, ed. D. S. Hunt, pp. 44-45: Mother Teresa, *Life in the Spirit: Reflections, Meditations, Prayers*, ed. K. Spink, p. 14.

1.2.2. *Spiritual Poverty*

Mother Teresa often spoke about the spiritually poor who must find a generous place in the Heart of Jesus and in our own hearts. These poor we can find everywhere because 'Calcutta is everywhere.' The deepest poverty is that which is hidden in one's own heart. We may not reduce it to the simple absence of material things necessary for survival.[23] In January 1976 after returning from America and Europe Mother Teresa made an observation about western countries: "They have material wealth, they lack spiritual values."[24] The spiritual poverty of the western world is much greater than the physical poverty of the poorest of the poor in Calcutta. In the West there are millions of people who suffer such terrible loneliness and emptiness.[25] The depth of spiritual poverty in the West is explained by her in the words:

> In the West you have another kind of poverty, spiritual poverty. This is far worse. People do not believe in God, do not pray. People do not care for each other. You have the poverty of people who are dissatisfied with what they

---

[23] Cf. O. Tanghe, *For the Least of My Brother: The Spirituality of Mother Teresa and Catherine Doherty*, translated by J. Mac Donald, pp. 31-32.

[24] Mother Teresa spoke these words to E. Le Joly during a conversation and he quoted in his book (E. Le Joly, *We do it for Jesus: Mother Teresa and the Missionaries of Charity*, p. 165). "There are many people who are spiritually poor. The spiritual poverty found in Europe, in America, is a heavy burden to bear. In these countries it is very difficult to convey a sense of God's love. . ." (Mother Teresa, *Love: A Fruit Always in Season – Daily Meditations*, ed. D. S. Hunt, p. 65; Mother Teresa, *Life in the Spirit: Reflections, Meditations, Prayers*, ed. K. Spink, p. 23).

[25] Cf. Mother Teresa, *Love: A Fruit Always in Season – Daily Meditations*, ed. D. S. Hunt, p. 226; cf. Mother Teresa, *Life in the Spirit: Reflections, Meditations, Prayers*, ed. K. Spink, pp. 13-14.

> have, who do not know how to suffer, who give in to despair.[26]

According to Mother Teresa these people are not hungry in the physical sense but they are hungry in another way. They know they need something more than money, yet they don't know what it is. What they are missing really is a living relationship with God.[27] Out of this conviction she taught that in the field of charity we cannot concentrate to relieve the people only from material poverty but also from spiritual poverty. This sort of spiritual poverty we can find every where; in the midst of the wealthy classes and in the midst of economically poor people. Therefore while helping out even the economically poor people, we are also obliged to relieve them from their spiritual poverty:

> All the desolation of the poor, not only their material poverty but their spiritual wounds as well, needs to be redeemed. We should share with them because only if we are united with them can we redeem them, bringing God to their lives and they, in turn, to God.[28]

The poor are not only the economically backward people of Calcutta or the many areas of misery and starvation in the Southern Hemisphere, or the handicapped, the unborn or the destitute of the industrialized world. They are also the numerous lonely and embittered people whom we meet daily on the street, on buses or trains, in department stores, in hospitals, in homes for the aged, in flats and high class

---

[26] Mother Teresa, *Love: A Fruit Always in Season – Daily Meditations*, ed. D. S. Hunt, p. 228; E. Le Joly, *Mother Teresa of Calcutta: A Biography*, pp. 227-228.

[27] Cf. Mother Teresa, *Love: A Fruit Always in Season – Daily Meditations*, ed. D. S. Hunt, p. 226; cf. Mother Teresa, *Life in the Spirit: Reflections, Meditations, Prayers*, ed. K. Spink, pp. 13-14.

[28] *Mother Teresa in Her Own Words*, compiled by J. L. González - Balado, p. 35.

living rooms. Often people with power and respect, with money and possessions are unhappy because they lack love and tenderness.[29] Poverty caused by the lack of love, seen in the West, is more severe than the material poverty we find in Calcutta:

> Think that the work of the Church in this developed and rich Western Hemisphere is more difficult than in Calcutta, South Yemen, or other areas where the needs of the people are reduced to the clothes needed to ward off the cold, or a dish of rice to curb their hunger; anything that will show them that someone loves them. In the West the problems the people have go much deeper; the problems are in the depths of their hearts.[30]

Mother Teresa was of the conviction that the greater kind of poverty is the state of being unwanted, unloved, and neglected. It means having no one to call one's own.[31] Thus

---

[29] Cf. O. Tanghe, *For the Least of My Brother: The Spirituality of Mother Teresa and Catherine Doherty,* translated by J. Mac Donald, p. 34.

[30] *Mother Teresa in her own words,* compiled by J. L. González - Balado, p. 36. "I find the poverty in the West much more difficult, much greater than the poverty I meet in India, in Ethiopia and in the Middle East, which is material poverty. For example, when a few months ago, before coming to Europe and America, I picked up a woman from the streets of Calcutta, dying of hunger, I had only to give her a plate of rice and I satisfied her hunger. But the lonely and the unwanted and the homeless, the shut-ins who are spending their lives in such terrible loneliness, who are known by the number of their room and not by their name! I think this is the greatest poverty that human being cannot bear and accept and go through" (Mother Teresa, *Love: A Fruit Always in Season – Daily Meditations*, ed. D. S. Hunt, p. 227; Mother Teresa Of Calcuta, *My Life for the poor,* eds. J. L. González – Balado and J. N. Playfoot, Harper & Row, New York 1985, p. 55).

[31] Cf. Mother Teresa, *One Heart Full of Love*, ed. J. L. González – Balado, p. 71.

poverty of heart is more difficult to relieve and to defeat. For example, she reminded the world that in the West there are many more broken homes, neglected children, and divorce on a huge scale.[32] According to her, to satisfy those who suffer from material poverty is easy. On the other hand to satisfy those who suffer from the poverty of heart is rather difficult. She illustrated this by saying that if one gives a little bit of rice to a poor person in India, that person feels satisfied and happy. The poor in Europe do not accept their spiritual poverty, and for many it is a source of despair.[33] She has witnessed the poverty of West in its deeper sense and once explained the seriousness of the situation:

> Each time I go to Europe and America I am struck by the unhappiness of so many people in those rich countries: so many broken homes, children not looked after by their parents. Their first duty is to work among their own people, bring together separated couples, build good homes where the children may receive their parent's love.[34]

When Jesus spoke about hunger He did not mean only physical hunger but also a hunger for love, for understanding, for warmth. He certainly experienced a lack of affection – He came among His own and was rejected. He knew the meaning of loneliness, rejection and of 'belonging nowhere'. This kind of hunger is very much prevalent in our world today; and it is destroying many lives,

---

[32] Cf. Mother Teresa, *Love: A Fruit Always in Season – Daily Meditations*, ed. D. S. Hunt, p. 228; cf. E. Le Joly, *Mother Teresa of Calcutta: A Biography*, p. 228.

[33] Cf. *Mother Teresa in Her Own Words,* compiled by J. L. González - Balado, p. 30.

[34] Mother Teresa spoke these words to E. Le Joly during the conversation and he quoted in his book (E. Le Joly, *We Do it for Jesus: Mother Teresa and the Missionaries of Charity*, p. 165).

many homes and many countries. Being dispossessed refers not only to not having a roof over our head but also not having someone who understands us and is kind to us. This kind of deprivation cries out for someone to open up his or her life and to take in the lonely, who has no family or human affection of any kind. Every human being who suffers in this way resembles Christ in His loneliness; and that is the hardest part, that's real hunger.[35] Thus the greatest poverty is the poverty of loneliness and unwantedness.[36] In search of the poor we need not go to a probably istant place, instead if we look around us we can find them in our home; persons hungry for love. So charity has to begin from one's own home. Mother Teresa once expressed in this regard:

> It is easy to love the people far away. It is not always easy to love those close to us. It is easier to give a cup of rice to relieve hunger than to relieve the loneliness and pain of someone unloved in our own home. Bring love into

---

[35] Cf. Mother Teresa, *Love: A Fruit Always in Season – Daily Meditations*, ed. D. S. Hunt, pp. 43-43, 158; cf. *Stories of Mother Teresa: Her Smile and Her Words*, ed. J. L. González – Balado, p. 51; cf. Mother Teresa Of Calcutta, *A gift for God: Prayers and Meditations*, compiled by M. Muggeridge, pp. 30-31.

[36] "Where are the old people? They are put in institutions. Why? Because they are unwanted, they are burden. I remember sometime ago I visited a very wonderful home for old people. They were about forty there and they had everything, but they were all looking towards the door. There was not a smile on their faces, and I asked the sister in charge of them: 'Sister, why are these people not smiling? Why are they looking towards the door?' And she, very beautifully, had to answer and give the truth: 'It is the same every day. They are longing for someone to come and visit them.' This is great poverty." (Mother Teresa, *Love: A Fruit Always in Season – Daily Meditations*, ed. D. S. Hunt, p. 64; Mother Teresa, *Life in the Spirit: Reflections, Meditations, Prayers*, ed. K. Spink, p. 72).

your home for this is where our love for each other must start.[37]

2. CHARITY IN ITS THEOLOGICAL ASPECTS

Charity is rooted in the love of God and man's love for God through the action of charity towards fellow brethren. The first action of charity is from the part of God and still He continues to shower His love towards mankind. Mother Teresa strongly believed that our holy faith is nothing but a Gospel of love, revealing to us God's love for men and claiming in return man's love for God.[38] Our mutual love is in a way a participation in God's love. Every act of charity enables us to have contact with God because love is the property of God; "God is love" (1Jn. 4:16). Again the teachings of Jesus Christ affirm that our charitable action towards our neighbour is equal to the charity done to him (Cf. Mt. 25: 25-31). Mother Teresa was also in the opinion that all our loving acts towards our neighbour enable us to have contact with God. Therefore we must live it in our daily life to understand the depth of this love and become united to God.[39] In order to achieve this mission of love in a better way we have to consider that we are in God, surrounded and encompassed by God, swimming in God.[40] She considered this union with God out of love to be the basic

---

[37] Mother Teresa, *Love: A Fruit Always in Season – Daily Meditations*, ed. D. S. Hunt, p. 129; Mother Teresa, *Life in the Spirit: Reflections, Meditations, Prayers*, ed. K. Spink, p. 39.

[38] Cf. *Little Book of Mother's Letters*, p. 61.

[39] Cf. O. Tanghe, *For the Least of My Brother: The spirituality of Mother Teresa and Catherine Doherty*, translated by J. Mac Donald, p. 101.

[40] Cf. Mother Teresa, *Life in the Spirit: Reflections, Meditations, Prayers*, ed. K. Spink, p. 30.

motive for the whole hearted free service to the poorest of the poor, the vow of charity:

> The more united we are to God, the greater will be our love and readiness to serve the poor wholeheartedly. Much depends on this union of hearts. The fruit of the love of God the Father for the Son and the Son for the Father produces God the Holy Ghost. So also the love of God for Missionaries of Charity and the love of the Missionaries of Charity for God should produce this whole-hearted free service for the poor.[41]

2.1. Christological Dimension

Jesus Christ is the incarnate love of God. His death on the cross is the manifestation of God's love for mankind, the most radical form of love through self sacrifice, in order to save humanity. By contemplating the pierced side of Christ we can understand this aspect of God's love for mankind. This is the starting point from which our definition of love must begin.[42]

Mother Teresa while teaching on charity made use of the Christological dimension of charity. She spoke about the need of the conviction of Christ's love for us and our love

---

[41] *Little Book of Mother's Letters*, p. 126; Mother Teresa, *Life in the Spirit: Reflections, Meditations, Prayers*, ed. K. Spink, p. 8. Edward Le Joly after having constant contact with Mother Teresa and her sisters expressed: "The Sister's fourth vow, by which they bind themselves to wholeheartedly free service of the poorest of the poor, is motivated by love. This love must be in imitation of the divine love, without ulterior motive, expecting nothing in return. The giver gives because it is good to give, to make other happy, to share the good things we have with others unable to return the gift" (E.Le Joly, *Mother Teresa: Messenger of God's Love*, p. 155).

[42] Cf. Benedict XVI, Encyclical Letter, *Deus Caritas Est*, 25 December 2006, no.12, in *AAS* 98 (2006).

for him which is the foundation for our sanctity. One of the ways to carry out this conviction is our acts of charity to others:

> Are we convinced of Christ's love for us and our love for him? This conviction is like the sunlight which makes the sap of life rise and the buds of sanctity bloom. This conviction is the rock on which sanctity is built. . . . We serve him under the distressing disguise of the poorest of the poor and everyone we meet.[43]

Mother Teresa explained how she reached a stage of deep conviction on charity, based on the love for Christ. The first step is that she had a faith in the presence of Christ in her. Secondly she had a desire to see God face to face. According to the teaching of Christ, she tried to meet him and serve him in the poor. She did not have any doubt in the statement of Jesus Christ about his presence in the poor. Mother Teresa reflected and grasped well the Gospel passage of St. Matthew on the theme of last judgement whereby Jesus affirms his presence in the poor and states that service done to them is equivalent to service done to Him (cf. Mt. 25: 31- 44). She believed firmly the resemblance of Christ in the poor and the needy. And whatever service is carried out to the poorest of the poor becomes a sign of love for Christ in concrete

---

[43] Mother Teresa, *Thirsting for God: A Year Book of Prayers, Meditations and Anecdotes*, compiled by A. D. Scolozzi, p. 163. The fundamental aspect of her faith that caused to form her conviction on charity can be seen in her following words: "Whatsoever you do the least of my brethren – you did it to me. This is my commandment that you love one another – suppress this commandment and the whole grand work of the Church on Christ falls in to ruins. For Jesus came on earth to give charity the rightful place in the hearts of men" (*Little Book of Mother's Letters*, p. 124).

action.[44] This belief developed in her a strong conviction about the need of charity towards the needy. Therefore she was able say to her admirers:

> To those who say they admire my courage, I have to tell them that I would not have any if I were not convinced that each time I touch the body of a leper, a body that reeks with a foul stench, I touch Christ's body, the same Christ I receive in the Eucharist.[45]

She affirmed that the basic motivation of charitable services by the Missionaries of Charity, is their deep conviction that each time they offer help to the poor they really offer help to Christ.[46] She advised her sisters to keep love for the poorest of the poor and made them aware that it is not a waste of time to feed the hungry, to visit and take care of the sick and dying, to open and receive the unwanted and homeless; rather it is a way for expressing our love for Christ.[47] Occasionally she strengthened them by encouraging words and reminding them of the presence of Christ in the poor; a strong motivation to perform acts of charity:

---

[44] Cf. Mother Teresa, *Total Surrender*, ed. A. D. Scolozzi, pp. 120-121; cf. Mother Teresa, *One Heart Full of Love*, ed. J. L. González – Balado, p. 3; cf. Mother Teresa, *Heart of Joy: The Transforming Power of Self-Giving*, ed. J. L. Gonzalez-Balado, p. 122; cf. Mother Teresa, *Life in Spirit: Reflections, Meditations, Prayer*, ed. K. Spink, p. 10; cf. Mother Teresa, *Love: A Fruit Always in Season – Daily Meditations*, ed. D. S. Hunt, p. 42.

[45] *Mother Teresa in her own words*, compiled by J. L. González - Balado, p. 115. "All I do is for Jesus. It is Jesus I serve in the poor, it is Jesus I serve twenty-four hours a day" (Mother Teresa, *Essential Writings*, selected with an introduction by J. Maalouf, p. 16; cf. E. Le Joly, *Mother Teresa: A Women in Love*, p. 36).

[46] Cf. *Mother Teresa in Her Own Words*, compiled by J. L. González - Balado, p. 36.

[47] Cf. Mother Teresa, *Jesus, The Word to be Spoken*, compiled by A. D. Scolozzi, p. 94.

> I know you all love the poor - otherwise you would not join – but let each one of us – try to make this love more kind, more charitable, more cheerful – let our eyes see more clearly in deep faith – the face of Christ in the face of the poor.[48]

The way to arrive at the conviction about the presence of Christ in the poor is the true interior life, which makes the active life burn forth and consume everything. The genuine interior life enables a person to find Jesus in the dark holes of the slums, in the most pitiful miseries of the poor – the God-man naked on the cross, mournful, despised by all, the man of suffering crushed like a worm by the scourging and the crucifixion.[49] One should have a pure heart to see Jesus in the person of the poorest of the poor. She went on to explain that the more repugnant the work, or the more disfigured or deformed the image of God in the person, the greater will be our faith and loving devotion in seeking the face of Jesus and lovingly ministering to Him in the distressing disguise.[50] She highlighted the pathetic situation of Christ in the present world who has no one to care for

---

[48] *Little Book of Mother's Letters*, p. 20. Mother Teresa once expressed the readiness of her sisters to charity: "We have many, many lepers who need care. You would be surprised to learn what happens when we ask the sisters of our congregation who among them is willing to work with the lepers. They all raise their hands. Even though the lepers are grotesquely disfigured and almost repulsive to look at, Christ is in them. He has said, 'You did it to me. I was sick, naked, given up for dead; and you did it to me'" (Mother Teresa, *One Heart Full of Love*, ed. J. L. González – Balado, p. 72).

[49] Cf. Mother Teresa, *Life in the Spirit: Reflections, Meditations, Prayers*, ed. K. Spink, pp. 30-31; cf. Mother Teresa, *Total Surrender*, ed. A. D. Scolozzi, p. 117.

[50] *MC's Constitutions*, Art. 70; *Little Book of Mother's Letters*, p. 126.

him, and she invited our attention to serve him in this condition. She also made it clear that if we have genuine love for Christ then we will be able to realise his presence in the needy and we will find them very easily:

> "Today Christ is in people who are unwanted, unemployed, uncared for, hungry, naked and homeless. They seem useless to the state or to society and nobody has time for them. It is you and I as Christians, worthy of the love of Christ if our love is true, we must find them and help them. They are there for the finding."[51]

The suffering presence of Christ is found all over the world in the form of the poor who suffer. In them the Son of God lives and dies; God presents His face.[52] If we want to console Christ then let us console Christ in the distressing disguise in the poor.[53] Similarly we can touch the suffering body of Christ by touching the sick and needy.[54] In case we reject those suffering souls in their misery indeed we reject Christ.[55]

---

[51] Mother Teresa, *Love: A Fruit Always in Season – Daily Meditations*, ed. D. S. Hunt, p. 43; Mother Teresa, *Life in Spirit: Reflections, Meditations, Prayer*, ed. K. Spink, p. 10.

[52] Cf. *Mother Teresa in Her Own Words*, compiled by J. L. González - Balado, p. 40.

[53] Cf. E.Le Joly, *Mother Teresa: Messenger of God's Love*, p. 113.

[54] Cf. *Mother Teresa in Her Own Words*, compiled by J. L. González - Balado, p. 38; "In our work amongst the poorest of the poor we are touching Jesus all the twenty-four hours" (Mother Teresa, *Love: A Fruit Always in Season – Daily Meditations*, ed. D. S. Hunt, p. 224; Mother Teresa, *Life in Spirit: Reflections, Meditations, Prayer*, ed. K. Spink, p. 55).

[55] "Jesus comes to meet us. To welcome him, let us go to meet him. He comes to us in the hungry, the naked, the lonely, the alcoholic, the drug, the prostitute, the street beggars. He may come to you or me in a father who is alone, in a mother, in a brother, or in a sister. If we reject them, if we do not go out to meet them, we reject Jesus himself" (*Mother Teresa in Her Own Words*, compiled by J. L. González - Balado, p. 41). Pope Benedict

These effects of charity are drawn from the words of Jesus. Mother Teresa expressed her deep trust in the words of Jesus by which she took a firm stand on charity:

> Jesus will not deceive us. He tells us, 'I was hungry and you gave me to eat.' Every time we are faced with such sacrifices for the poor, every time we are concerned about the poor – whether they are near or far away – we do it all for him. Every time you sacrifice something at great cost – every time you renounce something that appeals to you for the sake of the poor – you are feeding the hungry Christ. You are offering shelter to a homeless Christ. You do this when you help in caring for the poor around you.[56]

2.2. Vocational and Missionary Dimension

The call of charity begins at the very instance a person becomes a Christian. To be a true Christian means to become a person of charity; a true follower of Christ. The general call to all Christians is to give. It is accepted even by the faithful of other religions that a Christian is a person who gives. From the very beginning of the history of the Church the impression given by great men and women of Christianity has been the love of Christ and giving to others. Thus there is a common understanding that Christian means one who gives.[57] Mother Teresa said: "Love, an abundant

---

XVI in his first encyclical mentioned this view: "Love of neighbour is a path that leads to the encounter with God, and that closing our eyes to our neighbour also blinds us to God" (Benedict XVI, *Deus Caritas Est*, no.16).

[56] Mother Teresa, *One Heart Full of Love*, ed. J. L. González – Balado, pp. 72-73.

[57] Cf. *Mother Teresa in Her Own Words*, compiled by J. L. González - Balado, p. 29. "Some time ago a Hindu gentleman was asked, 'What is a Christian?' He gave an answer that was both very simple and surprising. "A Christian is someone who gives of himself. From the very start, we perceive that indeed to be a Christian is nothing other than to give of oneself for the

love, is the expression of our Christian religion."[58] Jesus said that the love we have for others will enable other people to recognize us as his disciples (cf. Jn. 13: 34-35), and the true love for our neighbour is to wish him well and do good for him. Further, by following the commandment of love by the disciples of Christ this commandment will have an everlasting effect.[59] She also went on to teach that charity is an obligation for all Christians:

> All Christians are bound by the commandment of God to love and serve their neighbour but we take upon ourselves a new obligation of devoting ourselves to work among the poor.[60]

The consecrated life of charity is Christ's call to MCs through his Church to labour for the salvation and sanctification of the poorest of the poor all over the world. It demands of one to love him wholeheartedly and freely in the poorest of the poor with whom he identifies himself, both in their own communities and in the people outside, and so make his presence known to them, loved and served by all. This call also expects them to make reparation for sins of hatred, coldness, lack of concern and love for him in the world today, in one another and in the people whom they serve.[61]

---

sake of Christ. God so loved the world that he gave us his Son. That was the first act of self-giving. His Son was given to us because he wanted to be one with us, like us in everything except sin" (Mother Teresa, *One Heart Full of Love,* ed. J. L. González – Balado, pp. 1, 2, 5; Mother Teresa, *Life in Spirit: Reflections, Meditations, Prayer,* ed. K. Spink, p. 53; Mother Teresa, *Love: A Fruit Always in Season – Daily Meditations,* ed. D. S. Hunt, p. 44).

[58] *Mother Teresa in Her Own Words,* compiled by J. L. González - Balado, p. 90.

[59] Cf. *Little Book of Mother's Letters,* pp. 124-125.

[60] *Ibid.,* p. 125.

[61] Cf. Mother Teresa, *Total Surrender,* ed. A. D. Scolozzi, pp. 80-81; cf. *MCs Constitutions,* Art. 68.

Mother Teresa strongly believed in the fact that the MCs are called to become men and women of charity as carriers of God's love. And this opportunity to do wonderful work among the poor and for the poor is a privilege and a gift from God.[62] She explained their distinct nature of vocation in the Church in the following words:

> Call of Jesus to satiate His thirst on the Cross for souls invites us to vow wholehearted and free service to Christ in the distressing disguise of the poor, giving us a distinct vocation in the Church today.[63]

Consecrated life is a vocation, which belongs to Jesus not to the poor. The Mission of charity is not out of mere love for the poor but, above all, out of love for Jesus. Jesus is seen in the poor and through serving a poor person one can achieve spiritual benefits, as service is being done to Jesus. There were certain confusions even among the MCs, regarding the emphasis on the poor and forgetting of the main goal. So Mother Teresa had to make them understand the basic point in the mission of charity.[64] She believed that vocation is

---

[62] Cf. Mother Teresa, *One Heart Full of Love,* ed. J. L. González - Balado, p. 70.

[63] *MCs Constitutions,* Art. 68.

[64] "It happened once, when the Congregation of the Missionary Brothers of Charity was first established, that a young brother came to me and said, 'Mother, I have a special vocation to work with the lepers. I want to give my life to them, my whole being. Nothing attracts me more than that.' I know for a fact that he truly loved those afflicted with leprosy. I, in turn, answered him, 'I think that you are somewhat wrong, brother. Our vocation consists in belonging to Jesus. The work is nothing but a means to express our love for him. That is why the work in itself is not important. What is important is for you to belong to Jesus. And he is the one who offers you the means to express that belonging" (*Mother Teresa in Her Own Words,* compiled by J. L. González - Balado, p. 117).

rooted in belonging to Jesus and in the firm conviction that nothing will separate her from the love of Christ. The criteria for a strong vocation are based on being possessed by Christ. She considered that her religious vocation as a Missionary of Charity is meaningful only when she is able to render wholehearted free service to the poorest of the poor with the conviction that Christ is being served.[65] While speaking about the service done to the poor as the fundamental aspect in the vocation of MCs and there is a need to be faithful in this specific call, she said:

> I pray to our Lord that if sisters are not to be faithful to their vocation, he may let the Institute die. God can do without us. The Church would go on existing without us. If the sisters are not faithful to their religious calling, our Lord may suppress our Congregation.[66]

A missionary must be a missionary of love was the main argument of Mother Teresa for becoming an ardent preacher of charity. The loving nature of God we have to spread through our actions and become carriers of God's love. Through the spreading of God's love on earth we can help souls repent wholeheartedly for sins, increase their generosity and their desire to suffer for Christ.[67] Mother Teresa was convinced of actions of her religious order in taking the love of God to others. So she expressed:

> We the Missionaries of Charity carry out an offensive of love, of prayer, of sacrifice on behalf of the poorest of the poor. We want to conquer the world through love, and

---

[65] Cf. Mother Teresa, *Essential Writings*, selected with an introduction by J. Maalouf, p. 36; cf. Mother Teresa, *One Heart Full of Love*, ed. J. L. González – Balado, pp. 15-16.

[66] Mother Teresa spoke these words to E. Le Joly during the conversation and he quoted in his book (E. Le Joly, *We Do it for Jesus: Mother Teresa and the Missionaries of Charity*, p. 163).

[67] Cf. *Little Book of Mother's Letters*, p. 61.

> thus bring to everyone's heart the love of God and the proof that God loves the world.[68]

Mother Teresa advised every member of her congregation to become a real carrier of God's love. She considered it as their mission. She expressed her confidence that a day would come when her congregation may become the carriers of God's love to all sorts of people.[69] She emphasised that a Missionary of Charity must be full of charity toward one's own soul and must spread this charity both among Christians and among people of other faith.[70] She was of the view that charity makes the MCs truly imitate Christ in their mission and by which they are able to contribute most effectively to the reign of Christ in all hearts.[71] Real love demands sacrifice for others as Jesus sacrificed his life for humanity. In her own words:

> True love causes pain. Jesus, in order to give us the proof of his love, died on the cross. A mother, in order to give birth to her baby, has to suffer. If you really love one another, you will not be able to avoid making sacrifices.[72]

There is a need for Christ-like action in the genuine service of poor; coming down to the level of the poor and knowing them well through the experience of their suffering, opening one's heart to love the poor and becoming living witnesses

---

[68] Mother Teresa, *Heart of Joy: The Transforming Power of Self-Giving*, ed. J. L. Gonzalez-Balado, p. 119.

[69] Cf. Mother Teresa, *One Heart Full of Love*, ed. J. L. González - Balado, p. 70.

[70] Cf. Mother Teresa, *Heart of Joy: The Transforming Power of Self-Giving*, ed. J. L. González-Balado, p. 99; cf. *Little book of Mother's Letters*, p. 62.

[71] Cf. *Little Book of Mother's Letters*, p. 61.

[72] *Mother Teresa in Her Own Words*, compiled by J. L. González - Balado, p. 45.

of God's mercy.[73] Christ Jesus had compassion on the multitudes of sufferers: he felt for the blind, the sick, the maimed, the hungry, the homeless, the captive and the lonely. He came to heal them, spoke to them in endearing terms, brought them hope, and told them that they counted before God. Yes, they are important, for God who created them out of love keeps loving them. Mother Teresa shared the compassion of Christ. It is His gift to her and she exemplified it both in words and action.[74]

Charity and the mission of preaching go hand in hand. Jesus was always concerned about the physical needs of his listeners and had compassion towards the multitude that followed after him. Some time he even missed his meals; he forgot to eat.[75] Jesus left us a beautiful example from his life and taught us how charity and missionary preaching is connected. This aspect is reflected well by her and expressed through the following words:

> How did he (Jesus) put his compassion into practice? He multiplied the loaves of bread and the fish to satisfy their hunger. He gave them food to eat until they couldn't eat any more, and twelve basketfuls were left over. Then he taught them. Only then did he tell them the good news. This is what we must often do in our work: we must first satisfy the needs of the body, so we can then bring Christ to the poor.[76]

---

[73] Cf. Mother Teresa, *No Greater Love,* ed. B. Benenate and J. Durepos, p. 102.

[74] Cf. E. Le Joly, *Mother Teresa: Messenger of God's Love,* pp. 116-117.

[75] Cf. Mother Teresa, *No Greater Love,* ed. B. Benenate and J. Durepos, p. 99.

[76] Mother Teresa, *One Heart Full of Love,* ed. J. L. González – Balado, p. 2.

Charity enables us to be ambassadors in the mission of peace. It is natural that war causes an increase in poverty and human suffering. Mother Teresa used to reach to the victims of war and offer her services in the best way possible. She, out of love and charity for humanity, always made an attempt to stop battles among the nations. She desired a peaceful atmosphere in the world that love and fraternity may flourish. In 1991 during the Gulf war through letters she pleaded national leaders to stop the war.[77]

The work of charity is a means to win over the hearts of many and create a good rapport between countries. There were always appreciations for the charitable services by MCs that paved the way for better relationship among nations. Mother Teresa remembered one such remark by an ambassador about the effect of charity:

> The Indian ambassador in Rome told the people, 'These sisters have done more in a short time to bring out two countries closer to each other by their influence of love than we have through official means'.[78]

---

[77] On January 2, 1991 Mother Teresa wrote a letter both to the President of the USA and to the President of Iraq: "I come to you with tears in my eyes and God's love in my heart to plead to you for the poor and those who will become poor if the war that we all dread and fear happens. I beg you with whole heart to work for, to labour for God's peace and to be reconciled with one another. You both have your cases to make and your people to care for but first please listen to the One who came into the world to teach us peace. . . PLEASE CHOOSE THE WAY OF PEACE" (MOTHER Teresa, "Letter to the President George Bush and President Saddam Hussein," in N. Chawla, *Mother Teresa*, Appendix III, pp. 217-218).

[78] Mother Teresa, *Jesus, The Word to be Spoken*, compiled by A. D. Scolozzi, p. 101.

The mission of charity can win over the hearts of national leaders. There were concrete examples whereby the MCs were allowed to remain in certain countries when, due to disturbed circumstances, all others were asked to quit the place. Thus charity enables the missionaries to remain as images of harmless peacemakers through loving service. Two such incidents recalled by Mother Teresa are as follows:

> In Addis Ababa, where the government is expelling missionaries in a few hours notice, the Governor said to me, 'Even if I have to send away everyone else, yet I will not let your sisters go, because I know and see that the sisters love and care for our poor people'.[79]

> 'Even though we might have to expel all missionaries,' the prime minister of Ethiopia told me, 'we will not allow your sisters to leave because I am told, and I have checked it myself to be true, that you truly love the poor and take care of them.'[80]

3. CHARITY IN THE DIMENSION OF A RELIGIOUS VOW

In general all religious orders have three vows; poverty, obedience and chastity. This distinguishes the religious from the secular orders and priests. But some religious communities have in addition a fourth vow, for example the Jesuits have a fourth vow: readiness to go anywhere in the world at the request of the Pope.[81] Mother Teresa, having a rapport with the Jesuits for a long period of her religious life, perhaps thought of having something special for her congregation too in the form of an additional vow. She

---

[79] Mother Teresa, *Total Surrender*, ed. A. D. Scolozzi, p. 133.

[80] *Mother Teresa in Her Own Words,* compiled by J. L. González - Balado, p. 37.

[81] Cf. E. Le Joly, *Mother Teresa: Messenger of God's Love*, pp. 151-152.

wanted to have charity as a new vow, something special to her congregation. She proposed a fourth vow – wholehearted free service to the poorest of the poor – for her congregation and got approval from the ecclesial authorities. This vow of charity differentiates her congregation from all other religious communities. She was very enthusiastic to tell about this vow during her interviews. Once she expressed it vigorously:

> We have something special in our congregation. We have a fourth vow we profess to offer wholehearted and free service to the poorest of the poor. We receive freely and we give freely, out of pure love for God.[82]

3.1. Charity as the Fourth Vow

The fourth vow of the MCs designed by Mother Teresa indicates that they cannot work for the rich; neither can they accept any money for the work they do. Theirs is a free service, and only to the poor.[83] During their religious profession together with other vows they profess this fourth vow, a solemn commitment, for the service to the poorest of the poor:

> Then comes our fourth vow, which consists in the solemn commitment we make to offer wholeheartedly a free service to the poorest poor – that is, to Christ under the humble appearances of the poor.[84]

---

[82] Mother Teresa, *One Heart Full of Love*, ed. J. L. González – Balado, p. 74.

[83] Cf. M. Muggeridge, *Something Beautiful for God: Mother Teresa of Calcutta*, p. 85; cf. Mother Teresa, *Heart of Joy: The Transforming Power of Self-Giving*, ed. J. L. Gonzalez-Balado, p. 55.

[84] Mother Teresa, *Heart of Joy: The Transforming Power of Self-Giving*, ed. J. L. Gonzalez-Balado, p. 103; cf. Mother Teresa Of Calcutta, *A gift for God: Prayers and Meditations*, compiled by M. Muggeridge, p. 36.

The purpose of charity as the fourth vow, included in the religious life of MCs, was to enable the members to be faithful to the original spirit of the religious order; to serve the poorest of the poor. This vow invites them to come forward to do hard things, not to look for easier and consoling apostolate, but to be firm in the basic intention of the foundation of the religious community, they must go to the poorest of the poor, the most abandoned, the neediest people, for the love of Jesus.[85]

3.1.1. Whole Hearted

The word "wholehearted" stands for the best of a person in the dedication of service, with full of love from the depths of one's own heart. Even if it becomes failure we have to do our best, our utmost.[86] Mother Teresa defined the word "wholehearted" in these words:

> Wholehearted means: with hearts burning with zeal and love for souls, with single minded devotion, wholly rooted in our deep union with God in prayer and fraternal love, that we give them not only our hands to serve, but also our hearts to love with kindness and humility, entirely at the disposal of the poor.[87]

It is not the quantity of service that counts but the love behind the service. And the word "wholehearted" would mean the fidelity to do small things with great love.[88] Mother Teresa discouraged the people donating to just get rid of something. Instead she was always of the opinion that giving something

---

[85] Cf. E. Le Joly, *Mother Teresa: Messenger of God's Love*, 151.

[86] Cf. *Little Book of Mother's Letters*, p. 128.

[87] Mother Teresa, *Total Surrender*, ed. A. D. Scolozzi, p. 81; *MCs Constitutions*, Art. 69.

[88] Cf. A. C. Savarimuthu, *Women of the Century: Mother Teresa*, p. 134.

must be with one's whole-heart.[89] Important, therefore, is the love we put in while giving to others. When we serve the poor we must experience the joy of giving.

3.1.2. Free Service

Whatever we have received from God as a free gift, we must give freely without taking any cost in return. There is nothing which we can claim to be our own. This also reminds us that we are totally dependent on divine providence. Therefore freely we have received and freely we must give.[90] The meaning of the word "free" stated in the constitution is as follows:

> Free means: joyfully and with eagerness; fearlessly and openly; freely giving what we have freely received; without accepting any return in cash or kind; without seeking any reward or gratitude.[91]

The fourth vow forces the MCs to do good to the poorest of the poor, those who cannot repay them. Even if the poor could contribute a tiny amount, a few crumbs or a few drops, the MCs may not accept any payment or compensation, nor any form of *quid pro quo.* Their service to their neighbour follows the pattern of God's love for us in its creative, salvific and sanctifying aspects.[92] According to Mother Teresa, the object matter of the vow consists of all action done for the poor provided it be free service; anything contrary would be a violation of this vow.[93] She emphasised that the

---

[89] Cf. Mother Teresa, *No Greater Love,* ed. B. Benenate and J. Durepos, p. 43.

[90] Cf. Mother Teresa, *Thirsting for God: A Year Book of Prayers, Meditations and Anecdotes*, compiled by A. D. Scolozzi, p. 100.

[91] *MCs Constitutions*, Art. 69.

[92] Cf. E. Le Joly, *Mother Teresa: Messenger of God's Love*, p. 155.

[93] Cf. *Little Book of Mother's Letters*, p. 125.

deliberate seeking of money-making service or voluntary consent to such transactions would be against the vow.[94] She explained it more clearly in another occasion:

> Since we devote ourselves to the poor and give wholehearted free service to them, it would be against the vow if a sister devoted her services to the rich with the aim of making money or even gave her free services to them habitually.[95]

Mother Teresa had a strong conviction to uphold, and remain firm to, the principle of totally free service to the poor. She did not yield to the vision of a bishop to take a small contribution from the poor as their contribution in order to teach the people self-help leading them to a sense of respectability and dignity. She reflected back this incident and said:

> Once a bishop wanted the sisters to make the people calling at our dispensary pay a small fee for their services. I refused to do so. We removed the sisters and the dispensary was closed.[96]

3.1.3. *The Poorest of the Poor*

Mother Teresa founded the new religious congregation with the intention to do service to the poorest of the poor; she was very strict in this matter of service *only* to the poor because through the fourth vow she has given a promise to Jesus.[97] Once Mother Teresa mentioned a long list of the poor

---

[94] Cf. *MCs Constitutions*, Art. 69.

[95] *Little Book of Mother's Letters*, pp. 125-126.

[96] Mother Teresa expressed this to E. Le Joly in an interview and he quoted in his book (E. Le Joly, *Mother Teresa: Messenger of God's Love*, p.152).

[97] "The Prime Minister of Yemen asked me, to start a sewing class for the daughters of the best families of the country. But I had to refuse. I did not know whether he would understand

toward whom charity has to be shown in which she also included each religious in the community as one among the poor.[98] Thus she gave importance of charity within the community. The reason for this reflection of charity in the community can be drawn from her following words:

> My vows bind me to my sister because she is much poorer than the poor outside. If I am not kind and do not smile to the poor outside, someone else will, but for my sister there is no one else.[99]

---

what our vows mean, so I said: we cannot accept because we gave our word to God to work only for the poor. When you give your word, you must keep it, mustn't you? He said: yes, of course. – Well we gave our word to God to work only for the poor, because they are more in need. So we must keep it; we cannot work for the children of the upper class. But I am sure you will find some other sisters to do that very well" (*Ibid.*, p.153).

[98] "The poorest of the poor, irrespective of caste, creed, or nationality are: the hungry, the thirsty, the naked, the homeless, the ignorant, the captives, the crippled, the leprosy sufferers, the alcoholics, the sick and dying destitutes, the unloved, the abandoned, the outcasts, all those who are a burden to human society, who have lost all hope and faith in life, and all hard-hearted, persistent sinners, those under the power of the evil one, those who are leading others to sin, error or confusion, the atheists, the erring, those in confusion and doubt, the tempted, the spiritually blind, the weak, lax, and ignorant, those not yet touched by the light of Christ, those hungry for the word and peace of God, the difficult, the repulsive, the rejected, the sorrowful and the souls in purgatory; and every Missionary of Charity by accepting to live the life of evangelical poverty and by the very fact of being sinners" (Mother Teresa, *Total Surrender*, ed. A. D. Scolozzi, p. 82).

[99] Mother Teresa, *Total Surrender*, ed. A. D. Scolozzi, p. 86. "This vow (4th vow) binds us equally to our sisters in the community and the Society as it does to the poorest of the poor outside" (*MCs Constitutions*, Art. 69).

3.2. Importance of the Fourth Vow

The fourth vow is an essential element for MCs and it is a fundamental point of their constitutions. It is the core of their existence and identity of their congregation. This vow brings them the freedom to dedicate themselves wholeheartedly to their aim; to seek out the down-trodden, the forsaken, the abandoned, the needy, the most suffering people. This enables them to have a participation in the self- abasement of Jesus as mentioned by St. Paul in his letter to Philippians (cf. Phil. 2: 5-8).[100] According to Mother Teresa this vow ensures double advantage for the religious who practices faithfully:

> We can give to the Lord who needs nothing, yet accepts our gift gratefully because it is made to one in need who represents him. When giving to the poor, we give to persons who cannot reward us or return the gift to us, so we earn merit for heaven, as promised by Jesus.[101]

Mother Teresa instructed that everyone in her congregation is bound to work for the poor habitually and all sins against charity in that devotedness to the poor, are also sins against the fourth vow. For example, it would be against the vow if, on account of laziness and want of love for the poor, a sick person died of neglect through their fault.[102]

While speaking about the importance of the fourth vow Mother Teresa mentioned three things that are protected by this vow, in the consecrated life of MCs: to ensure faithfulness to their calling, to safeguard their poverty and

---

[100] Cf. E. Le Joly, *Mother Teresa: Messenger of God's Love*, pp. 152-153.

[101] Mother Teresa expressed this to E. Le Joly in an interview and he quoted in his book (*Ibid.*, pp. 114-115).

[102] Cf. *Little Book of Mother's Letters*, pp. 125-126.

to force them to trust fully in God.[103] This vow obliges them also for commitment toward the poor and enables them to live in total divine providence. Therefore she considered the fourth vow to be very important for MCs.[104] In other words this vow gives them a firm foundation and true identity in the main charism of the congregation. How charity in the form of a fourth vow plays a great role for the existence of the MCs is expressed by her in a metaphorical way:

> Charity for the poor must be a burning flame in our society; and just as when a fire ceases to burn, it gives us less usefulness and heat so the society, the day it loses grip on charity towards the poor will lose its usefulness and there will be no life. To be able to do this with greater fervour in our society we take a fourth vow that of devoting oneself to the service of the poor.[105]

In some cases, the fourth vow may limit the availability of the MCs and prevent them from assuring tasks beneficial to souls. But the vow is necessary to safeguard their particular character and their aim which finally serves the common good, since they care for the more deprived, the more neglected section of mankind.[106]

---

[103] Cf. E. Le Joly, *Mother Teresa: Messenger of God's Love*, 152.

[104] "This is why the fourth vow we profess in our congregation is so important. We commit ourselves to offer wholehearted, free service to the poorest of the poor. Through this vow we freely commit ourselves to the poorest of the poor. We are at their service. We become totally dependent on God's providence, and that providence has been wonderful to us. Christ has kept this word" (Mother Teresa, *One Heart Full of Love*, ed. J. L. González – Balado, p. 96).

[105] *Little Book of Mother's Letters*, p. 125: Mother Teresa, *Heart of Joy: The Transforming Power of Self-Giving*, ed. J. L. Gonzalez-Balado, p. 130.

[106] Cf. E. Le Joly, *Mother Teresa: Messenger of God's Love*, 153.

3.3. The Fourth Vow in Relation with Other Vows

There is an inner relationship between charity and other vows. The vow of charity is the fruit of chastity and an unavoidable element for the existence of other two vows; poverty and obedience. In the words of Mother Teresa:

> The vow of charity is a fruit of our union with Christ, just as a child is the fruit of the sacrament of matrimony. Just as a lamp cannot live without oil, so also a vow of charity cannot live without the vows of poverty and obedience.[107]

3.3.1. Charity and Chastity

A religious enters into a spousal union with Jesus through the vow of chastity. Jesus becomes the only one whom a religious makes a life partner, in place of a husband/ wife in the married life.[108] Entire love is concentrated on Jesus and being charitable to others through contemplating the presence of Jesus in them, love for Jesus is being actualised. Mother Teresa advised her sisters to begin charity in their respective community; love and respect for every one in the community. In this regard she expressed:

---

[107] Mother Teresa, *Heart of Joy: The Transforming Power of Self-Giving*, ed. J. L. González-Balado, p. 77; *Little Book of Mother's Letters*, p. 5.

[108] "My sisters, what a great and wonderful vocation is ours, but must know it to be able to love it and if you love it you will keep your word to God – 'I want to be the spouse of Jesus crucified.' Offer to God every word you say, every movement you make, every thought you think as a act of love. To be able to become a true M.C. we must more and more fall in love with God. Love Him with all the powers of body and soul. Let it not be said that a woman in the world loves her husband better than we do Christ. This love is our right and privilege – as woman we have been created to love" (*Little Book of Mother's Letters*, pp. 55-56).

> Be kind and loving with each other for you cannot love Christ in His distressing disguise, if you cannot love Jesus in the heart of your sisters. . . . Look up – wake up – be brave – and generous. Be what Jesus has accepted you to be - His spouse. Love one another, love your 'sister'. In the midst of 'sister' is your sister superior.[109]

Whole hearted and free service to Christ in the distressing disguise of the poor is an overflow of MC's love for God and the first fruits of their cleaving to Him with undivided love in chastity.[110] A genuine love of a person can be measured by his attitude towards the other in the midst of unpleasant and difficult situations. There will be many to love in the pleasant state of a person, but in the state of difficulty it is rare that someone turns to love. Mother Teresa taught that love for Christ as a spouse should remain equal even in his most disgusting appearance in the poor; indeed, we should show more love in such situations. She said:

> Love of God must give rise to a total service. The more disgusting the work is, the greater must love be, as it takes succour to the Lord disguised in the rags of the poor.[111]

---

[109] *Ibid.*, p. 5.

[110] Cf. *MCs Constitutions*, Art. 68.

[111] Mother Teresa, *Heart of Joy: The Transforming Power of Self-Giving*, ed. J. L. González-Balado, p. 130. Christ as the spouse and the need to him in all situations Mother Teresa once said: "We are at his disposal. If he wants you to be sick in bed, if he wants you to proclaim his word in the street, if he wants you to clean the toilets all day, that's all right, everything is all right. We must say, 'I belong to you. You can do whatever you like.' This is our strength, and this is the joy of the Lord" (Mother Teresa, *Jesus, The Word to be Spoken*, compiled by A. D. Scolozzi, p. 41).

3.3.2. *Charity and Obedience*

The norms and conditions of the fourth vow, wholehearted service for the poorest of the poor, are practiced in accordance with the vow of obedience. Thus obedience is the string which connects all other vows. The vow of obedience is affected whenever negligence is shown in any other vows. It is to say that the breaking of the vow of charity is also equal to breaking the vow of obedience because the vow of charity is taken in obedience. In the words of Mother Teresa: "we shall give free service according to obedience."[112] The love towards superiors, an act of charity, has to be performed by obedience to them:

> Love your superiors – be one with them – be loyal to them. The society will be what you together with you superior make it; Fervent or tepid – a fruitful branch or a dry branch."[113]

The relationship between the vow of poverty and the vow of charity will be seen in the following two subtitles.

4. POVERTY STRENGTHENS THE ROLE OF CHARITY

The life of voluntary poverty leads us to have the freedom of charity. Charity enables a more intimate and personal love for Jesus. In the action of charity there is a chance to know each other better and this knowledge leads us to love. The love developed through proper understanding and knowledge will lead to kind, joyful and peaceful service. Thus the life of religious poverty, after experiencing the hardships of the poor and a properly formed love for the poor, leads one to do service to the poorest of the poor with

---

[112] *Little Book of Mother's Letters*, p. 126; Mother Teresa, *Jesus, The Word to be Spoken*, compiled by A. D. Scolozzi, p. 94.

[113] *Little Book of Mother's Letters*, p. 6.

a joyful heart.[114] How religious poverty strengthens the role of charity is discussed here below in four subheadings: vow of poverty safeguards the vow of charity, the life of poverty to understand the poor, the life of poverty to welcome and win over the hearts of the poor, and identification with the poor as an effective means of charity.

4.1. Vow of Poverty Safeguards the Vow of Charity

Profoundness in religious poverty enables charity. Charity is compared with a living flame and the brightness of the flame depends upon the condition of the fuel, which is religious poverty. Detachment from earthly motives, and complete unity with the will of God, paves the way for the wholehearted free service to the poorest of the poor.[115] If a person is weak in practicing the religious vow of poverty then he will also be weak in free service to the poorest of the poor. In other words, the strength of religious poverty has a role to play in creating a solid motivation in the heart for the mission of charity. She emphasised that faithfulness to the vow of poverty enables one to be faithful in the vow of charity. Mother Teresa said:

> Let us renew our love for the poor. We will be able to do so only if we are faithful to the poverty we have vowed, that we have chosen.[116]

---

[114] Cf. Mother Teresa, *Thirsting for God: A Year Book of Prayers, Meditations and Anecdotes,* compiled by A. D. Scolozzi, p. 48.

[115] Cf. *Little Book of Mother's Letters,* p. 126; cf. Mother Teresa, *Jesus, The Word to be Spoken,* compiled by A. D. Scolozzi, p. 94; cf. Mother Teresa, *Life in the Spirit: Reflections, Meditations, Prayers,* ed. K. Spink, pp. 7-8; cf. Mother Teresa, *No Greater Love,* ed. B. Benenate and J. Durepos, p. 31.

[116] Mother Teresa, *Jesus, The Word to be Spoken,* compiled by A. D. Scolozzi, p. 102; Mother Teresa, *Thirsting for God: A Year Book of Prayers, Meditations and Anecdotes,* compiled by A. D. Scolozzi, p. 123.

Mother Teresa affirmed, "Before God, all of us are poor."[117] The sense of our nothingness and humility lead us to the development of a spirit of fraternal charity.[118] All that we have is from God and there is nothing to claim as our own. This realization enables us to be charitable towards others. Freedom from selfishness and the courage of poverty leads to charity. Mother Teresa said:

> To love, it is necessary to give. To give, it is necessary to be free from selfishness, to have the courage of poverty.[119]

Love for the poor and consequent charity has to come out of the sacrifice of material comforts from one's own life; then it is real love and genuine charity.[120] Becoming one among the poorest of the poor through voluntary poverty allows the growth of charity.[121] This spirit of poverty should be seen in the entire life of the religious, especially in selecting the areas of service. In the life of the MC's we can notice a kind of detachment from attractive, pleasure giving and money fetching jobs. This spirit of poverty paves the way to dedicate their life only for the poorest of the poor; the specific way of charity envisaged by Mother Teresa. Thus religious poverty facilitates better performances in the service of charity. In her words:

---

[117] Mother Teresa, *Heart of Joy: The Transforming Power of Self-Giving*, ed. J. L. Gonzalez-Balado, p. 62; *Mother Teresa in Her Own Words*, compiled by J. L. González - Balado, p. 41.

[118] Cf. Mother Teresa, *Thirsting for God: A Year Book of Prayers, Meditations and Anecdotes*, compiled by A. D. Scolozzi, p. 160.

[119] *Ibid.*, p. 153.

[120] Cf. *Little book of Mother's letters*, p. 5. "We must do our utmost to keep our sight clear and free from the world, so that our service to the poor may become one generous act of love" (*Little Book of Mother's Letters*, p. 127).

[121] Cf. Mother Teresa, *Heart of Joy: The Transforming Power of Self-Giving*, ed. J. L. Gonzalez-Balado, p. 137.

> We renounce the natural inclination to work for and with the rich and more attractive people and also the pleasure of bringing to the community financial help through the work we do for the people.[122]

4.2. The Life of Poverty to Understand the Poor

Knowledge about the suffering of others may create compassion and desire to help them in their plight. The gravity of this good will increase when knowledge is derived from the experience of their hardship. In other words knowledge leads to love and love to service of the poor and the suffering ones.[123] Mother Teresa was of the opinion that in order to understand and be able to help the poor we have to experience hardships by living as they live.[124] Theoretical knowledge is not sufficient to get the real picture of a phenomenon. Rather, practical knowledge is indispensable, and comes to the need of voluntary poverty in order to serve the poor. In this regard Mother Teresa said:

> To know the problem of poverty intellectually is not to understand it. It is not by reading, taking a walk in the slums, admiring and regretting, that we come to understand it and to discover what it has of bad and good. We have to dive into it, live it, share it.[125]

---

[122] *Little Book of Mother's Letters*, p. 125.

[123] Cf. Mother Teresa, *Heart of Joy: The Transforming Power of Self-Giving*, ed. J. L. González-Balado, pp. 101,109; cf. Mother Teresa, *One Heart Full of Love*, ed. J. L. González – Balado, p. 74.

[124] Cf. Mother Teresa, *Heart of Joy: The Transforming Power of Self-Giving*, ed. J. L. González – Balado, p. 65; cf. Mother Teresa, *No Greater Love*, ed. B. Benenate and J. Durepos, p. 97; cf. G. Goree and J. Barbier, *Love Without Boundaries*, translated by P. Speakman, p. 62; cf. K. Spink, *Mother Teresa: An Authorised Biography*, p. 44; cf. J. L. González – Balado, *Always the Poor - Mother Teresa: Her Life and Message*, pp. 32, 82.

[125] Mother Teresa, *Love: A Fruit Always in Season – Daily Meditations*, ed. D. S. Hunt, p. 224; Mother Teresa, *Life in the*

Jesus took upon him a life of poverty in order to understand the poor and left us a lesson to be followed in our mission of charity. Experiencing the life of poverty is a must to serve the poor and give Christ to the poor.

> To understand the poor, we must know what poverty is and why Jesus made himself poor. If we understand our poverty, our smallness, our weakness, our littleness, then we will be able to serve the poor and give Christ to the poor.[126]

In referring to her religious order, Mother Teresa expressed how important it is for the sisters to lead the life of the poor in order to understand them well and to serve them in a better way.[127] The better the knowledge about the miseries of the poor the better service can be rendered for them. Therefore sisters have their vow of poverty and commit themselves to practice it in a radical way. On this matter she once said:

> In our community we choose poverty: we want to know the poor, to understand them. To that end we have to know what poverty is all about.[128]

4.3. The Life of Poverty to Welcome and Win Over the Hearts of the Poor

In the context of charity and the need to interrelate with the poor, religious communities should be aware of creating

---

Spirit: Reflections, Meditations, Prayer, ed. K. Spink, pp. 55-56; Mother Teresa, *The Joy in Loving*, compiled by J. Chalika and E. Le Joly, p. 315.

[126] Mother Teresa, *Thirsting for God: A Year Book of Prayers, Meditations and Anecdotes*, compiled by A. D. Scolozzi, p. 180.

[127] Cf. Mother Teresa, *Heart of Joy: The Transforming Power of Self-Giving*, ed. J. L. González-Balado, p. 108; cf. Mother Teresa, *One Heart Full of Love*, ed. J. L. González – Balado, pp. 12, 43.

[128] Mother Teresa, *Heart of Joy: The Transforming Power of Self-Giving*, ed. J. L. González – Balado, p. 9.

such a situation where poor people should not remain at a distance. The religious house should create an atmosphere in which the poor are able to come to the house without any inhibitions. When a house is decorated with rich furniture and made more beautiful with costly materials, then the poor would feel a difficulty to enter, and a fear that their poverty would be dishonoured. Then the service to the poorest of the poor becomes difficult as they keep a distance from the religious community. Mother Teresa instructed her sisters:

> We must not occupy our time in trying to make our houses beautiful and attractive. May God keep us free of convents with rich furniture, where the poor would feel strange to enter for fear that their poverty would be a dishonour.[129]

The practice of voluntary poverty becomes a means to win over the hearts of the poor which is necessary for a better performance of charity to the poor. In the process of helping the poor, if religious are able to go down to the level of the poor in material comforts, then their action will be more effective. This is because it touches the hearts of the poor and religious get a place in their heart. When the poor come to know that religious have chosen the minimum facilities for their sake, it enables the poor people to open their hearts, leading to a genuine rapport with them.[130] Convinced on this matter Mother Teresa said:

---

[129] *Ibid.*, p. 129.

[130] "Poverty is necessary because we are working with the poor. When they complain about the food, we can say, we eat the same. They say, 'It was so hot last night, we could not sleep.' We can reply, 'We also felt very hot.' The poor have to wash for themselves, go barefoot; we do the same. We have to go down and lift them up. It opens the heart of the poor when we can say we live the same way they do. Sometimes they only have one bucket of water. It is the same with us. The poor have to stand in line; we do too. Food, clothing, everything must be like that

> The heart of the poor opens to us when we can show that we live with them. We must humble ourselves in order to lift them up.[131]

Unless religious live in the freedom of true poverty, poor people may reject them because of their riches.[132] Therefore, in the ministry of charity, voluntary poverty is an essential element. Mother Teresa was very strong in this view and she used to answer her critics with full vigour and enthusiasm, as they questioned her about the severity of their religious poverty. Once she answered to a journalist:

> We have freely chosen that, and this is the difference between us and the poor. How could they believe in us if our life were any different? If we had everything that money can buy, that the world can give, how could they relate to us? What language could I use with them? But now, if someone were to say to me: 'I am dying of the heat today,' I could respond: 'Come and see how hot it is in my room'.[133]

4.4. Identification with the Poor as an Effective Means of Charity

While teaching the values of religious poverty, Mother Teresa always stressed the importance of identification with

---

of the poor" (Mother Teresa, *No Greater Love,* ed. B. Benenate and J. Durepos, p. 98; Mother Teresa, *Total Surrender*, ed. A. D. Scolozzi, p. 57).

[131] Mother Teresa, *Essential Writings*, selected with an introduction J. Maalouf, p. 110; L. Gjergji, *Mother Teresa: To Live, to Love, to Witness – Her Spiritual Way*, p. 53.

[132] Cf. Mother Teresa, *Thirsting for God: A Year Book of Prayers, Meditations and Anecdotes,* compiled by A. D. Scolozzi, p. 80.

[133] Mother Teresa answered this to a Journalist of Time Magazine as he asked her about the sharp criticism of the severity of life she imposes on herself and her Sisters. Later F. Zambonini collected this and quoted in his book (F. Zambonini, *Teresa of Calcutta: A Pencil in God's Hand*, p. 122).

the poor,[134] to experience the hardships of the poor and be effective in the mission of serving the poorest of the poor. She wanted her sisters to feel as the poor feel; feel their poverty before God, know what it is to live without security, depending on God for tomorrow.[135] Once she exhorted a few questions in this regard for their reflection:

> We are at service of the poor. But are we capable, are we willing to share the poverty of the poor? Do we identify with the poor whom we serve? Do we really feel in solidarity with them? Do we share with them just like Jesus shares with us?[136]

---

[134] "What does it mean for us to be the poorest of the poor? Do we know what it means to be hungry and thirsty, lonely and unloved? Do we know what it means to be sick and unwanted, homeless and misunderstood? Do the poor really know us? Do they love us? Are they happy in our presence?" (Mother Teresa, *Thirsting for God: A Year Book of Prayers, Meditations and Anecdotes,* compiled by A. D. Scolozzi, p. 123).

[135] Cf. Mother Teresa, *Love: A Fruit Always in Season – Daily Meditations,* ed. D. S. Hunt, p. 157; cf. E. Le Joly, *Mother Teresa of Calcutta: A Biography,* Harper and Row Publishers, San Francisco 1983, p. 221; cf. E. LE Joly, *Mother Teresa Messenger of God's Love,* p. 113; cf. J. MONIZ, *No Greater Service: Mother and the Mahatma,* p. 60.

[136] *Mother Teresa in Her Own Words,* compiled by J. L. González - Balado, p. 40. The identification with the poor is not a mere figure of speech for MCs. Every sister is allowed to have three saris – one to wear, another to wash, and a third one to mend. Two sets of underclothes, a pair of sandals, a small crucifix, a rosary, a bucket, metal spoon and rimmed plate, a canvas bag and a prayer book complete their belongings. They eat the same food, wear the same clothes, possess very little, and are not permitted to have a fan or anything to mitigate life in Bengal's sweltering heat and the clamour and discordances of the street outside even at their prayers, lest they should forget for a single second why they are there and where they belong (Cf. J. Moniz, *No Greater Service: Mother and the Mahatma,* p. 61).

Religious can win over the confidence of the poor and share their suffering by identification with them in their plight. Voluntary poverty is an entrance into the life of the poor, to understand them well and give Christ's message. This entrance also helps to console them and also enables them to convert their suffering for the salvation of the world. Thus religious can save the poor and the suffering through the identification. This idea was well manifested in her teachings as she said:

> We shall befriend the friendless and comfort the sick and sorrowful by our real love and personal concern for them, identifying ourselves with them in their pain and sorrow and by praying with them for God's healing and comfort and by encouraging them to offer their sufferings to the Lord for the salvation of the whole world.[137]

Living the utter lowliness and self-effacement of Christ leads one to identify oneself with the poor and yet remain joyfully faithful to the humble works among the poorest of the poor. This also leads one to share the sufferings of the poor for whom service is rendered.[138] Without our suffering, our task would not be of Jesus. We have to follow Jesus in executing our mission. Jesus offered his help by sharing our life, our loneliness, our agony, our death. He did this in order to save us, as it was his mission on earth. We too must share the afflictions of the poor because only by becoming one with the poor will we be able to save them.[139] This view is well explained in her following words:

---

[137] Mother Teresa, *No Greater Love,* ed. B. Benenate and J. Durepos, p. 62.

[138] Cf. *MCs Constitutions,* Art. 6.

[139] Cf. Mother Teresa, *Heart of Joy: The Transforming Power of Self-Giving,* ed. J. L. González – Balado, p. 59.

> All the unhappiness of the poor – their material poverty, their spiritual abandonment – may be redeemed if we share their suffering. Only by remaining united with them will we be able to save them.[140]

5. CHARITY STRENGHTENS RELIGIOUS POVERTY

The persons for whom the charitable services are rendered are the poorest of the poor. The contact with the poor opens the eyes of the person who is involved in these services with regard to the miseries and deep poverty of the people outside. This gives an inspiration for the necessity of actual poverty by the people who have taken the vow of poverty. The experience of the actual situation is a more powerful teacher than the theories learned in the class rooms during formation, to become a religious. The concrete situations of poverty seen outside the religious communities also create great impact on the level of conscience against the comparative luxuries of life in the religious communities. Besides the inspiration for a better life of poverty, charitable activity also helps provide spiritual enlightenment on the

---

[140] *Ibid.*, p. 83. How Mother Teresa personally united with the poor can be very well understood from her words: "My community are the poor. Their security is mine. Their health is my health. My home is the home of the poor; not just of the poor, but of those who are the poorest of the poor. Of those to whom one tries not to get too close for fear of catching something, for fear of the dirt, or because they are covered in germs and disease. Of those that do no go to pray because they can't leave their houses naked. Of those that no longer eat because they haven't the strength. Of those that fall in the streets, knowing that they are going to die, while the living walk by their sides ignoring them. Of those who no longer cry, because they have no tears left. Of the untouchables" (Mother Teresa, *Love: A Fruit Always in Season – Daily Meditations*, ed. D. S. Hunt, p. 159; Mother Teresa, *My Life for the Poor*, eds. J. L. González – Balado and J. N. Playfoot, p. 10).

level of religious poverty; the available peace and joy in the midst of poverty.

5.1. Vow of Charity Safeguards the Vow of Poverty

Mother Teresa stated in an interview that, while introducing the fourth vow, one of the aims was to safeguard the vow of poverty. She was of the understanding that in the history of the Church the decline in fervour of religious orders usually started with a slackening of the spirit of poverty, with excessive possessions and personal spending by individual members. Therefore, she insisted that MC's are to accept no salary for any work, no material reward, enter into no contract, receive no pension or security. Not being paid, not earning, not possessing, forces them to rely on God alone, to show perfect trust.[141] In this respect she taught that by this vow one becomes equal to the poor with regard to the utter dependence on God for one's sustenance. MCs make a solemn commitment in the form of the fourth vow to offer wholeheartedly a free service to the poorest poor, depending exclusively on divine providence, to posses nothing even though they possess everything as they possess Christ.[142]

Commitment to do service in the line of charity becomes a necessity to practice voluntary poverty in one's own personal life to become more effective in the mission of charity. Therefore MCs lead a life of poverty, and how service of charity demands of them the life of poverty was expressed by Mother Teresa in these words:

---

[141] Cf. E. Le Joly, *Mother Teresa: Messenger of God's Love*, p. 152.

[142] Cf. Mother Teresa, *Heart of Joy: The Transforming Power of Self-Giving*, ed. J. L. González-Balado, p. 103.

> Every Missionary of Charity is the poorest of the poor. That is why we can do anything. Whatever is given to the poor is the same for us. We wear the kind of clothes they wear. But ours is a choice. We chose that way to understand the poor, we must know what is poverty. Otherwise we will speak another language, no?[143]

5.2. Charity as a Motivation for Religious Poverty

The inner urge towards charity and love for the poor leads to detachment from wealth, as it comes without any chance to cleave onto one's life. In this way charity enables a person to be faithful in religious poverty. Mother Teresa always waited to give away immediately whenever something valuable reached her hand; to give a lesson to others on charity as well as the need for spiritual detachment. She applied this principle even to the great honours she received and gave a lesson to the world:

> We raffled the car that Pope Paul VI gave me in Bombay. With the money we collected, we created a great centre for lepers that we have named City of Peace. With the money received from the John XXIII award, we created another rehabilitation centre for lepers called Gift of Peace. With the Nobel Peace Prize money, we built homes for the poor because I only accepted the prize in the name of and as a representative of the poor.[144]

Humility is an essential element in religious poverty. Mother Teresa was of the opinion that charity leads to humility. She wished to have charity among the sisters in the community, accepting one another when they are different, and creating

---

[143] Mother Teresa, *Essential Writings*, selected with an introduction by J. Maalouf, pp. 110-111; N. Chawla, *Mother Teresa: The Authorized Biography*, p. 209.

[144] *Mother Teresa in Her Own Words*, compiled by J. L. González - Balado, p. 89.

an atmosphere of unity through charity. The exercise of charity can instil in them the need to become humble.[145]

The mission of charity helps a person to come closer to the miseries of the poor and it generates a prick of conscience about one's own extravagance while others are suffering to keep their body and soul together. From this emerges a real sense of moral conscience to withdraw from a luxurious life and come forward to help the poor by the savings of sacrifice. Mother Teresa said:

> The goods of this world are the free gifts of God and that no one has a right to superfluous wealth as long as there are some who are suffering.[146]

When some one accumulates more than one's need, then some others are to undergo the deprivation of their share. Can anyone claim that he is strong both in mind and body so much so whatever he earned out his hard effort are his property? Does man have control over his life span? Can he decide the stability of his wealth and property? If man has no control over his life span and the losing of his wealth then he has to agree that whatever he has is the property of God. Poverty is created by wrong distribution in the social system and the selfishness of some people. Therefore Mother Teresa said: "God has not created poverty; it is we who have created it."[147]

---

[145] Cf. E. Le Joly, *We Do it for Jesus: Mother Teresa and the Missionaries of Charity*, p. 167.

[146] Mother Teresa, *Heart of Joy: The Transforming Power of Self-Giving*, ed. J. L. Gonzalez-Balado, p. 64.

[147] *Ibid.*, p. 62; *Mother Teresa in Her Own Words*, compiled by J. L. GONZÁLEZ - Balado, p. 41.

5.3. Life of the Poor as a Source of Inspiration for Religious Poverty

Mother Teresa also taught the world how the life of poor people can become for others an inspirational source in practicing religious poverty.[148] She was of the opinion that rich people cannot even think of leading a life without food and clothing, whereas there are millions of poor people who can live without such things. To affirm this view she narrated an incident. One day a very rich man came to the home of the dying destitutes in Calcutta. Upon departing he expressed his realization how poor he was.[149] Even in the midst of hardships and difficulties due to lack of material comforts the poor are happy and contented with their situation. While practicing poverty a person should have this disposition of satisfaction and joy. To convey this message Mother Teresa said:

> The poorest of the poor are free, happy and without the aggression of those who aspire or can aspire to many things. The poor of the third world can teach us contentment."[150]

---

[148] Cf. E. LE Joly, *Mother Teresa: Messenger of God's Love*, p. 113.

[149] Cf. Mother Teresa, *One Heart Full of Love*, ed. J. L. González - Balado, pp. 127-128.

[150] Mother Teresa, *Life in the Spirit: Reflections, Meditations, Prayers*, ed. K. Spink, p. 51. Mother Teresa enumerated an example to support this view: "I'll give you an example of what happened to me recently. I went out with my sisters in Calcutta to seek out the sick and dying. We picked up about forty people that day. One woman, covered in a dirty cloth, was very ill and I could see it. So I just held her hand and tried to comfort her. She smiled weakly at me and said, 'thank you'. Then she died. She was more concerned to give to me than to receive from me. I put myself in her place and I thought what I would have done. I am sure I would have said: 'I am dying, I am hungry, call a doctor, call a Father, call somebody.' But what she did was so beautiful. That woman was more concerned with me than I was with her" (*Ibid.*).

> We can learn from the poor how to accept a difficult situation of adversity, to be content with few material goods, to appreciate very much the little we have.[151]

Mother Teresa called upon the attention of religious to learn from the poor to accept difficult situations and hardships, to be satisfied with a few material goods, to make much of little. Having little, they feel small, unimportant, dependent, and ready to receive.[152] She always admitted with gratitude how the life of the poor became a genuine inspirational source for her to be in the spirit of poverty. The contact with the poor, while engaged on charity, changed her life and helped her to understand the teachings of Jesus. This also made her certain of her own nothingness and the right attitude in the midst of poverty. Once she expressed these sentiments of her heart in the words:

> I have learned from the poor how poor I myself am. They give me infinitely more than I give them: their joy (they are content with everything), their zest for life, their receptiveness, their way of accepting things.[153]

5.4. Experience of God and Spiritual Enlightenment from the Poor

The experience of God is also possible from misery and poverty. It is the attitude with which one looks at a particular situation. Mother Teresa made even these struggles of the poor an inspirational source of poverty, as there is the presence of God hidden in it. The life with the poor in the line of charity enables a person to have the experience of

---

[151] Mother Teresa, Mother Teresa, *Essential Writings*, selected with an introduction by J. Maalouf, p. 109; L. Gjergji, *Mother Teresa: To Live, to Love, to Witness – Her Spiritual Way*, p. 51.

[152] Cf. E. Le Joly, *Mother Teresa: Messenger of God's Love*, p. 115.

[153] Mother Teresa, *One Heart Full of Love*, ed. J. L. González – Balado, p. 127.

God. Travelling in the train with the poor people in the lower class of train in India effects solidarity with the poor people and it gives, according to Mother Teresa, an experience of God.[154] In the words of E. Le Joly: "The poor, as a group, are closer to God, more detached from human comforts, from material things. Having fewer obstacles on the way, they are generally God-fearing, God-worshipping, and accept what comes to them as the will of God."[155]

We can have the presence of Christ in the midst of miseries, poverty, sufferings, etc. In the month of December 1988 there was an earthquake in Armenia, and Mother Teresa and sisters went to serve the victims. When she returned she was explaining how she experienced the birth of Jesus in the midst of the suffering victims of the earthquake. To a question asked of her about how she celebrated her Christmas among the victims of the earthquake, she answered:

> Mary and Joseph looked for a place where Jesus could be born. They found it in Armenia. Jesus was born in poverty; he had nothing but hay and a stable. The poverty of Christ and the suffering of the Armenian people are united. Armenia was Golgotha – death; but then it became Bethlehem and the world hastened to it, as the shepherds and the Three Kings had done.[156]

---

[154] Cf. O. Tanghe, *For the Least of My Brother: The Spirituality of Mother Teresa and Catherine Doherty*, translated by J. Mac Donald, p. 17.

[155] E. Le Joly, *Mother Teresa: Messenger of God's Love*, p. 113.

[156] Mother Teresa answered this to F. Zambonini to his question. "How was her Christmas among the victims of the earthquake in Armenia?" In the month of December 1988 Mother Teresa and Sisters had been to Armenia to serve the earthquake victims and when she returned to Rome the writer interviewed her. Later he quoted her answer in his book (F. Zambonini, *Teresa of Calcutta: A Pencil in God's Hand*, p. 116).

Poverty can intensify a thirst for Jesus. By seeing the misery of people, religious realize the value of their consecrated life. It can also lead them to a real sense of poverty in which they must live:

> Calcutta is every where. We can discover Calcutta with its misery and sin everywhere, Father. Only then will we realize that we are all destined for higher, nobler things. The things that we often allow to clutter our hearts can only serve to intensify our thirst for Jesus. This thirst is the poverty in which we all must live.[157]

The poor are also capable to teach by their faith, their resignation, their patience in suffering. They also give the religious a chance to serve Jesus by allowing them to serve them.[158] According to Mother Teresa, in heaven we will be able see how much we owe to the poor for helping them to love God better because of them.[159]

---

[157] Mother Teresa spoke these words to O. Tanghe in an interview and he quoted in his book (O. Tanghe, *For the Least of My Brother: The Spirituality of Mother Teresa and Catherine Doherty*, translated by J. Mac Donald, p. 11).

[158] Cf. Mother Teresa, *Love: A Fruit Always in Season – Daily Meditations*, ed. D. S. Hunt, p. 63; cf. E. Le Joly, *Mother Teresa of Calcutta: A Biography*, p. 220.

[159] Cf. Mother Teresa, *Love: A Fruit Always in Season – Daily Meditations*, ed. D. S. Hunt, p. 63; cf. Mother Teresa, *My Life for the Poor*, eds. J. L. González – Balado and J. N. Playfoot, p. 97.

Conclusion

Renunciation is an essential element in the consecrated life, and it is a condition put forward by Jesus for those who wish to become his true disciples. In accordance with this condition, each person belonging to a religious order takes the vow of poverty. Religious poverty is one of the three evangelical counsels. These are understood as the virtues of discipleship, so much so, that evangelical poverty becomes a Christian virtue of discipleship. Often one leaves everything with the true spirit of renunciation at the threshold of one's vocation, but in the course of time one accumulates more than what he or she had left behind. There are many rationalisations used to justify these acquisitions. Thus one attempts to clear the guilt of conscience. In many religious orders poverty is binding only upon individuals and not the community as such; in the name of the community they can have various kinds of modern comforts. Young people have become selective in entering the religious or priestly life by looking at the degree of future hardships. In this respect, Blessed Mother Teresa lived and taught a strict religious poverty. Her teaching on evangelical poverty was the subject matter of this research, and we have seen the effectiveness and practicality of her teachings concerning this virtue. Thus this theme provides a great opportunity for the modern world to reflect upon and return to the genuine spirit of religious poverty.

A LIFE OF WITNESS IN POVERTY

In the first chapter we have examined in detail the way Blessed Mother Teresa practised religious poverty in her life. Her renunciation of material comforts to enter into a religious life and its radical form in the second stage of her religious life is self explanatory. They show her genuine spirit of religious poverty. We also have seen the way she was strengthened by the inspiration from Sacred Scripture, lives of saints, devotion to the Eucharist and life of prayer. A deep intimacy with Jesus through these religious observances helped her to remain untouched by worldly inclinations and be ever faithful to religious poverty in its true sense. All these enabled her to be strong in living a life of radical poverty. We have explored her trust in divine providence and detachment from money in carrying out the mission without losing the spirit of poverty. Though financial assistance from all over the world poured into her mission on an enormous scale, she remained untouched and was never deflected from her radical poverty. She had proposed special criteria to accept the donations for the work of the poor, that they should touch the life of the donor and should not be accepted unless needed immediately. Special care had been taken not to lose the spirit of poverty while accepting any gifts.

Through a study of the life of Blessed Mother Teresa, one can discover in her a deep conviction and preference for voluntary poverty in the religious life. Her life had become equal to the volumes of books about her from which we can draw inspiration. She was convinced that she could not live apart from the poor to answer the call within the call: to become poor and serve the poorest of the poor. She had to dispossess herself of everything in order to be one with the poor. Her life of poverty was a consequence of her great love of Jesus and the fruit of her love for the poorest of the poor. In pursuing willingly such an arduous life, Mother Teresa exhibited great abandonment to and deep trust in the providence of God. She began all alone with a faith that moved mountains. She won the admiration and love and recognition from all over the world for her austere life and works for the poor. God worked wonderful and great things through this humble instrument during her life on earth and even after her death. The fruit of it is that today she is a Blessed shining star in heaven.

In the life of Bl. Mother Teresa, one can see the vow of poverty as the most important of all the three evangelical vows. She taught more through her exemplary life than through her spoken words or written works. Her spirit for imitating the poor Jesus and practicing poverty to the highest degree is something marvellous. Her conviction about poverty guided her profound trust in the Providence of God and remained the same from the beginning of her religious life to the end of her life. Christ-like poverty, especially its self-emptying aspect, is seen very strongly in her life. Inspired by the spirit of kenosis from the life of Christ, she always tried to identify with the poorest of the poor in order to be more effective in her mission. "Christ became poor for our sake" (2Cor. 8:9). Her life-style, her readiness to live with minimum facilities, her humble demeanour etc., are witness to her religious poverty. She always remained a living model of evangelical poverty, and her followers learned a great deal from her exemplary life. Her constant effort and struggle to maintain her congregation with the rule of strict poverty is something more than praiseworthy. She did so through her timely intervention and corrections, whenever her sisters tended to go astray.

QUINTESSENCE OF HER DOCTRINE ON POVERTY

In the second chapter we have analysed the teachings of Blessed Mother Teresa on religious poverty as an effective means of following Christ with its four dimensions: the call of Christ, the life of Christ, the teaching of Christ and the mission of Christ. In this section we dealt with the Christological nature of religious poverty. The demand of voluntary poverty, in various dimensions of Christ's call, was seen in detail. To be a disciple of Jesus, voluntary poverty is indispensable. The emphasis on poverty made by Jesus while he called his disciples and sent them for a mission necessitates its importance in the life of religious. Similarly, poverty has a great importance in the call of Christ towards holiness and eternal life. She was of the opinion that away from the practice of poverty following the call of Christ can not be realised. The need to follow the poor life of Christ was emphasised very much by her as something expected from the religious. Christ, who practiced poverty from birth to death, and especially his self-emptying aspect, is the model of poverty the religious are to follow.

Religious poverty has its foundation in the teachings of Christ. She gave a special emphasis to the loving trust in God as taught by Jesus Christ. According to her, preoccupation with the future leads to the longing for money; the longing for money leads to the comforts that money can provide; and the result will be that religious are busy with very many things and endless dissatisfaction. Practice of voluntary poverty for the love of Jesus can be a solution to this and we can thereby lead a happy life. She taught that religious must never get into the habit of being preoccupied with the future. There is no reason to do so. God is there.

Preaching the good news to the poor requires a certain amount of voluntary poverty on the part of missionaries, the method Jesus practised through his Incarnation and taught his disciples to follow.

In the third chapter we have made an analysis to understand the vision of Blessed Mother Teresa with regard to the vow of poverty with its various characteristics and significance in the religious life. Evangelical poverty for Blessed Mother Teresa was a freely chosen renunciation for the love of Christ and the poor whom she served. She considered it as a joyful freedom and dowry to Jesus. She taught her followers to practice poverty with cheerfulness, as it is a state of emptiness providing a freedom from material pre-occupations. This study also enabled us to know how she explored an interrelation between the vow of poverty and other religious vows. She highlighted the elements of renunciation in the vow of chastity in order to enter into a genuine spousal relationship with Jesus. The vow of poverty is related to obedience in connection with its profession and maintenance in obedience to the superior. She very well brought out the interrelationship and interdependence among the vows for their existence. It is very interesting to note that the strict observances of the vow of poverty safeguard the religious life. Similarly, negligence in the practice of this vow can become the cause of losing one's own vocation to religious life.

Finally, in the fourth chapter we have analysed the relation between religious poverty and the virtue of charity and arrived at the conclusion that religious poverty and charity support each other. She taught the importance of charity in its various aspects, especially its theological and religious dimensions. She affirmed the fundamental aspect of reciprocal love between Christ and human being. She emphasised the assurance of Christ that the service done to other brethren is equal to the service done unto him. Christ's voluntary poverty out of love for mankind and his teachings on love lead us to understand the Christological foundation of charity. This also can lead to the proper understanding about the interrelation between charity and poverty. She urged the attention of religious in following the mission of Christ by becoming carriers of God's love. In this process voluntary poverty becomes a true sign of love for the poor. The mission of charity was the specific call Blessed Mother Teresa received in the second stage of her religious vocation and accordingly she founded a new congregation with the name of Missionaries of Charity. In addition to the three vows common to all religious orders, she introduced a fourth vow of charity; namely wholehearted free service to the poorest of the poor.

Fidelity to the vow of poverty leads the religious to have fidelity to the vow of charity. From this research we could understand how the vow of charity is strengthened and protected by the strict observances of poverty. When religious lead a life of a higher standard than the poor with whom they intend to work, then it is difficult to relate to them; and it also creates a distance from them. Instead, when religious experience the lack of material things in their life, they will be able to understand the difficulties of the poor, who suffer more substantial deprivations in their life. This has a double effect. It creates in the religious a proper understanding of the hardships of the poor; and secondly, their simple life will create among the poor an awareness that the sacrifices that religious undergo are for their sake. Similarly, charitable services to the poorest of the poor enable a religious to remain faithful to the practice of poverty.

Evangelical poverty for Blessed Mother Teresa was a freely chosen renunciation for the love of Christ and the poor whom she served. She also stressed identification with the poor in the spirit of kenosis from the life Christ, leading one towards the virtue of humility. She found a great interrelationship between vows, to the extent that when one is slighted, the others are affected. The life of the members in her congregations, and their fast growth in numbers, is the real proof of the effectiveness of her teachings of evangelical poverty. Apart from its strictness, another peculiarity of her teachings about poverty is its obligation not only to individuals but also to the community; whereas, in other religious orders, the vow of poverty usually binds only individuals.

The life and teachings of Blessed Mother Teresa on religious poverty once again proved its importance in consecrated life and remains a guide to whoever wishes to practice it in a better way. This research has enabled us to affirm that voluntary poverty is very essential to the religious life, as it is related to the other religious vows and has a great role to play in one's remaining faithful to the vocation to be a religious. Every religious has to give special attention to maintaining genuine poverty in the spirit of sacrifice. Let me conclude with the inspiring words of Blessed Mother Teresa to the religious to maintain the vow of poverty in their consecrated life: "We must always try to be poorer still and discover new ways to live our vows of poverty."[1]

---

[1] Mother Teresa, *Love: A Fruit Always in Season – Daily Meditations*, ed. D. S. Hunt, p. 160; Mother Teresa, *The Love of Christ: Spiritual Counsels*, eds. G. Goree and J. Barbier, p. 106.

Bibliography

I. Sources

A. Primary Sources[1]

Constitutions and Directory and Testament of the Society of the Missionaries of Charity – Fathers, Tijuana 1992.

Constitutions of the Missionaries of Charity, 54 Circular Road, Private Printer, Calicut, India 1988.

Explanation of the Original Constitution: Missionaries of Charity, unpublished.

Mother's Instructions: Let us Make Our society Something Beautiful for God, (3 Volumes). Printed as a gift to the Missionaries of Charity by the Knights of Columbus, for private circulation, no date.

Mother's Letters: Unpublished.

B. Secondary Sources[2]

In the Heart of the World, ed. Benenate, Becky, New World Library, California 1997.

---

[1] In the primary sources we have made use of some unpublished documents. The details of these documents are not available. They are meant only for private circulation among Missionaries of Charity. In the secondary sources we have mentioned the published books in the name of Mother Teresa. Her words are compiled, edited and published by some authors.

[2] In the secondary sources we have mentioned the published books in the name of Mother Teresa. Her words are compiled, edited and published by some authors. And these are arranged in an alphabetic order of the names of compiler and editors.

No Greater Love, eds. Benenate, Becky, and Durepos J., New World Library, Novato 1997.

Daily Readings with Mother Teresa, ed. Bertodano, T., Fount, London 1993.

The Joy in Loving, eds. Chaliha, J. and Le Joly, E., Viking Penguin, New York 1997.

Words to Love by Mother Teresa, ed. Cunningham Frank, J., Ave Maria Press, Notre Dame, Indiana 1983.

Prayer Times with Mother Teresa: A new Adventure in Prayer Involving Scripture, Mother Teresa and You, eds. Egan, E. and Egan, K., Image Books, New York 1989.

Living the Word, eds. Egan, E. and Egan, K., Fount Paperbacks, London 1990.

Blessed are You, eds. Egan, E., and Egan, K., Fount Paperbacks, London 1992.

Suffering into Joy, eds. Egan, E. and Egan, K., Servant Publication, Ann Arbor 1994.

Essential Writings, ed. Ellsberg, R., Orbis books, New York 2001.

One Heart Full of Love, ed. Gonzalez – Balado J. L., Servant Publications, Ann Arbour, Michigan 1984.

My Life for the poor, eds. Gonzalez – Balado, J. L and J. N. Playfoot, Harper & Row, New York 1985.

Heart of Joy, ed. Gonzalez – Balado, J. L., Fount Paperbacks, London 1988.

Loving Jesus, ed. Gonzalez – Balado, J. L., Translated by Labastida, S., Servant Publications, Ann Arbor, Michigan 1991.

In My Own Words, compiled by Gonzalez – Balado, J. L., Liguori Publications, Liguori 1996.

In Her Own Words, ed. Gonzalez – Balado J. L., St. Pauls, Bandra, Mumbai 1997.

For the Love of God: Mother Teresa of Calcutta, eds. Goree, G. and Barbier, J., Translated by P. Speakman, Veritas publications, Dublin 1974.

Love of Christ, eds. Goree, G. and Barbier, J., Translated by John A. Otto, Harper & Collins, London 1982.

Passage Way to Heaven: A Pilgrims Diary, ed. Hess, R., Sacred Heart League, Walls 1987.

Love: A Fruit Always in Season -Daily Meditations, ed. Hunt D. S., Ignatius Press, San Francisco 1989.

Mothers founding Grace: A Selection from the Documentary Sources, ed. Kolodiejchuk, B., Postulation of the cause of beatification and canonization of Mother Teresa, Vatican City 2001.

The Best Gift is Love: Meditations by Mother Teresa, ed. Lovett, Sean-Patrick, Fount, London 1993.

Essential Writings, selected with an introduction by Maalouf, J., Orbis Books, Mary Knoll, N. Y. 2001.

A Gift for God: Prayers and Meditations, compiled by Muggeridge M., Harper & Row, New York 1975.

A Life for God, Compiled by Neff, L., Servant Publications, Michigan, 1995.

Speaking from the Heart, introduction by O'connor, Cardinal J., Scepter Publisher, Princeton 1986.

The Blessings of Love, ed. Sabbag N., Servant Publications, Michigan 1996.

Mother Teresa: Total Surrender, ed. Scolozzi, A. D., Servant Books, Ohio 1985.

Thirsting for God: A Yearbook of Prayer, Meditations & Anecdotes, compiled by Scolozzi, A. D., Servant Books, Ohio 2000.

Jesus the Word to be Spoken: Prayers and Meditations for Every Day of the Year, compiled by Scolozzi, A. D., Claretian Publications, Bangalore 2004.

In the Silence of the Heart: Meditations by Mother Teresa, Compiled by Spink, K., SPCK, London 1988.

Life in the Spirit: Reflections, Meditations,Prayers, ed. Spink K., Harper & Row, San Francesco 1983.

A Simple Path, compiled by Vardey, L., Rider, London 1995.

A Fruitful Branch on the Vine, Jesus, compiled by Varia O., translated by Guerneri L., Arnoldo Mondadori, Milano 1998.

II. STUDIES

A. Books

Allegri, R., *Teresa of the poor: The Story of Her life*, Servant Publications, Ann Arbour, Michigan 1996.

Aloor, J., *Suffering and Serving for Jesus in the Life and Apostolate of Mother Teresa*, Ph.D. diss., Pontifical University of St. Thomas Aquinas, Rome 2000.

Cardinal, M., *Blessed Mother Teresa of Calcutta: The Making of a Saint*, Novalis CBC Radio-Canada, Toronto 2003.

Chawala, N., *Mother Teresa*, Gulmohur, New Delhi 1992.

Chetcuti, P., *Choosing to Serve the Destitute*, Irish Messenger Publications, Dublin 1980.

Collopy, M., *Works of Love are Works of Peace, Mother Teresa of Calcutta and the Missionaries of Charity*, Ignatius press, San Francisco 1996.

Coniiker, J. F., *Peaceful Seed Living*, The Apostolate for Family Consecration, Kenosha, USA 1978.

Conroy, S., *Mother Teresa's Lessons of Love and Secrets of Sanctity*, Our Sunday Visitor Publishing Division, Indiana 2003.

Crimp, S., *Touched by a Saint: Personal encounters with Mother Teresa*, Sorin Books, Notre Dame 2000.

D'cunha, Fr. S., *Mother of the Motherless: A short Sketch of the Life and Work of Mother Teresa*, St. Paul Publications, Bangalore 1978.

Doig, D., *Mother Teresa: Her People and Her Work*, Collins, Glasgow 1976.

Drouin, L. H., *Mother Teresa: We are too*, St. Paul Journal, Alberta 1982.

Egan, E., *Such a Vision of the Street*, Sedgwick & Jackson, London 1985.

Feldmann, C., *Mother Teresa: Love Stay*, The crossroad Publishing Company, New York 1998.

Gallagher, J., *Mother Teresa*, Catholic Truth Society, London 2003.

Gallela, P., *Christian Charity as Witnessed by Mother Teresa of Calcutta*, Ph.D. diss., Pontifical University of St. Thomas Aquinas, Rome 1999.

Ganss, G. E., *Formula of the Institute*, The Institute of Jesuit Sources, St. Louis 1970.

__________, *The Constitutions of the Society of Jesus*, The Institute of Jesuit Sources, St. Louis 1970.

Ghosh, G., *Mother Teresa: the Apostle of Love,* Rupa & Co, New Delhi 2002.

Gjergji, L., *Mother Teresa: Her Life, Her Works,* New City Press, New York 1991.

__________, *Mother Teresa: To Live, to Love, to Witness,* Translated by Jordan, A., New City Press, New York 1998.

Gonzalez – Balado, J. L., *Always the poor – Mother Teresa: Her life and Message,* Liguori Publications, Missouri 1980.

__________, *Stories of Mother Teresa: Her Smile and her Words,* Translated by Diaz, O., Ligouri Publications, Ligouri, Missouri 1983.

__________, *Mother Teresa: Her Life, Her Work, Her Message,* Liguori Publications, Liguori 1997.

Gonzalez – Balado, J. L., & Janet, N. Playfoot (eds.), *My Life for the Poor: Mother Teresa of Calcutta,* Ballantine Books, New York 1993.

Goree, G. and Barbier, J., *Love without Boundaries: Mother Teresa of Calcutta,* Translated by Speakman, P., Our Sunday Visitor, Indiana 1976.

Hitchens, C., *The Missionary Position: Mother Teresa in Theory and Practice,* Indus, New Delhi 1996.

J. Jeremias, *Jerusalem in the Time of Jesus,* SCM Press, London 1969.

Le Joly, E., *Servant of Love,* Harper & Row, New York 1977.

__________, *We do it for Jesus: Mother Teresa and Missionaries of Charity,* Oxford University Press, Calcutta 1977.

__________, *A Women in Love,* Harper & Row, New York 1977.

__________, *Jesus said 'I Thirst': A Spiritual Dialogue modelled on the Song of Songs,* Jaya guru Printers, Calcutta 1981.

__________, *Mother Teresa of Calcutta: A Biography,* Harper and Row Publishers, San Francisco 1983.

__________, *Mother Teresa: Messenger of God's Love,* (New edition), St. Paul's, Mumbay 1988.

__________, *Mother Teresa: The Glorious Years,* St. Paul's, Bombay 1989.

Maalouf, J., *Praying with Mother Teresa: The Word Among us,* USA 2000.

Mcgovern, J., *To give the Love of Christ: A Portrait of Mother Teresa and the Missionaries of Charity*, Paulist Press, New York 1978.

Missionaries Of Charity, *Come Be My Light: Blessed Mother Teresa of Calcutta*, Official Commemorative Edition, Rome 2003.

Moniz, J., *No Greater Service: Mother and the Mahatma*, Better Yourself Books, Bombay 1998.

Muggeridge, M., *Something Beautiful for God: Mother Teresa*, Ballantine Books, New York 1971.

Mundackal, T. T., *Blessed Mother Teresa*, Ligouri Publications, Missouri 1998.

__________, *Listen to Mother Teresa*, Asian Trading Corporation, Bangalore 2001.

O'connor, J., *Speaking from the Heart: Mother Teresa of Calcutta*, Scepter Publishers, New Jersey 1986.

Palumbo, E., *Mother Teresa: Angel of God*, Resurrection Press, New Jersey 2000.

Pambady, C., *Mother Theresa*, Josco Books, Mannanam 2003.

Porter, D., *Mother Teresa: The Early Years*, SPCK, London 1986.

Royle, R., *Mother Teresa*, Bloomsbury, London 1992.

Savarimuthu, A., *Spirituality of Mother Teresa of Calcutta*, Ph.D. diss., Pontifical University of St. Thomas Aquinas, Rome 1999.

__________, *Mother Teresa: Woman of the Century*, Asian Trading Corporation, Bangalore 2000.

Scolozzi, A. D., *Mother Teresa: Contemplative in the Heart of the World*, Servant Books, Ann Arbor, Michigan 1985.

Sebba, A., *Mother Teresa Beyond the Image*, Doubleday, New York 1997.

__________, A., *Mother Teresa*, (Illustrated Paul Crompton), Julia MacRae Books, London 1982.

Simson, P., *Poverty, Celibacy, Obedience*, Gaba Publications, Kenya 1976.

Spink, K., *For the Brotherhood of Man under the Fatherhood of God: Mother Teresa of Calcutta, Her Missionaries of Charity and her Co – Workers*, Colour Library International, New Malden 1981.

__________, *The Miracle of Love: Mother Teresa of Calcutta, her Missionaries of Charity and her Co-Workers*, Harper & Row, San Francisco 1982.

__________, *Words to Love by*, Ave Maria Press, Notre Dame 1983.

__________, *I need Souls Like you: Sharing in the Work of Mother Teresa through Prayer and Suffering*, Harper & Row Publishers, San Francisco 1984.

__________, *A Chain of Love: Mother Teresa and Her Suffering Disciples*, SPCK, London 1984.

__________, *Mother Teresa: An Authorised Biography*, Harper and Collins, London 1997.

Tanghe, O., *For the Least of my Brothers: The Spirituality of Mother Teresa and Catherine Doherty*, Translated by mac Donald, J., Alba House, New York 1989.

Tully, M., *Mother*, Form Asia Books Limited, Hong Kong 1992.

Vazhakala, S., *Life with Mother Teresa*, Servant Books, Ohio 2004.

Wright, P., *Mother Teresa's Prescription: Finding Happiness and Peace in Service*, Ave Maria Press, Notre Dame, Indiana 2006.

Zamboni, F., *Teresa of Calcutta: A Pencil in God's Hand*, Translated by Jordan, A., Alba House, New York 1993.

B. Articles

Chittister, J., "Vows", in *The New Dictionary of Catholic Spirituality*, ed. M. downey, The Liturgical Press, Minnesota 1993, p. 1011.

Dede, J. F., "Vows: impediment to marriage", in *New Catholic Encyclopaedia*, The Catholic University of America, Gale, New York 2003, vol. 14, p. 758.

Driscoll, M. S., "Chastity", in *The New Dictionary of Catholic Spirituality*, ed. M. Downey, The Liturgical Press, Minnesota 1993, p. 147.

Gallen, J. F., "Religious Poverty Re-examined" in *Review for Religious*, 37 (1978) 739.

Karokaran, A., "Discipleship: A Participation in Jesus' sending", in *Review for Religious*, 58 (1999), p. 618.

Mass, R., "Obedience" in *The New Dictionary of Catholic Spirituality*, ed. M. Downey, pp. 709-710.

Mother Teresa, "Women Religious and Mission", in *Consecrated Life at the Frontiers of Mission*, ed. M. Bianchi, Pontifical Missionary Union, Roma 1994.

Neuner, J., "Mother Teresa's Charism", in *Review for Religious*, 60, 5 (September - October 2001) 479- 493.

__________, "Mother Teresa's Charism", in *Vidyajyoti Journal of Theological Reflection*, (March 2001) 179-192.

O'riordan, S., "Chastity: Asceticism of Chastity", in *New Catholic Encyclopaedia*, The Catholic University of America, Gale, New York 2003, vol. 3, p. 444.

www.ingramcontent.com/pod-product-compliance
Ingram Content Group UK Ltd.
Pitfield, Milton Keynes, MK11 3LW, UK
UKHW041840190726
13854UKWH00002B/638

9 788184 650624